Roots of Strategy

Roots of Strategy

The 5 Greatest Military Classics of All Time

Containing
THE ART OF WAR, by Sun Tzu, 500 B. C.
THE MILITARY INSTITUTIONS OF THE
ROMANS, by Vegetius, 390 A. D.
MY REVERIES UPON THE ART OF WAR,
by Marshal Maurice de Saxe, 1732
THE INSTRUCTION OF FREDERICK THE
GREAT FOR HIS GENERALS, 1747
THE MILITARY MAXIMS OF NAPOLEON

Edited by
BRIG. GEN. THOMAS R. PHILLIPS
U.S. Army

Stackpole Books

First paperback printing, March 1985

Published by
STACKPOLE BOOKS
5067 Ritter Road
Mechanicsburg, PA 17055
www.stackpolebooks.com

Printed in the United States of America

Library of Congress Cataloging-in-Publication Data
Main entry under title:

Roots of strategy.

    Reprint. Originally published: Harrisburg,
Pa. : Military Service Pub. Co., 1940.
    Includes index.
    Contents: The art of war / by Sun Tzu — The military institutions of the Romans / by Vegetius — My reveries on the art of war / by Marshal Maurice de Saxe — [etc.]
    1. Strategy—Addresses, essays, lectures.
2. Military art and science—Addresses, essays, lectures.
I. Phillips, Thomas Raphael, 1892–
U161.R66   1985   355'.02   84–26826
ISBN 0-8117-2194-9 (pbk.)

EDITOR'S FOREWORD

This collection contains the most influential military classics written prior to the nineteenth century. *The Art of War* by Sun Tzu is not only the oldest military work in existence but is unquestionably the greatest military classic in any language. It has had little influence in the western world but has guided Chinese and Japanese military thought for 2400 years.

The period of the Renaissance in Europe was also a period of military renaissance. And it was to the ancients that the European soldiers turned for instruction. Gustavus Adolphus was an ardent student of Xenophon. In the early eighteenth century, Chevalier Folard's commentaries on Polybius were the most influential military work of the period. During all this return to the ancients, *The Military Institutions of the Romans,* by Vegetius, took the place of what we today would call field service regulations. In the Dark Ages, Vegetius' work was circulated in manuscript form, but only the parts of it dealing with the attack and defense of fortified places were considered of value. As skill in war advanced those portions of Vegetius dealing with tactics, training, and organization became greatly appreciated.

It was through study of the ancients that Maurice de Saxe arrived at the innovations in marching and organization that cleared the way for improvements in the art of war made by Frederick the Great and Napoleon. Frederick the Great's *Instruction for His Generals* was soon overshadowed by the fame of Napoleon. As a consequence, it has not had great influence on military thought outside of Germany. In Germany, the principles expounded by Frederick the Great, as distinguished from details of operations no longer applicable, are still influential. No appreciation of German military ideals can be accurate unless the *Instructions* have been read.

The Maxims of Napoleon are the distilled wisdom of the greatest warrior of the western world. Since the time of Napoleon, one writer on warfare has exerted or may exert an influence as great as those in this collection. Clausewitz' great work, *On War*, can be considered to have supplied the abstract theories for the conduct of the Franco-Prussian War of 1870 and World War I. Admiral Castex, of France, has also produced strategical studies of significance.

Little as modern historians like to admit it, great nations have been built by war, and it has been by war that they have been overthrown. Much history has been stultified by the failure of civilian students to pay any attention to the modification of military ideas and the improvements in military possibilities. Thus, it was Napoleon's ability to use the military possibilities of his time that set the course of history in Europe. Today, the dark clouds of war again seem to be lowering and threaten to make more profound changes and deal greater destruction than ever before.

It is hoped that this volume, containing the most influential military works of the past, may increase appreciation of the effect of military ideas on the course of history and the fate of nations, and assist in demonstrating the historical importance of military thought.

Thomas R. Phillips
1940

CONTENTS

Synopsis of Contents

THE ART OF WAR
by Sun Tzu

Written about 500 B. C., this is the oldest military work in existence and probably the finest ever written. Sun Tzu's book still is held in great esteem in China and in even greater reverence in Japan. Chinese literature is thought compressed; consequently THE ART OF WAR deals with principles and fundamentals which are ageless. To the military student able to adapt its principles to conditions of modern warfare, it even now, two thousand four hundred years after its preparation, is quite up to date and a most valuable guide to the conduct of war. Sun Tzu said: *"There is no instance of a country having been benefited from a long war."* Sun Tzu explains how to estimate the situation quite as well as the most modern texts. *"All warfare is based on deception,"* he proclaims and proceeds to explain how to deceive and surprise the enemy by methods as good today as they were in China five hundred years before Christ.

THE MILITARY INSTITUTIONS OF THE ROMANS
By Vegetius

Vegetius' compilation of the military wisdom and customs of the Romans has been the most influential military work written in the western world. Compiled

9

for the Emperor Valentinian II about 390 A. D., just before Rome was captured and burned by Alaric, King of the Goths, it was circulated in manuscript for a thousand years and served the purpose of a field service and training regulations throughout Europe. As soon as printing was discovered it was published in Italian, French, German, Dutch, and English within the space of sixteen years. Caxton printed the first English edition in 1489. To Vegetius can be attributed the organization of the modern division, even to ponton equipment, a description of which is given in his book. The disciplinary practices of our own army can be traced to him. It was from study of Vegetius that Marshal de Saxe rediscovered cadenced marching, an art that had been lost in European armies for a thousand years. *"In war,"* wrote Vegetius, *"discipline is superior to strength; but if that discipline is neglected there is no longer any difference between the soldier and the peasant."* And he proceeds to explain how to insure discipline. No officer can understand our own military institutions who has failed to read Vegetius.

MY REVERIES
UPON
THE ART OF WAR
by Field Marshal Maurice de Saxe

One of the greatest generals of all time, and a military radical, wrote this protest and call for reform. *"War,"* he wrote, *"is a science covered with shadows in whose obscurity one cannot move with an assured step. Routine and prejudice, the natural result of ignorance, are its foundation and support.*" And then he proceeds to indicate the reforms in organization, discipline and strategy required to build effective armies. His work had much to do with the advances in military art made by Napoleon. De Saxe is one of the great links in military development between Vegetius and Napoleon. Many of his propositions now are military commonplaces, but when written they were considered absurd. He understood the human heart, interested himself in his soldiers and, unique in his time, did not treat them like cannon-fodder. The modern soldier still can learn from him and no one can understand the evolution of armies who has not read the famous REVERIES.

THE SECRET INSTRUCTIONS OF FREDERICK THE GREAT TO HIS GENERALS

In an unimportant battle, February 21, 1760, Major General Czetteritz, of the Prussian army, was captured. In examining his baggage a small volume entitled *Military Instructions for the Generals* was discovered. This was the instruction for the generals of Frederick the Great, which they were religiously bound to keep secret. It was duly prized and immediately translated into English, French, Polish and Russian. In it is synthesized the wisdom of the great soldier-king. Prussian discipline and Prussian military methods were adapted from it by all armies, for it contained the secrets of Frederick's military success. Next to Clauswitz this small volume is the most influential work in founding the German military system of today. Most of the great Frederick's observations apply to modern war. Understanding of German military success and the development of German methods is impossible without this book.

THE MILITARY MAXIMS OF NAPOLEON

Napoleon's Maxims need no recommendation. Stonewall Jackson carried them in his haversack and consulted them constantly throughout his campaigns. This little volume contains a fairly complete exposition, in Napoleon's own words, of the grand principles of war. They are now out of print and purchasable only in this edition of the greatest military classics.

Sun Tzu

ON THE ART OF WAR

The Oldest Military Treatise in the World
Translated from the Chinese

by

LIONEL GILES, M. A.

*Assistant in the Department of Oriental Books and
Manuscripts in the British Museum*

INTRODUCTION

Written about 500 B. C., THE ART OF WAR by Sun
Tzu is the oldest military treatise in the world. Highly
compressed, it is devoted to principles and still retains
its original value. To the military student able to adapt
its principles to modern warfare, it even now, two thousand four hundred years after its preparation, is a valuable guide for the conduct of war. Although the chariot
has gone and weapons have changed, this ancient master
holds his own, since he deals with fundamentals, with
the influence of politics and human nature on military
operations. He shows in a striking way how unchanging
these principles are.

Sun Tzü Wu, according to Ssü-ma Ch'ien, was a
native of the Ch'i state. His ART OF WAR brought
him to the notice of Ho Lu, King of Wu. Ho Lu said
to him: "I have carefully perused your thirteen chapters.
May I submit your theory to a slight test?"

Sun Tzu replied: "You may."

Ho Lu asked: "May the test be applied to women?"

The answer was again in the affirmative. So arrangements were made to bring 180 ladies out of the palace.
Sun Tzu divided them into two companies and placed
one of the King's favorite concubines at the head of
each.

He then bade them all to take spears in their hands,
and addressed them thus: "I presume you know the
difference between front and back, right hand and left

hand?" The girls replied: "Yes." Sun Tzu went on: "When I say 'Eyes front,' you must look straight ahead. When I say 'Left turn,' you must face towards your left hand. When I say 'About turn,' you must face right around towards the back." Again the girls assented.

The words of command having been thus explained, he set up the halberds and battle-axes in order to begin the drill. Then, to the sound of drums, he gave the order, "Right turn." But the girls only burst out laughing. Sun Tzu said: "If the words of command are not clear and distinct, if orders are not thoroughly understood, then the general is to blame."

So he started drilling them again, and this time gave the order, "Left turn." Whereupon the girls once more burst into fits of laughter. Sun Tzu said: "If the words of command are not clear and distinct, if orders are not thoroughly understood, the general is to blame. But if his orders *are* clear, and the soldiers nevertheless disobey, then it is the fault of their officers." So saying, he ordered the leaders of the two companies to be beheaded.

Now the King of Wu was watching the scene from the top of a raised pavilion; and when he saw that his favorite concubines were about to be executed, he was greatly alarmed and hurriedly sent down the following message: "We are now quite satisfied as to our general's ability to handle troops. If we are bereft of these two concubines, Our meat and drink will lose their savor. It is Our wish that they shall not be beheaded."

Sun Tzu replied: "Having once received His Majesty's commission to be general of his forces, there are certain commands of His Majesty which, acting in that capacity, I am unable to accept." Accordingly, he had the two ladies beheaded, and straightway installed the pair next in order as leaders in their places.

When the execution was over, the drum was sounded for the drill once more. And the girls went through all the evolutions, turning to the right or to the left, marching ahead or wheeling back, kneeling or standing, with perfect accuracy and precision, not venturing to utter a sound.

Then Sun Tzu sent a messenger to the King, saying: "Your soldiers, Sire, are now properly drilled and disciplined, and ready for Your Majesty's inspection. They can be put to any use that their sovereign may desire; bid them go through fire and water, and they will not disobey." But the King replied: "Let our general cease drilling and return to camp. As for Us, We have no wish to come down and inspect the troops."

Thereupon, Sun Tzu said: "The King is only fond of words and cannot translate them into deeds." After that Ho Lu saw that Sun Tzu was one who knew how to handle an army, and finally appointed him general. In the west he defeated the Ch'u state and forced his way into Ying, the capital. To the north, he put fear into the states of Ch'i and Chin, and spread his fame abroad amongst the feudal princes. And Sun Tzu shared the might of the king.

This narrative may be apocryphal, but Sun Tzu says in his book: "There are commands of the sovereign which must not be obeyed."

The tactics and strategy of Sun Tzu place high value on maneuver. He advises the avoidance of battle unless all considerations are favorable. Victory is won by indirect methods. The holding force and the enveloping force are the direct and indirect elements of the army. "In all fighting the direct method may be used for joining battle, but indirect methods will be needed to secure victory." And he adds that indirect tactics are as inexhaustible as Heaven and Earth, as unending as the flow of rivers and streams. "All men," he repeats, "can see the tactics whereby I conquer, but what none can see is the strategy out of which victory is evolved." The victorious strategist seeks battle after the victory has been won, while he who is destined to defeat first fights and seeks victory afterwards.

"All warfare is based on deception." When able to attack the general must seem unable; when using his forces, he should appear inactive. Tactical dispositions should mask strength with weakness. And conversely, the skillful opponent should be judged, not by appearances, but by the more precise information obtained from spies.

The five kinds of spies are listed and their use is treated in detail. Inward spies are officials of the enemy. Sun Tzu could well understand how the German aviators were able to bomb Polish headquarters every time it was moved in September, 1939. Converted spies are enemy spies who have been bought off.

Estimation and calculation are given a wholly modern place in gaining victory. Ponder and deliberate before you make a move. Sun Tzu claims he can forecast victory or defeat by the seven items of his estimate. His large attention to terrain is also in accord with modern practice. "The natural formation of the country is the soldier's best ally."

Nor does he forget the importance of discipline and the need for gaining the loyalty of his soldiers. "Regard your soldiers as your children, and they will follow you into the deepest valleys; look on them as your own beloved sons, and they will stand by you unto death." Men must be gradually led to discipline. "If soldiers are punished before they have grown attached to you, they will not prove submissive. If, when the soldiers have become attached to you, punishments are not enforced, they (the soldiers) will be useless."

No page of Sun Tzu's book can be read without finding the distilled wisdom of a great soldier written with the aphoristic distinctness of Chinese literature.

THE ART OF WAR is the greatest military classic of the Chinese. It has had innumerable commentators and has been plagiarized throughout its existence. It is held in even greater reverence in Japan than in China, where the low estate of the soldier prevented the literary recognition it warrants.

The text of the ART OF WAR has been transcribed without omission from the translation by Lionel Giles, M. A., Assistant in the Department of Oriental Books and Manuscripts in the British Museum. It was published by Luzac & Co., London, in 1910. The critical notes of the translator, which comprise the larger portion of his book, have been omitted. Other translations in English and French are lacking both in accuracy and the crystalline language which Dr. Giles has given his work. Grateful acknowledgment is made to Dr. Giles and Luzac & Co. for their generous permission to include his translation in this collection.

SUN TZU
On The
ART OF WAR

1

LAYING PLANS. Sun Tzu said: The art of war is of vital importance to the state.

It is a matter of life and death, a road either to safety or to ruin. Hence it is a subject of inquiry which can on no account be neglected.

The art of war is governed by five constant factors, to be taken into account in one's deliberations, when seeking to determine the conditions obtaining in the field.

These are: (1) The Moral Law; (2) Heaven; (3) Earth; (4) The Commander; (5) Method and Discipline.

The Moral Law causes the people to be in complete accord with their ruler, so that they will follow him regardless of their lives, undismayed by any danger.

Heaven signifies night and day, cold and heat, times and seasons.

Earth comprises distances, great and small; danger and security; open ground and narrow passes; the chances of life and death.

The Commander stands for the virtues of wisdom, sincerity, benevolence, courage and strictness.

By *Method and Discipline* are to be understood the

marshaling of the army in its proper subdivisions, the gradations of rank among the officers, the maintenance of roads by which supplies may reach the army, and the control of military expenditure.

These five heads should be familiar to every general; he who knows them will be victorious; he who knows them not will fail.

Therefore, in your deliberations, when seeking to determine the military conditions, let them be made the basis of a comparison, in this wise:

(1) Which of the two sovereigns is imbued with the Moral law?

(2) Which of the two generals has most ability?

(3) With whom lie the advantages derived from Heaven and Earth?

(4) On which side is discipline most rigorously enforced?

(5) Which army is the stronger?

(6) On which side are officers and men most highly trained?

(7) In which army is there the greater constancy both in reward and punishment?

By means of these seven considerations I can forecast victory or defeat.

The general that harkens to my counsel and acts upon it, will conquer—let such a one be retained in command! The general that harkens not to my counsel nor acts upon it, will suffer defeat—let such a one be dismissed! While heeding the profit of my counsel, avail yourself also of any helpful circumstances over and beyond the ordinary rules. According as circumstances are favorable, one should modify one's plans.

All warfare is based on deception. Hence, when able to attack, we must seem unable; when using our forces, we must seem inactive; when we are near, we must make the enemy believe that we are away; when far away, we must make him believe we are near. Hold out baits to entice the enemy. Feign disorder, and crush him.

If he is secure at all points, be prepared for him. If he is superior in strength, evade him. If your opponent is of choleric temper, seek to irritate him. Pretend to be weak, that he may grow arrogant.

If he is taking his ease, give him no rest. If his forces are united, separate them. Attack him where he is unprepared, appear where you are not expected. These military devices, leading to victory, must not be divulged beforehand.

Now the general who wins a battle makes many calculations in his temple ere the battle is fought. The general who loses a battle makes but few calculations beforehand. Thus do many calculations lead to victory, and few calculations to defeat: How much more no calculation at all! It is by attention to this point that I can see who is likely to win or lose.

2

WAGING WAR. Sun Tzu said: In the operations of war, where there are in the field a thousand swift chariots, as many heavy chariots, and a hundred thousand mail-clad soldiers, with provisions enough to carry them a thousand *li**, the expenditure at home and at the front, including entertainment of guests, small items such as glue and paint, and sums spent on chariots and armour, will reach the total of a thousand ounces of silver per day. Such is the cost of raising an army of 100,000 men.

When you engage in actual fighting, if victory is long in coming, the men's weapons will grow dull and their ardour will be damped. If you lay siege to a town, you will exhaust your strength. Again, if the campaign is protracted, the resources of the State will not be equal to the strain.

Now, when your weapons are dulled, your ardour damped, your strength exhausted and your treasure spent, other chieftains will spring up to take advantage of your extremity. Then no man, however wise, will be able to avert the consequences that must ensue.

Thus, though we have heard of stupid haste in war, cleverness has never been associated with long delays. There is no instance of a country having been benefited from prolonged warfare.

It is only one who is thoroughly acquainted with the evils of war that can thoroughly understand the profitable way of carrying it on. The skillful soldier does not raise a second levy, neither are his supply-wagons loaded more than twice. Bring war material with you from home, but forage on the enemy. Thus the army will have food enough for its needs.

Poverty of the state exchequer causes an army to be

* 2.78 modern li make one mile.

maintained by contributions from a distance. Contributing to maintain an army at a distance causes people to be impoverished.

On the other hand, the proximity of an army causes prices to go up; and high prices cause the people's substance to be drained away.

When their substance is drained away, the peasantry will be afflicted by heavy exactions.

With this loss of subsistance and exhaustion of strength, the homes of the people will be stripped bare and three-tenths of their incomes will be dissipated; while Government expenses for broken chariots, worn-out horses, breast-plates and helmets, bows and arrows, spears and shields, protective mantlets, draught-oxen and heavy wagons, will amount to four-tenths of its total revenue.

Hence a wise general makes a point of foraging on the enemy. One cartload of the enemy's provisions is equivalent to twenty of one's own, and likewise a single picul of his provender is equivalent to twenty from one's own store.

Now in order to kill the enemy, our men must be roused to anger; that there may be advantage from defeating the enemy, they must have their rewards.

Therefore in chariot fighting, when ten or more chariots have been taken, those should be rewarded who took the first. Our own flags should be substituted for those of the enemy, and the chariots mingled and used in conjunction with ours. The captured soldiers should be kindly treated and kept. This is called, using the conquered foe to augment one's own strength.

In war, then, let your great object be victory, not lengthy campaigns.

Thus it may be known that the leader of armies is the arbiter of the people's fate, the man on whom depends whether the nation shall be in peace or peril.

3

ATTACK BY STRATAGEM. Sun Tzu said: In the practical art of war, the best thing of all is to take the enemy's country whole and intact; to shatter and destroy it is not so good. So, too, it is better to capture an army entire than to destroy it, to capture a regiment, a detachment or a company entire than to destroy them.

Hence to fight and conquer in all your battles is not supreme excellence; supreme excellence consists in breaking the enemy's resistance without fighting.

Thus the highest form of generalship is to baulk the enemy's plans; the next best is to prevent the junction of the enemy's forces; the next in order is to attack the enemy's army in the field; and the worst policy of all is to besiege walled cities.

The rule is, not to besiege walled cities if it can possibly be avoided. The preparation of mantlets, movable shelters, and various implements of war, will take up three whole months; and the piling up of mounds over against the walls will take three months more.

The general, unable to control his irritation, will launch his men to the assault like swarming ants, with the result that one-third of his men are slain, while the town remains untaken. Such are the disastrous effects of a siege.

Therefore the skillful leader subdues the enemy's troops without any fighting; he captures their cities without laying siege to them; he overthrows their kingdom without lengthy operations in the field.

With his forces intact he will dispute the mastery of the Empire, and thus, without losing a man, his triumph will be complete. This is the method of attacking by stratagem.

It is the rule in war, if our forces are ten to the enemy's one, to surround him; if five to one, to attack him; if twice as numerous, to divide our army into two.

If equally matched, we can offer battle; if slightly inferior in numbers, we can avoid the enemy; if quite unequal in every way, we can flee from him. Hence, though an obstinate fight may be made by a small force, in the end it must be captured by the larger force.

Now the general is the bulwark of the state: if the bulwark is complete at all points, the state will be strong; if the bulwark is defective, the state will be weak.

There are three ways in which a ruler can bring misfortune upon his army:

(1) By commanding the army to advance or to retreat, being ignorant of the fact that it cannot obey. This is called hobbling the army.

(2) By attempting to govern an army in the same way as he administers a kingdom, being ignorant of the conditions which obtain in an army. This causes restlessness in the soldier's minds.

(3) By employing the officers of his army without discrimination, through ignorance of the military principle of adaptation to circumstances. This shakes the confidence of the soldiers.

But when the army is restless and distrustful, trouble is sure to come from other feudal princes. This is simply bringing anarchy into the army, and flinging victory away.

Thus we may know that there are five essentials for victory: (1) He will win who knows when to fight and when not to fight. (2) He will win who knows how to handle both superior and inferior forces. (3) He will win whose army is animated by the same spirit throughout all ranks. (4) He will win who, prepared himself, waits to take the enemy unprepared. (5) He will win who has military capacity and is not interfered with by the sovereign. Victory lies in the knowledge of those five points.

Hence the saying: If you know the enemy and know yourself, you need not fear the result of a hundred battles. If you know yourself but not the enemy, for every victory gained you will also suffer a defeat. If you know neither the enemy nor yourself, you will succumb in every battle.

4

TACTICAL DISPOSITIONS. Sun Tzu said: The good fighters of old, first put themselves beyond the possibility of defeat, and then waited for an opportunity of defeating the enemy.

To secure ourselves against defeat lies in our own hands, but the opportunity of defeating the enemy is provided by the enemy himself.

Thus the good fighter is able to secure himself against defeat, but cannot make certain of defeating the enemy.

Hence the saying: One may *know* how to conquer without being able to do it.

Security against defeat implies defensive tactics; ability to defeat the enemy means taking the offensive.

Standing on the defensive indicates insufficient strength; attacking, a superabundance of strength.

The general who is skilled in defense hides in the most secret recesses of the earth; he who is skilled in attack flashes forth from the topmost heights of heaven. Thus on the one hand we have ability to protect ourselves; on the other, a victory that is complete.

To see victory only when it is within the ken of the common herd is not the acme of excellence. Neither is it the acme of excellence if you fight and conquer and the whole Empire says, "Well done!"

To lift an autumn hair is no sign of great strength; to see sun and moon is no sign of sharp sight; to hear the noise of thunder is no sign of a quick ear. What the ancients called a clever fighter is one who not only wins, but excels in winning with ease.

Hence his victories bring him neither reputation for wisdom nor credit for courage. He wins his battles by making no mistakes. Making no mistakes is what establishes the certainty of victory, for it means conquering an enemy that is already defeated.

Hence the skillful fighter puts himself into a position which makes defeat impossible, and does not miss the moment for defeating the enemy.

Thus it is that in war the victorious strategist seeks battle after the victory has been won, whereas he who is destined to defeat first fights and afterwards looks for victory.

The consummate leader cultivates the moral law, and strictly adheres to method and discipline; thus it is in his power to control success.

In respect of military method, we have, firstly, Measurement; secondly, Estimation of quantity; thirdly, Calculation; fourthly, Balancing of chances; fifthly, Victory.

Measurement owes its existence to Earth; Estimation of quantity to Measurement; Calculation to Estimation of Quantity; Balancing of chances to Calculation; and Victory to Balancing of chances.

A victorious army opposed to a routed one, is as a pound's weight placed in the scale against a single grain. The onrush of a conquering force is like the bursting of pent-up waters into a chasm a thousand fathoms deep. So much for tactical dispositions.

5

ENERGY. Sun Tzu said: The control of a large force is the same in principle as the control of a few men: it is merely a question of dividing up their numbers.

Fighting with a large army under your command is nowise different from fighting with a small one: it is merely a question of instituting signs and signals.

To ensure that your whole host may withstand the brunt of the enemy's attack and remain unshaken—this is effected by maneuvers direct and indirect.

That the impact of your army may be like a grindstone dashed against an egg—that is effected by the science of weak points and strong.

In all fighting, the direct method may be used for joining battle, but indirect methods will be needed in order to secure victory.

Indirect tactics, efficiently applied, are inexhaustible as Heaven and Earth, unending as the flow of rivers and streams; like the sun and moon, they end but to begin anew; like the four seasons, they pass but to return once more.

There are not more than five musical notes, yet the combinations of these five give rise to more melodies than can ever be heard. There are not more than five primary colors, yet in combination they produce more hues than can ever be seen. There are not more than five cardinal tastes, yet combinations of them yield more flavours than can ever be tasted.

In battle, there are not more than two methods of attack—the direct and indirect; yet these two in combination give rise to an endless series of maneuvers. The direct and indirect lead on to each other in turn. It is like moving in a circle—you never come to an end. Who can exhaust the possibilities of their combination?

The onset of troops is like the rush of a torrent which will even roll stones along its course.

The quality of decision is like the well-timed swoop

of a falcon which enables it to strike and destroy its victim.

Therefore the good fighter will be terrible in his onset, and prompt in his decision.

Energy may be likened to the bending of a cross-bow; decision, to the releasing of the trigger.

Amid the turmoil and tumult of battle, there may be seeming disorder and yet no real disorder at all; amid confusion and chaos, your array may be without head or tail, yet it will be proof against defeat.

Simulated disorder postulates perfect discipline; simulated fear postulates courage; simulated weakness postulates strength.

Hiding order beneath the cloak of disorder is simply a question of subdivision; concealing courage under a show of timidity presupposes a fund of latent energy; masking strength with weakness is to be effected by tactical dispositions.

Thus one who is skillful at keeping the enemy on the move maintains deceitful appearances, according to which the enemy will act.

By holding out baits, he keeps him on the march; then with a body of picked men he lies in wait for him.

The clever combatant looks to the effect of combined energy, and does not require too much from individuals. Hence his ability to pick out the right men and to utilize combined energy.

When he utilizes combined energy, his fighting men become as it were like unto rolling logs or stones. For it is the nature of a log or stone to remain motionless on level ground, and to move when on a slope; if four cornered, to come to a standstill, but if round-shaped to go rolling down.

Thus the energy developed by good fighting men is as the momentum of a round stone rolled down a mountain thousands of feet in height. So much on the subject of energy.

6

WEAK POINTS AND STRONG. Sun Tzu said: Whoever is first in the field and awaits the coming of the enemy, will be fresh for the fight; whoever is second in the field and has to hasten to the battle, will arrive exhausted.

Therefore the clever combatant imposes his will on the enemy, but does not allow the enemy's will to be imposed on him.

By holding out advantages to him, he can cause the enemy to approach of his own accord; or by inflicting damage, he can make it impossible for the enemy to draw near.

If the enemy is taking his ease, he can harass him; if well supplied he can starve him out; if quietly encamped, he can force him to move.

Appear at points which the enemy must hasten to defend; march swiftly to places where you are not expected.

An army may march great distances without distress if it marches through country where the enemy is not.

You can be sure of succeeding in your attacks if you attack places which are not defended. You can insure the safety of your defense if you hold only positions that cannot be attacked.

Hence the general is skillful in attack whose opponent does not know what to defend; and he is skillful in defense whose opponent does not know what to attack.

O divine art of subtlety and secrecy! Through you we learn to be invisible, through you inaudible; and hence hold the enemy's fate in our hands.

You may advance and be absolutely irresistible, if you make for the enemy's weak points; you may retire and be safe from pursuit if your movements are more rapid than those of the enemy.

If we wish to fight, the enemy can be forced to an engagement even though he be sheltered behind a high rampart and a deep ditch. All we need to do is to attack some other place which he will be obliged to relieve.

If we do not wish to fight, we can prevent the enemy from engaging us even though the lines of our encampment be merely traced on the ground. All we need to do is to throw something odd and unaccountable in his way.

By discovering the enemy's dispositions and remaining invisible ourselves, we can keep our forces concentrated while the enemy must be divided.

We can form a single united body, while the enemy must split up into fractions. Hence there will be a whole pitted against separate parts of a whole, which means that we shall be many to the enemy's few.

And if we are thus able to attack an inferior force with a superior one, our opponents will be in dire straits.

The spot where we intend to fight must not be made known; for then the enemy will have to prepare against a possible attack at several different points; and his forces being thus distributed in many directions, the numbers we shall have to face at any given point will be proportionately few.

For should the enemy strengthen his van, he will weaken his rear; should he strengthen his rear, he will weaken his van; should he strengthen his left, he will weaken his right; should he strengthen his right, he will weaken his left. If he sends reinforcements everywhere, he will be everywhere weak.

Numerical weakness comes from having to prepare against possible attacks; numerical strength, from compelling our adversary to make these preparations against us.

Knowing the place and time of the coming battle, we may concentrate from great distances in order to fight.

But if neither time nor place be known, then the left wing will be impotent to succor the right, the right equally impotent to succor the left, the van unable to relieve the rear, or the rear to support the van. How much more so if the furthest portions of the army are anything under a hundred *li* apart, and even the nearest are separated by several *li*.

Though according to my estimate the soldiers of Yüeh exceed our own in number, that shall advantage them nothing in the matter of victory. I say then that victory can be achieved.

Though the enemy be stronger in numbers, we may

prevent him from fighting. Scheme so as to discover his plans and the likelihood of their success.

Rouse him, and learn the principle of his activity or inactivity. Force him to reveal himself, so as to find out his vulnerable spots.

Carefully compare the opposing army with our own, so that you may know where strength is superabundant and where it is deficient.

In making tactical dispositions, the highest pitch you can attain is to conceal them; conceal your dispositions and you will be safe from the prying of the subtlest of spies, from the machinations of the wisest brains.

How victory may be produced for them out of the enemy's own tactics—that is what the multitude cannot comprehend.

All men can see these tactics whereby I conquer, but what none can see is the strategy out of which victory is evolved.

Do not repeat the tactics which have gained you one victory, but let your methods be regulated by the infinite variety of circumstances.

Military tactics are like unto water; for water in its natural course runs away from high places and hastens downwards. So in war, the way to avoid what is strong is to strike what is weak.

Water shapes its course according to the ground over which it flows; the soldier works out his victory in relation to the foe whom he is facing.

Therefore, just as water retains no constant shape, so in warfare there are no constant conditions.

He who can modify his tactics in relation to his opponent and thereby succeed in winning, may be called a heaven-born captain.

The five elements* are not always equally prominent; the four seasons make way for each other in turn. There are short days and long; the moon has its periods of waning and waxing.

7

MANEUVERING. Sun Tzu said: In war, the general receives his commands from the sovereign.

Having collected an army and concentrated his forces, he must blend and harmonize the different elements thereof before pitching his camp.

After that, comes the tactical maneuvering, than which there is nothing more difficult. The difficulty of tactical maneuvering consists in turning the devious into the direct, and misfortune into gain.

Thus, to take a long circuitous route, after enticing the enemy out of the way, and though starting after him, to contrive to reach the goal before him, shows knowledge of the artifice of *deviation*.

Maneuvering with an army is advantageous; with an undisciplined multitude, most·dangerous.

If you set a fully equipped army in march in order to snatch an advantage, the chances are that you will be too late. On the other hand, to detach a flying column for the purpose involves the sacrifice of its baggage and stores.

---

*Water, fire, wood, metal, earth.

Thus if you order your men to roll up their buff-coats, and make forced marches without halting day or night, covering double the usual distance at a stretch, doing a hundred *li* in order to wrest an advantage, the leaders of your three divisions will fall into the hands of the enemy.

The stronger men will be in front, the jaded ones will fall behind, and on this plan only one-tenth of your army will reach its destination.

If you march fifty *li* in order to outmaneuver the enemy, you will lose the leader of your first division, and only half your force will reach its goal.

If you march thirty *li* with the same object, two-thirds of your army will arrive.

We may take it then that an army without its baggage train is lost; without provisions it is lost; without bases of supply it is lost.

We cannot enter into alliances until we are acquainted with the designs of our neighbors.

We are not fit to lead an army on the march unless we are familiar with the face of the country—its mountains and forests, its pitfalls.

We shall be unable to turn natural advantages to account unless we make use of local guides.

In war, practice dissimulation, and you will succeed. Move only if there is a real advantage to be gained.

Whether to concentrate or to divide your troops must be decided by circumstances.

Let your rapidity be that of the wind, your compactness that of the forest. In raiding and plundering be like fire, in immovability like a mountain.

Let your plans be dark and impenetrable as night and when you move, fall like a thunderbolt.

When you plunder a countryside, let the spoil be divided amongst your men; when you capture new territory, cut it up into allotments for the benefit of the soldiery.

Ponder and deliberate before you make a move.

He will conquer who has learnt the artifice of deviation. Such is the art of maneuvering.

The *Book of Army Management* says: On the field of battle the spoken word does not carry far enough: hence the institution of gongs and drums. Nor can ordinary objects be seen clearly enough: hence the institution of banners and flags.

Gongs and drums, banners and flags, are means whereby the ears and eyes of the host may be focussed on one particular point.

The host thus forming a single united body, it is impossible either for the brave to advance alone, or for the cowardly to retreat alone. This is the art of handling large masses of men.

In night-fighting, then, make much use of signal fires and drums, and in fighting by day, of flags and banners, as a means of influencing the ears and eyes of your army.

A whole army may be robbed of its spirit; a commander-in-chief may be robbed of his presence of mind.

Now a soldier's spirit is keenest in the morning; by noonday it has begun to flag; and in the evening his mind is bent only on returning to camp.

A clever general, therefore, avoids an army when its

spirit is keen, but attacks it when it is sluggish and inclined to return. This is the art of studying moods.

Disciplined and calm, to await the appearance of disorder and hubbub amongst the enemy—this is the art of retaining self possession.

To be near the goal while the enemy is still far from it, to wait at ease while the enemy is toiling and struggling, to be well fed while the enemy is famished—this is the art of husbanding one's strength.

To refrain from intercepting an enemy whose banners are in perfect order, to refrain from attacking an army drawn up in calm and confident array—this is the art of studying circumstances.

It is a military axiom not to advance uphill against the enemy, nor to oppose him when he comes downhill.

Do not pursue an enemy who simulates flight; do not attack soldiers whose temper is keen.

Do not swallow a bait offered by the enemy. Do not interfere with an army that is returning home.

When you surround an army leave an outlet free. Do not press a desperate foe too hard.

Such is the art of warfare.

8

VARIATION OF TACTICS. Sun Tzu said: In war, the general receives his commands from the sovereign, collects his army and concentrates his forces.

When in difficult country do not encamp. In country where high roads intersect join hands with your allies.

Do not linger in dangerously isolated positions. In hemmed-in situations, you must resort to stratagem. In a desperate position, you must fight.

There are roads which must not be followed, armies which must not be attacked, towns which must not be besieged, positions which must not be contested, commands of the sovereign which must not be obeyed.

The general who thoroughly understands the advantages that accompany variation of tactics knows how to handle his troops.

The general who does not understand these may be well acquainted with the configuration of the country, yet he will not be able to turn his knowledge to practical account.

So, the student of war who is unversed in the art of varying his plans, even though he be acquainted with the Five Advantages will fail to make the best use of his men.

Hence in the wise leader's plans, considerations of advantage will be blended together. If our expectation of advantage be tempered in this way, we may succeed in accomplishing the essential part of our schemes.

If, on the other hand, in the midst of difficulties we are always ready to seize an advantage, we may extricate ourselves from misfortune.

Reduce the hostile chiefs by inflicting damage on them; make trouble for them, and keep them constantly engaged; hold out specious allurements, and make them rush to any given point.

The art of war teaches us to rely not on the likelihood of the enemy's not coming, but on our own readiness to receive him; not on the chance of his not attacking, but rather on the fact that we have made our position unassailable.

There are five dangerous faults which may affect a general: (1) Recklessness, which leads to destruction; (2) cowardice, which leads to capture; (3) a hasty temper that can be provoked by insults; (4) a delicacy of honor that is sensitive to shame; (5) over-solicitude for his men, which exposes him to worry and trouble. These are the five besetting sins of a general, ruinous to the conduct of war.

When an army is overthrown and its leader slain, the cause will surely be found among the five dangerous faults. Let them be a subject of meditation.

9

THE ARMY ON THE MARCH. Sun Tzu said: We now come to the question of encamping the army, and observing signs of the enemy. Pass quickly over mountains, and keep in the neighborhood of valleys.

Camp in high places. Do not climb heights in order to fight. So much for mountain warfare.

After crossing a river, you should get far away from it.

When an invading force crosses a river in its onward march, do not advance to meet it in mid-stream. It will be best to let the army get across and then deliver your attack.

If you are anxious to fight, you should not go to meet the invader near a river which he has to cross.

Moor your craft higher up than the enemy and facing the sun. Do not move upstream to meet the enemy. So much for river warfare.

In crossing salt-marshes, your sole concern should be to get over them quickly, without any delay.

If forced to fight in a salt-marsh, you should have the water and grass near you, and get your back to a clump of trees. So much for operations in salt-marshes.

In dry, level country, take up an easily accessible position with rising ground to your right and on your rear, so that the danger may be in front, and safety lie behind. So much for campaigning in flat country.

These are the four useful branches of military knowledge which enabled the Yellow Emperor to vanquish four several sovereigns.

All armies prefer high ground to low, and sunny places to dark. If you are careful of your men, and camp on hard ground, the army will be free from disease of every kind, and this will spell victory.

When you come to a hill or a bank, occupy the sunny side, with the slope on your right rear. Thus you will at once act for the benefit of your soldiers and utilize the natural advantages of the ground.

When, in consequence of heavy rains up-country, a river which you wish to ford is swollen and flecked with foam, you must wait until it subsides. Country in which there are precipitous cliffs with torrents running between, deep natural hollows, confined places, tangled thickets, quagmires and crevasses, should be left with all possible speed and not approached.

While we keep away from such places, we should get the enemy to approach them; while we face them, we should let the enemy have them on his rear.

If in the neighborhood of your camp there should be any hilly country, ponds surrounded by aquatic grass, hollow basins filled with reeds, or woods with thick undergrowth, they must be carefully routed out and searched; for these are places where men in ambush or insidious spies are likely to be lurking.

When the enemy is close at hand and remains quiet, he is relying on the natural strength of his position.

When he keeps aloof and tries to provoke a battle, he is anxious for the other side to advance.

If his place of encampment is easy of access, he is tendering a bait.

Movement amongst the trees of a forest shows that the enemy is advancing. The appearance of a number of screens in the midst of thick grass means that the enemy wants to make us suspicious.

The rising of birds in their flight is the sign of an ambuscade. Startled beasts indicate that a sudden attack is coming.

When there is dust rising in a high column, it is the sign of chariots advancing; when the dust is low, but spread over a wide area, it betokens the approach of infantry. When it branches out in different directions, it shows that parties have been sent out to collect firewood. A few clouds of dust moving to and fro signify that the army is encamping.

Humble words and increased preparations are signs

that the enemy is about to advance. Violent language and driving forward as if to the attack are signs that he will retreat.

When the light chariots come out and take up a position on the wings, it is a sign that the enemy is forming for battle.

Peace proposals unaccompanied by a sworn covenant indicate a plot.

When there is much running about it means that the critical moment has come.

When some are seen advancing and some retreating, it is a lure.

When soldiers stand leaning on their spears, they are faint from want of food.

If those who are sent to draw water begin by drinking themselves, the army is suffering from thirst.

If the enemy sees an advantage to be gained and makes no effort to secure it, the soldiers are exhausted.

If birds gather on any spot, it is unoccupied. Clamour by night betokens nervousness.

If there is disturbance in the camp, the general's authority is weak. If the banners and flags are shifted about, sedition is afoot. If the officers are angry, it means that the men are weary.

When an army feeds its horses with grain and kills its cattle for food, and when the men do not hang their cooking pots over the camp-fires, showing that they will not return to their tents, you may know that they are determined to fight to the death.

The sight of men whispering together in small knots

and speaking in subdued tones points to dissatisfaction amongst the rank and file.

Too frequent rewards signify that the enemy is at the end of his resources; too many punishments betray a condition of dire distress.

To begin by bluster, but afterwards to take fright at the enemy's numbers, shows supreme lack of intelligence.

When convoys are sent with compliments in their mouths, it is a sign that the enemy wishes for a truce.

If the enemy's troops march up angrily and remain facing ours for a long time without either joining battle or taking themselves off again, the situation is one that demands great vigilance and circumspection.

If our troops are no more in number than the enemy, that is amply sufficient; it means that no direct attack can be made. What we can do is simply to concentrate all our available strength, keep a close watch on the enemy, and obtain reinforcements.

He who exercises no forethought but makes light of his opponents is sure to be captured by them.

If soldiers are punished before they have grown attached to you, they will not prove submissive; and, unless submissive, they will be practically useless. If, when the soldiers have become attached to you, punishments are not enforced, they will still be useless.

Therefore soldiers must be treated in the first instance with humanity, but kept under control by means of iron discipline. This is a certain road to victory.

If in training soldiers commands are habitually enforced, the army will be well disciplined.

If a general shows confidence in his men but always insists on his orders being obeyed, the gain will be mutual.

10

TERRAIN. Sun Tzu said: We may distinguish six kinds of terrain, to wit: (1) Accessible ground; (2) entangling ground; (3) temporizing ground; (4) narrow passes; (5) precipitous heights; (6) positions at a great distance from the enemy.

Ground which can be freely traversed by both sides is called *accessible*. With regard to ground of this nature, be before the enemy in occupying the raised and sunny spots, and carefully guard your line of supplies. Then you will be able to fight with advantage.

Ground which can be abandoned but is hard to reoccupy is called *entangling*. From a position of this sort, if the enemy is unprepared, you may sally forth and defeat him. But if the enemy is prepared for your coming, and you fail to defeat him, then, return being impossible, disaster will ensue.

When the position is such that neither side will gain by making the first move, it is called *temporizing* ground. In a position of this sort, even though the enemy should offer us an attractive bait, it will be advisable not to stir forth, but rather to retreat, thus enticing the enemy in his turn; then, when part of his army has come out, we may deliver our attack with advantage.

With regard to *narrow passes* if you can occupy them first, let them be strongly garrisoned and await the advent of the enemy. Should the enemy forestall you in occupying a pass, do not go after him if the pass is fully garrisoned, but only if it is weakly garrisoned.

With regard to *precipitous heights*, you should occupy the raised and sunny spots, and there wait for him to come up. If the enemy has occupied them before you, do not follow him, but retreat to entice him away.

If you are situated at a great distance from the enemy, and the strength of the two armies is equal, it is not easy to provoke a battle, and fighting will be to your disadvantage.

These six are the principles connected with Earth. The general who holds a responsible post must study them.

Now an army is exposed to six several calamities, not arising from natural causes, but from faults for which the general is responsible. These are: (1) flight; (2) insubordination; (3) collapse; (4) ruin; (5) disorganization; (6) rout.

Other conditions being equal, if one force is hurled against another ten times its size, the result will be the *flight* of the former.

When the common soldiers are too strong and their officers too weak, the result is *insubordination*. When the officers are too strong and the common soldiers too weak, the result is *collapse*.

When the higher officers are angry and insubordinate, and on meeting the enemy give battle on their own account from a feeling of resentment, before the commander-in-chief can tell whether or not he is in a position to fight, the result is *ruin*.

When the general is weak and without authority; when his orders are not clear and distinct; when there are no fixed duties assigned to officers and men, and the ranks are formed in a slovenly haphazard manner, the result is utter *disorganization.*

When a general, unable to estimate the enemy's strength, allows an inferior force to engage a larger one, or hurls a weak detachment against a powerful one, and neglects to place picked soldiers in the front rank, the result must be a *rout.*

These are six ways of courting defeat, which must be carefully noted by the general who has attained a responsible post.

The natural formation of the country is the soldier's best ally; but a power of estimating the adversary, of controlling the forces of victory, and of shrewdly calculating difficulties, dangers and distances, constitutes the test of a great general.

He who knows these things, and in fighting puts his knowledge into practice, will win his battles. He who knows them not, nor practices them, will surely be defeated.

If fighting is sure to result in victory, then you must fight, even though the ruler forbid it; if fighting will not result in victory, then you must not fight even at the ruler's bidding.

The general who advances without coveting fame and retreats without fearing disgrace, whose only thought is to protect his country and do good service for his sovereign, is the jewel of the kingdom.

Regard your soldiers as your children, and they will follow you into the deepest valleys; look on them as your own beloved sons, and they will stand by you even unto death.

If, however, you are indulgent, but unable to make your authority felt; kind-hearted but unable to enforce your commands; and incapable, moreover, of quelling disorder, then your soldiers must be likened to spoilt children; they are useless for any practical purpose.

If we know that our own men are in a condition to attack, but are unaware that the enemy is not open to attack, we have gone only halfway towards victory.

If we know that the enemy is open to attack, but are unaware that our own men are not in a condition to attack, we have gone only halfway towards victory.

If we know that the enemy is open to attack, and also know that our own men are in a condition to attack, but are unaware that the nature of the ground makes fighting impracticable, we have gone only halfway towards victory.

Hence the experienced soldier, once in motion, is never bewildered; once he has broken camp, he is never at a loss.

Hence the saying: If you know the enemy and know yourself, your victory will not stand in doubt; if you know Heaven and know Earth, you may make your victory complete.

11

THE NINE SITUATIONS. Sun Tzu said: The art of

war recognizes nine varieties of ground: (1) Dispersive ground; (2) facile ground; (3) contentious ground; (4) open ground; (5) ground of intersecting highways; (6) serious ground; (7) difficult ground; (8) hemmed-in ground; (9) desperate ground.

When a chieftain is fighting in his own territory, it is dispersive ground.

When he has penetrated into hostile territory, but to no great distance, it is facile ground.

Ground the possession of which imports great advantage to either side is contentious ground.

Ground on which each side has liberty of movement is open ground.

Ground which forms the key to three contiguous states, so that he who occupies it first has most of the Empire at his command, is ground of intersecting highways.

When an army has penetrated into the heart of a hostile country, leaving a number of fortified cities in his rear, it is serious ground.

Mountain forests, rugged steeps, marshes and fens—all country that is hard to traverse, this is difficult ground.

Ground which is reached through narrow gorges, and from which we can retire only by tortuous paths, so that a small number of the enemy would suffice to crush a large body of our men, this is hemmed-in ground.

Ground on which we can only be saved from destruction by fighting without delay, is desperate ground.

On dispersive ground, therefore, fight not. On facile ground, halt not. On contentious ground, attack not.

On open ground, do not try to block the enemy's way. On ground of intersecting highways, join hands with your allies.

On serious ground, gather in plunder.

On hemmed-in ground, resort to stratagem. On desperate ground, fight.

Those who were called skillful leaders of old knew how to drive a wedge between the enemy's front and rear; to prevent co-operation between his large and small divisions; to hinder the good troops from rescuing the bad, the officers from rallying their men.

When the enemy's men were scattered, they prevented them from concentrating; even when their forces were united, they managed to keep them in disorder.

When it was to their advantage, they made a forward move; when otherwise, they stopped still.

When asked how to cope with a great host of the enemy in orderly array and on the point of marching to the attack, I should say: "Begin by seizing something which your opponent holds dear; then he will be amenable to your will."

Rapidity is the essence of war; take advantage of the enemy's unreadiness, make your way by unexpected routes, and attack unguarded spots.

The following are the principles to be observed by an invading force: the further you penetrate into a country, the greater will be the solidarity of your troops, and thus the defenders will not prevail against you.

Make forays in fertile country in order to supply your army with food.

Carefully study the well-being of your men, and do not overtax them. Concentrate your energy and hoard your strength. Keep your army continually on the move and devise unfathomable plans.

Throw your soldiers into positions whence there is no escape, and they will prefer death to flight. Officers and men alike will put forth their uttermost strength.

Soldiers when in desperate straits lose the sense of fear. If there is no place of refuge, they will stand firm. If they are in the heart of a hostile country, they will show a stubborn front. If there is no help for it, they will fight hard.

Thus, without waiting to be marshaled, the soldiers will be constantly on the *qui vive;* without waiting to be asked, they will do your will; without restrictions, they will be faithful; without giving orders, they can be trusted.

Prohibit the taking of omens, and do away with superstitious doubts. Then, until death comes, no calamity need be feared.

If our soldiers are not overburdened with money, it is not because they have a distaste for riches; if their lives are not unduly long, it is not because they are disinclined to longevity.

On the day they are ordered out to battle, your soldiers may weep, those sitting up bedewing their garments, and those lying down letting the tears run down their cheeks. But let them once be brought to bay, and they will display the courage of a Chu or a Kuei.

The skillful tactician may be likened to the *shuai-jan.*

Now the shuai-jan is a snake that is found in the Ch'ang mountains. Strike at its head and you will be attacked by its tail; strike at its tail, and you will be attacked by its head; strike at its middle, and you will be attacked by head and tail both.

Asked if an army can be made to imitate the shuai-jan, I should answer, yes. For the men of Wu and the men of Yüeh are enemies; yet if they are crossing a river in the same boat and are caught by a storm, they will come to each other's assistance just as the left hand helps the right.

Hence it is not enough to put one's trust in the tethering of horses, and the burying of chariot wheels in the ground.

The principle on which to manage an army is to set up one standard of courage which all must reach.

How to make the best of both strong and weak—that is a question involving the proper use of ground.

Thus the skillful general conducts his army just as though he were leading a single man, willy-nilly, by the hand.

It is the business of a general to be quiet and thus ensure secrecy; upright and just, and thus maintain order.

He must be able to mystify his officers and men by false reports and appearances, and thus keep them in total ignorance.

By altering his arrangements and changing his plans, he keeps the enemy without definite knowledge. By shifting his camp and taking circuitous routes, he prevents the enemy from anticipating his purpose.

At the critical moment, the leader of an army acts like one who has climbed up a height and then kicks away the ladder behind him. He carries his men deep into hostile territory before he shows his hand.

He burns his boats and breaks his cooking pots; like a shepherd driving a flock of sheep, he drives his men this way and that, and none knows whither he is going.

To muster his host and bring it into danger:—this may be termed the business of the general.

The different measures suited to the nine varieties of ground; the expediency of aggressive or defensive tactics; and the fundamental laws of human nature, are things that must most certainly be studied.

When invading hostile territory, the general principle is, that penetrating deeply brings cohesion; penetrating but a short way means dispersion.

When you leave your own country behind, and take your army across neighbouring territory, you find yourself on critical ground. When there are means of communication on all four sides, the ground is one of intersecting highways.

When you penetrate deeply into a country, it is serious ground. When you penetrate but a little way, it is facile ground.

When you have the enemy's strongholds on your rear, and narrow passes in front, it is hemmed-in ground. When there is no place of refuge at all, it is desperate ground.

Therefore, on dispersive ground, I would inspire my men with unity of purpose. On facile ground, I would see that there is close connection between all parts of my army.

On contentious ground, I would hurry up my rear.

On open ground, I would keep a vigilant eye on my defenses. On ground of intersecting highways, I would consolidate my alliances.

On serious ground, I would try to ensure a continuous stream of supplies. On difficult ground, I would keep pushing on along the road.

On hemmed-in ground, I would block any way of retreat. On desperate ground, I would proclaim to my soldiers the hopelessness of saving their lives. For it is the soldier's disposition to offer an obstinate resistance when surrounded, to fight hard when he cannot help himself, and to obey promptly when he has fallen into danger.

We cannot enter into alliance with neighbouring princes until we are acquainted with their designs. We are not fit to lead an army on the march unless we are familiar with the face of the country—its mountains and forests, its pitfalls and precipices, its marshes and swamps. We shall be unable to turn natural advantages to account unless we make use of local guides.

To be ignorant of any one of the following four or five principles does not befit a warlike prince.

When a warlike prince attacks a powerful state, his generalship shows itself in preventing the concentration of the enemy's forces. He overawes his opponents, and their allies are prevented from joining against him.

Hence he does not strive to ally himself with all and

sundry, nor does he foster the power of other states. He carries out his own secret designs, keeping his antagonists in awe. Thus he is able to capture their cities and over-throw their kingdoms.

Bestow rewards without regard to rule, issue orders without regard to previous arrangements and you will be able to handle a whole army.

Confront your soldiers with the deed itself; never let them know your design. When the outlook is bright, bring it before their eyes; but tell them nothing when the situation is gloomy.

Place your army in deadly peril, and it will survive; plunge it into desperate straits, and it will come off in safety.

For it is precisely when a force has fallen into harm's way that it is capable of striking a blow for victory.

Success in warfare is gained by carefully accommodating ourselves to the enemy's purpose.

By persistently hanging on the enemy's flank, we shall succeed in the long run in killing the commander-in-chief. This is called ability to accomplish a thing by sheer cunning.

On the day that you take up your command, block the frontier passes, destroy the official tallies and stop the passage of all emissaries.

Be stern in the council chamber, so that you may control the situation.

If the enemy leaves a door open, you must rush in.

Forestall your opponent by seizing what he holds dear, and subtly contrive to time his arrival on the ground.

Walk in the path defined by rule, and accommodate yourself to the enemy until you can fight a decisive battle.

At first, then, exhibit the coyness of a maiden, until the enemy gives you an opening; afterwards emulate the rapidity of a running hare, and it will be too late for the enemy to oppose you.

12

THE ATTACK BY FIRE.   Sun Tzu said: There are five ways of attacking with fire. The first is to burn soldiers in their camp; the second is to burn stores; the third is to burn baggage-trains; the fourth is to burn arsenals and magazines; the fifth is to hurl dropping fire amongst the enemy.

In order to carry out an attack with fire, we must have means available; the material for raising fire should always be kept in readiness.

There is a proper season for making attacks with fire, and special days for starting a conflagration.

The proper season is when the weather is very dry; the special days are those when the moon is in the constellations of the Sieve, the Wall, the Wing or the Crossbar; for these are all days of rising wind.

In attacking with fire, one should be prepared to meet five possible developments:

(1) When fire breaks out inside the enemy's camp, respond at once with an attack from without.

(2) If there is an outbreak of fire, but the enemy's soldiers remain quiet, bide your time and do not attack.

(3) When the force of the flames has reached its height, follow it up with an attack, if that be practicable; if not stay where you are.

(4) If it is possible to make an assault with fire from without, do not wait for it to break out within, but deliver your attack at the favorable moment.

(5) When you start a fire, be to windward of it. Do not attack from the leeward.

A wind that rises in the daytime lasts long, but a night breeze soon fails.

In every army, the five developments connected with fire must be known, the movements of the stars calculated, and watch kept for the proper days.

Hence those who use fire as an aid to the attack show intelligence; those who use water as an aid to the attack gain an accession of strength.

By means of water an enemy may be intercepted but not robbed of all his belongings.

Unhappy is the fate of one who tries to win his battles and succeed in his attacks without cultivating the spirit of enterprise; for the result is waste of time and general stagnation.

Hence the saying: The enlightened ruler lays his plans well ahead; the good general cultivates his resources.

Move not unless you see an advantage; use not your troops unless there is something to be gained; fight not unless the position is critical.

No ruler should put troops into the field merely to gratify his own spleen; no general should fight a battle simply out of pique.

If it is to your advantage to make a forward move, make a forward move; if not, stay where you are.

Anger may in time change to gladness; vexation may be succeeded by content.

But a kingdom that has once been destroyed can never come again into being; nor can the dead ever be brought back to life.

Hence the enlightened ruler is heedful, and the good general full of caution. This is the way to keep a country at peace and an army intact.

13

THE USE OF SPIES.   Sun Tzu said: Raising a host of a hundred thousand men and marching them great distances entails heavy loss on the people and a drain on the resources of the state. The daily expenditure will amount to a thousand ounces of silver. There will be commotion at home and abroad, and men will drop down exhausted on the highways. As many as seven hundred thousand families will be impeded in their labor.

Hostile armies may face each other for years, striving for victory which is decided in a single day. This being so, to remain in ignorance of the enemy's condition simply because one grudges the outlay of a hundred ounces of silver in honours and emoluments, is the height of inhumanity.

One who acts thus is no leader of men, no present help to his sovereign, no master of victory.

Thus, what enables the wise sovereign and the good

general to strike and conquer, and achieve things beyond the reach of ordinary men, is *foreknowledge.*

Now this foreknowledge. cannot be elicited from spirits; it cannot be obtained inductively from experience, nor by any deductive calculation.

Knowledge of the enemy's dispositions can only be obtained from other men.

Hence the use of spies, of whom there are five classes: (1) Local spies; (2) inward spies; (3) converted spies; (4) doomed spies; (5) surviving spies.

When these five kinds of spy are all at work, none can discover the secret system. This is called "divine manipulation of the threads." It is the sovereign's most precious faculty.

Having *local spies* means employing the services of the inhabitants of a district.

Having *inward spies,* making use of officials of the enemy.

Having *converted spies,* getting hold of the enemy's spies and using them for our own purposes.

Having *doomed spies,* doing certain things openly for purposes of deception, and allowing our own spies to know of them and report them to the enemy.

Surviving spies, finally, are those who bring back news from the enemy's camp.

Hence it is that with none in the whole army are more intimate relations to be maintained than with spies. None should be more liberally rewarded. In no other business should greater secrecy be preserved. Spies cannot be usefully employed without certain intuitive sagacity.

They cannot be properly managed without benevolence and straightforwardness.

Without subtle ingenuity of mind, one cannot make certain of the truth of their reports. Be subtle! and use your spies for every kind of business.

If a secret piece of news is divulged by a spy before the time is ripe, he must be put to death together with the man to whom the secret was told.

Whether the object be to crush an army, to storm a city, or to assassinate an individual, it is always necessary to begin by finding out the names of the attendants, the aides-de-camp, the door-keepers and sentries of the general in command. Our spies must be commissioned to ascertain these.

The enemy's spies who have come to spy on us must be sought out, tempted with bribes, led away and comfortably housed. Thus they will become converted spies and available for our service.

It is through the information brought by the converted spy that we are able to acquire and employ local and inward spies.

It is owing to his information, again, that we can cause the doomed spy to carry false tidings to the enemy.

Lastly, it is by his information that the surviving spy can be used on appointed occasions.

The end and aim of spying in all its five varieties is knowledge of the enemy; and this knowledge can only be derived, in the first instance, from the converted spy. Hence it is essential that the converted spy be treated with the utmost liberality.

Of old, the rise of the Yin dynasty was due to I Chih who had served under the Hsia. Likewise, the rise of the Chou dynasty was due to Lü Ya who had served under the Yin.

Hence it is only the enlightened ruler and the wise general who will use the highest intelligence of the army for purposes of spying, and thereby they achieve great results. Spies are a most important element in war, because on them depends an army's ability to move.

The Military Institutions of the Romans

(*DE RE MILITARI*)

By Flavius Vegetius Renatus

Translated from the Latin

by

Lieutenant John Clarke

INTRODUCTION

The most influential military treatise in the western world from Roman times to the 19th Century was Vegetius' DE RE MILITARI. Its impressions on our own traditions of discipline and organization are everywhere evident.

The Austrian Field Marshal, Prince de Ligne, as late as 1770, called it a golden book and wrote: "A God, said Vegetius, inspired the legion, but for myself, I find that a God inspired Vegetius." Richard Coeur de Lion carried DE RE MILITARI everywhere with him in his campaigns, as did his father, Henry II of England. Around 1000 A. D. Vegetius was the favorite author of Foulques the Black, the able and ferocious Count of Anjou. Numerous manuscript copies of Vegetius circulated in the time of Charlemagne and one of them was considered a necessity of life by his commanders. A manuscript Vegetius was listed in the will of Count Everard de Frejus, about 837 A. D., in the time of Ludwig the Just.

In his *Memoirs*, Montecuculli, the conqueror of the Turks at St. Gotthard, wrote: "However, there are spirits bold enough to believe themselves great captains as soon as they know how to handle a horse, carry a lance at charge in a tournament, or as soon as they have read the precepts of Vegetius." Such was the reputation of Vegetius for a thousand years.

Manuscript copies dating from the 10th to the 15th

centuries are extant to the number of 150. DE RE MILITARI was translated into English, French, and Bulgarian before the invention of printing. The first printed edition was made in Utrecht in 1473. It was followed in quick succession by editions in Cologne, Paris and Rome. It was first published in English by Caxton, from an English manuscript copy, in 1489.

Flavius Vegetius Renatus was a Roman of high rank. In some manuscripts he is given the title of count. Raphael of Volterra calls him a Count of Constantinople. Little is known of his life. It is apparent from his book that he had not had extensive practical experience as a soldier. He states quite frankly that his purpose was to collect and synthesize from ancient manuscripts and regulations the military customs and wisdom that made ancient Rome great. According to his statement, his principal sources were Cato the Elder, Cornelius Celsus, Paternus, Frontinus, and the regulations and ordinances of Augustus, Trajan and Hadrian.

The Emperor Valentinian, to whom the book is dedicated, is believed to be the second emperor of that name. He evidently was not Valentinian I, since his successor, Gratian, is named in the book. Between the reign of Valentinian II and Valentinian III, Rome was taken and burned by Alaric, King of the Goths, an event that unquestionably would have been mentioned had it occurred before the book was written. Vegetius mentions the defeat of the Roman armies by the Goths, but probably refers to the battle of Adrianople where Valens, the colleague of Valentinian I, was killed.

It is a paradox that DE RE MILITARI, which was to become a military bible for innumerable generations of European soldiers, was little used by the Romans for whom it was written. The decay of the Roman armies had progressed too far to be arrested by Vegetius' pleas for a return to the virtues of discipline and courage of the ancients. At the same time Vegetius' hope for a revival of the ancient organization of the legion was impracticable. Cavalry had adopted the armor of the foot soldier and was just commencing to become the principal arm of the military forces. The heavy armed foot-soldier, formerly the backbone of the legion, was falling a victim of his own weight and immobility, and the light-armed infantry, unable to resist the shock of cavalry, was turning more and more to missile weapons. By one of the strange mutations of history, when later the cross-bow and gun-powder deprived cavalry of its shock-power, the tactics of Vegetius again became ideal for armies, as they had been in the times from which he drew his inspiration.

Vegetius unceasingly emphasized the importance of constant drill and severe discipline and this aspect of his work was very tiresome to the soldiers of the middle ages, the feudal system lending itself but poorly to discipline. "Victory in war," he states in his opening sentence, "does not depend entirely upon numbers or mere courage; only skill and discipline will insure it." His first book is devoted to the selection, training and discipline of recruits. He insists upon the utmost meticulousness in drill. "No part of drill is more essential in action than for soldiers to keep their ranks with the greatest exactness." His description of the many arms which the Roman soldier was required to become expert in reminds one of the almost innumerable duties of the present day infantryman. Recruits were to be hardened so as to be able to march twenty miles in half a summer's day at ordinary step and twenty-four miles at quick step. It was the ancient regulation that practice marches of this distance must be made three times a month.

The second book deals with the organization and officers of the legion, the ancient system of promotion, and how to form the legion for battle. We find the Romans provided for soldier's deposits, just as is done in the American army today; that guard and duty rosters were kept in those days as now; and that the Roman system of guard duty is only slightly different from our manual for interior guard duty. The field music is described and is an ornamental progenitor of that in use in United States. The legion owed its success, according to Vegetius, to its arms and its machines, as well as to the bravery of its soldiers. The legion had fifty-five ballista for throwing darts and ten onagri, drawn by oxen, for throwing stones. Every legion carried its ponton equipment, "small boats hollowed out of a single piece of timber, with long cables or chains to fasten them together." And in addition were "whatever is necessary for every kind of service, that the encampments may have all the strength and conveniences of a fortified city." Trains of workmen were provided to perform all the duties now performed by the various services in armies.

The third book deals with tactics and strategy and it was this portion of Vegetius that influenced war in the Middle Ages so greatly. He explains the use of reserves, attributing this invention to the Spartans, from whom the Romans adopted it. "It is much better to have several bodies of reserves than to extend your front too much"— an injunction as good today as when it was written. Encircling pursuit is described. The terrain is not overlooked. "The nature of the ground is often of more consequence than courage." The enemy should be estimated carefully. "It is essential to know the character of the enemy and of their principal officers—whether they be rash or cautious, enterprising or timid, whether they fight from careful calculation or from chance."

Vegetius' work is filled with maxims that have become a part of our everyday life. "He, therefore, who aspires to peace should prepare for war." "The ancients preferred discipline to numbers." "In the midst of peace, war is looked upon as an object too distant to merit consideration." "Few men are born brave; many become so through training and force of discipline."

Vegetius was a reformer who attempted to restore the degenerate Romans of the 4th Century to the military virtues of the ancients, whom he never ceases to laud. His little book was made short and easy to read, so as not to frighten, by a too arduous text, the readers whom he hoped to convince. He constantly gives the example of the "Ancients" to his contemporaries. The result is a sort of perfume of actuality, which had much to do with his success. It still is interesting reading and still is the

subject of modern commentaries. No less than forty
have appeared in Germany in the 19th and 20th centuries. *Revue Militare Generale* (France) and our own
Infantry Journal carried articles on Vegetius in 1938.
Dankfried Schenk published an interesting article in *Klio*
in 1930, which gives Vegetius the highest place among
the writers of his time.

The present edition includes the first three books of
Vegetius' work, omitting only repetitions. The fourth
and fifth books, both very brief, deal with the attack and
defense of fortified places and with naval operations.
These are of interest only to military antiquarians and for
that reason have not been included. The present translation was made by Lieutenant John Clarke and published in London in 1767. It is the best available in
English and has been edited only to the minimum extent
necessary to conform to modern usage.

An excellent discussion of Vegetius can be found in
Warfare, by Spaulding, Nickerson and Wright, page
294, et sequens, Harcourt Brace & Co., 1925. Delpech,
La Tactique au 13me Siecle, Paris, 1886, gives the best
account of the influence of Vegetius on European military thought. Hans Delbruck's discussion of Vegetius
in *Geschichte der Kriegskunft*, Vol. II, Berlin, 1921, although brief, is very acute.

PREFACE TO BOOK I

To the Emperor Valentinian

It has been an old custom for authors to offer to their Princes the fruits of their studies in belles letters, from a persuasion that no work can be published with propriety but under the auspices of the Emperor, and that the knowledge of a Prince should be more general, and of the most important kind, as its influence is felt so keenly by all his subjects. We have many instances of the favorable reception which Augustus and his illustrious successors conferred on the works presented to them; and this encouragement of the Sovereign made the sciences flourish. The consideration of Your Majesty's superior indulgence for attempts of this sort, induced me to follow this example, and makes me at the same time almost forget my own inability when compared with the ancient writers. One advantage, however, I derive from the nature of this work, as it requires no elegance of expression, or extraordinary share of genius, but only great care and fidelity in collecting and explaining, for public use, the instructions and observations of our old historians of military affairs, or those who wrote expressly concerning them.

My design in this treatise is to exhibit in some order the peculiar customs and usages of the ancients in the choice and discipline of their new levies. Nor do I presume to offer this work.to Your Majesty from a supposition that you are not acquainted with every part of its contents; but that you may see that the same salutary dispositions and regulations which your own wisdom prompts You to establish for the happiness of the Empire, were formerly observed by the founders thereof; and that Your Majesty may find with ease in this abridgement whatever is most useful on so necessary and important a subject.

BOOK I

The Selection and Training of New Levies

THE ROMAN DISCIPLINE THE CAUSE OF THEIR GREAT-
NESS. Victory in war does not depend entirely upon
numbers or mere courage; only skill and discipline will
insure it. We find that the Romans owed the conquest
of the world to no other cause than continual military
training, exact observance of discipline in their camps
and unwearied cultivation of the other arts of war. Without these, what chance would the inconsiderable numbers of the Roman armies have had against the multitudes
of the Gauls? Or with what success would their small
size have been opposed to the prodigious stature of the
Germans? The Spaniards surpassed us not only in numbers, but in physical strength. We were always inferior
to the Africans in wealth and unequal to them in deception and stratagem. And the Greeks, indisputably, were
far superior to us in skill in arts and all kinds of knowledge.

But to all these advantages the Romans opposed unusual care in the choice of their levies and in their military training. They thoroughly understood the importance of hardening them by continual practice, and of
training them to every maneuver that might happen in
the line and in action. Nor were they less strict in punishing idleness and sloth. The courage of a soldier is height-
ened by his knowledge of his profession, and he only
wants an opportunity to execute what he is convinced
he has been perfectly taught. A handful of men, inured

75

to war, proceed to certain victory, while on the contrary numerous armies of raw and undisciplined troops are but multitudes of men dragged to slaughter.

THE SELECTION OF RECRUITS. To treat our subject with some method, we shall first examine what provinces or nations are to be preferred for supplying the armies with recruits. It is certain that every country produces both brave men and cowards; but it is equally as certain that some nations are naturally more warlike than others, and that courage, as well as strength of body, depends greatly upon the influence of the different climates.

We shall next examine whether the city or the country produces the best and most capable soldiers. No one, I imagine, can doubt that the peasants are the most fit to carry arms for they from their infancy have been exposed to all kinds of weather and have been brought up to the hardest labor. They are able to endure the greatest heat of the sun, are unacquainted with the use of baths, and are strangers to the other luxuries of life. They are simple, content with little, inured to all kinds of fatigue, and prepared in some measure for a military life by their continual employment in their country-work, in handling the spade, digging trenches and carrying burdens.

In cases of necessity, however, they are sometimes obliged to make levies in the cities. And these men, as soon as enlisted, should be taught to work on entrenchments, to march in ranks, to carry heavy burdens, and to bear the sun and dust. Their meals should be coarse and moderate; they should be accustomed to lie sometimes in the open air and sometimes in tents. After this, they should be instructed in the use of their arms. And if any long expedition is planned, they should be encamped as far as possible from the temptations of the city. By these precautions their minds, as well as their bodies, will properly be prepared for the service.

I realize that in the first ages of the Republic, the Romans always raised their armies in the city itself, but this was at a time when there were no pleasures, no luxuries to enervate them. The Tiber was then their only bath, and in it they refreshed themselves after their exercises and fatigues in the field by swimming. In those days the same man was both soldier and farmer, but a farmer who, when occasion arose, laid aside his tools and put on the sword. The truth of this is confirmed by the instance of Quintius Cincinnatus, who was following the plow when they came to offer him the dictatorship. The chief strength of our armies, then, should be recruited from the country. For it is certain that the less a man is acquainted with the sweets of life, the less reason he has to be afraid of death.

THE PROPER AGE FOR RECRUITS. If we follow the ancient practice, the proper time for enlisting youth into the army is at their entrance into the age of puberty. At this time instructions of every kind are more quickly imbibed and more lastingly imprinted on the mind. Besides this, the indispensable military exercises of running and leaping must be acquired before the limbs are too much stiffened by age. For it is activity, improved by continual practice, which forms the useful and good soldier. Formerly, says Sallust, the Roman youth, as soon as they were of an age to carry arms, were trained in the strictest manner in their camps to all the fatigues and exercises of war. For it is certainly better that a soldier, perfectly disciplined, should, through emulation, repine at his not being yet arrived at a proper age for action, than have the mortification of knowing it is past. A sufficient time is also required for his instruction in the different branches of the service. It is no easy matter to train the horse or foot archer, or to form the legionary soldier to every part of the drill, to teach him not to quit his post, to keep ranks, to take a proper aim and throw his missile weapons with force, to dig trenches, to plant palisades, how to manage his shield, glance off the blows of the enemy, and how to parry a stroke with dexterity. A soldier, thus perfect in his business, so far from showing any backwardness to engage, will be eager for an opportunity of signaling himself.

THEIR SIZE. We find the ancients very fond of procuring the tallest men they could for the service, since the standard for the cavalry of the wings and for the infantry of the first legionary cohorts was fixed at six feet, or at least five feet ten inches. These requirements might easily be kept up in those times when such numbers followed the profession of arms and before it was the fashion for the flower of Roman youth to devote themselves to the civil offices of state. But when necessity requires it, the height of a man is not to be regarded so much as his strength; and for this we have the authority of Homer, who tells us that the deficiency of stature in Tydeus was amply compensated by his vigor and courage.

78

SIGNS OF DESIRABLE QUALITIES. Those employed to superintend new levies should be particularly careful in examining the features of their faces, their eyes, and the make of their limbs, to enable them to form a true judgment and choose such as are most likely to prove good soldiers. For experience assures us that there are in men, as well as in horses and dogs, certain signs by which their virtues may be discovered. The young soldier, therefore, ought to have a lively eye, should carry his head erect, his chest should be broad, his shoulders muscular and brawny, his fingers long, his arms strong, his waist small, his shape easy, his legs and feet rather nervous than fleshy. When all these marks are found in a recruit, a little height may be dispensed with, since it is of much more importance that a soldier should be strong than tall.

TRADES PROPER FOR NEW LEVIES. In choosing recruits regard should be given to their trade. Fishermen, fowlers, confectioners, weavers, and in general all whose professions more properly belong to women should, in my opinion, by no means be admitted into the service. On the contrary, smiths, carpenters, butchers, and huntsmen are the most proper to be taken into it. On the careful choice of soldiers depends the welfare of the Republic, and the very essence of the Roman Empire and its power is so inseparably connected with this charge, that it is of the highest importance not to be intrusted indiscriminately, but only to persons whose fidelity can be relied on. The ancients considered Sertorius' care in this point as one of the most eminent of his military qualifications. The soldiery to whom the defense of the Empire is consigned and in whose hands is the fortune of war, should, if possible, be of reputable families and unexceptionable in their manners. Such sentiments as may be expected in these men will make good soldiers. A sense of honor, by preventing them from behaving ill, will make them victorious.

But what good can be expected from a man by nature a coward, though ever so well disciplined or though he has served ever so many campaigns? An army raised without proper regard to the choice of its recruits was never yet made good by length of time; and we are now convinced by fatal experience that this is the source of all our misfortunes. So many defeats can only be imputed to the effects of a long peace which has made us negligent and careless in the choice of our levies and to the inclination so prevalent among the better sort in preferring the civil posts of the government to the profession of arms and to the shameful conduct of the superintendents, who, through interest or connivance, accept many men which those who are obliged to furnish substitutes for the army choose to send, and admit such men into the service as the masters themselves would not even keep for servants. Thus it appears that a trust of such importance should be committed to none but men of merit and integrity.

THE MILITARY MARK. The recruit, however, should not receive the military mark* as soon as enlisted. He must first be tried if fit for service; whether he has sufficient activity and strength; if he has capacity to learn his

---

*This mark was imprinted on the hands of the soldiers, either with a hot iron, or in some other manner. It was indelible.

duty; and whether he has the proper degree of military courage. For many, though promising enough in appearance, are found very unfit upon trial. These are to be rejected and replaced by better men; for it is not numbers, but bravery which carries the day.

After their examination, the recruits should then receive the military mark, and be taught the use of their arms by constant and daily exercise. But this essential custom has been abolished by the relaxation introduced by a long peace. We cannot now expect to find a man to teach what he never learned himself. The only method, therefore, that remains of recovering the ancient customs is by books, and by consulting the old historians. But they are of little service to us in this respect, as they only relate the exploits and events of wars, and take no notice of the objects of our present enquiries, which they considered as universally known.

INITIAL TRAINING. The first thing the soldiers are to be taught is the military step, which can only be acquired by constant practice of marching quick and together. Nor is anything of more consequence either on the march or in the line than that they should keep their ranks with the greatest exactness. For troops who march in an irregular and disorderly manner are always in great danger of being defeated. They should march with the common military step twenty miles in five summer-hours, and with the full step, which is quicker, twenty-four miles in the same number of hours. If they exceed this pace, they no longer march but run, and no certain rate can be assigned.

But the young recruits in particular must be exercised in running, in order to charge the enemy with great vigor; occupy, on occasion, an advantageous post with greater expedition, and prevent the enemy in their designs upon the same; that they may, when sent to reconnoiter, advance with speed, return with greater celerity and more easily come up with the enemy in a pursuit.

Leaping is another very necessary exercise, to enable them to pass ditches or embarrassing eminences of any kind without trouble or difficulty. There is also another very material advantage to be derived from these exercises in time of action; for a soldier who advances with his javelin,. running and leaping, dazzles the eyes of his adversary, strikes him with terror, and gives him the fatal stroke before he has time to put himself on his defense. Sallust, speaking of the excellence of Pompey the Great in these particulars, tells us that he disputed the superiority in leaping with the most active, in running with the most swift, and in exercises of strength with the most robust. Nor would he ever have been able to have opposed Sertorius with success, if he had not prepared both himself and his soldiers for action by continual exercises of this sort.

To Learn to Swim. Every young soldier, without exception, should in the summer months be taught to swim; for it is sometimes impossible to pass rivers on bridges, but the flying and pursuing army both are often obliged to swim over them. A sudden melting of snow or fall of rain often makes them overflow their banks, and in such a situation, the danger is as great from ignorance in swimming as from the enemy. The ancient Romans, therefore, perfected in every branch of the military art by a continued series of wars and perils, chose the Field of Mars as the most commodious for their exercises on account of its vicinity to the Tiber, that the youth might therein wash off the sweat and dust, and refresh themselves after their fatigues by swimming. The cavalry also as well as the infantry, and even the horses and the servants of the army should be accustomed to this exercise, as they are all equally liable to the same accidents.

THE POST-EXERCISE. We are informed by the writings of the ancients that, among their other exercises, they had that of the post. They gave their recruits round bucklers woven with willows, twice as heavy as those used on real service, and wooden swords double the weight of the common ones. They exercised them with these at the post both morning and afternoon.

This is an invention of the greatest use, not only to soldiers, but also to gladiators. No man of either profession ever distinguished himself in the circus or field of battle, who was not perfect in this kind of exercise. Every soldier, therefore, fixed a post firmly in the ground, about the height of six feet. Against this, as against a real enemy, the recruit was exercised with the above mentioned arms, as it were with the common shield and sword, sometimes aiming at the head or face, sometimes at the sides, at others endeavoring to strike at the thighs or legs. He was instructed in what manner to advance and retire, and in short how to take every advantage of his adversary; but was thus above all particularly cautioned not to lay himself open to his antagonist while aiming his stroke at him.

NOT TO CUT, BUT TO THRUST WITH THE SWORD.   They were likewise taught not to cut but to thrust with their swords. For the Romans not only made a jest of those who fought with the edge of that weapon, but always found them an easy conquest. A stroke with the edges, though made with ever so much force, seldom kills, as the vital parts of the body are defended both by the bones and armor. On the contrary, a stab, though it penetrates but two inches, is generally fatal. Besides in the attitude of striking, it is impossible to avoid exposing the right arm and side; but on the other hand, the body is covered while a thrust is given, and the adversary receives the point before he sees the sword. This was the method of fighting principally used by the Romans, and their reason for exercising recruits with arms of such a weight at first was, that when they came to carry the common ones so much lighter, the greater difference might enable them to act with greater security and alacrity in time of action.

THE DRILL CALLED ARMATURA.   The new levies also should be taught by the masters at arms the system of drill called armatura, as it is still partly kept up among us. Experience even at this time convinces us that soldiers, perfect therein, are of the most service in engagements. And they afford certain proofs of the importance and effects of discipline in the difference we see between those properly trained in this branch of drill and the other troops. The old Romans were so conscious of its usefulness that they rewarded the masters at arms with a double allowance of provision. The soldiers who were backward in this drill were punished by having their allowance in barley. Nor did they receive it as usual, in wheat, until they had, in the presence of the prefect, tribunes, or other principal officers of the legion, showed sufficient proofs of their knowledge of every part of their study.

No state can either be happy or secure that is remiss and negligent in the discipline of its troops. For it is not profusion of riches or excess of luxury that can influence our enemies to court or respect us. This can only be effected by the terror of our arms. It is an observation of Cato that misconduct in the common affairs of life may be retrieved, but that it is quite otherwise in war, where errors are fatal and without remedy, and are followed by immediate punishment. For the consequences of engaging an enemy, without skill or courage, is that part of the army is left on the field of battle, and those who remain receive such an impression from their defeat that they dare not afterwards look the enemy in the face.

THE USE OF MISSILE WEAPONS. Besides the aforementioned exercise of the recruits at the post, they were furnished with javelins of greater weight than common, which they were taught to throw at the same post. And the masters at arms were very careful to instruct them how to cast them with a proper aim and force. This practice strengthens the arm and makes the soldier a good marksman.

THE USE OF THE BOW. A third or fourth of the youngest and fittest soldiers should also be exercised at the post with bows and arrows made for that purpose only. The masters for this branch must be chosen with care and must apply themselves diligently to teach the men to hold the bow in a proper position, to bend it with strength, to keep the left hand steady. to draw the right with skill, to direct both the attention and the eye to the object, and to take their aim with equal certainty either on foot or on horseback. But this is not to be acquired without great application, nor to be retained without daily exercise and practice.

The utility of good archers in action is evidently demonstrated by Cato in his treatise on military discipline. To the institution of a body of troops of this sort Claudius owed his victory over an enemy who, till that time, had constantly been superior to him. Scipio Africanus, before his battle with the Numantines, who had made a Roman army ignominiously pass under the yoke, thought he could have no likelihood of success except by mingling a number of select archers with every century.

THE SLING. Recruits are to be taught the art of throwing stones both with the hand and sling. The inhabitants of the Balearic Islands are said to have been the inventors of slings, and to have managed them with surprising dexterity, owing to the manner of bringing up their children. The children were not allowed to have their food by their mothers till they had first struck it with their sling. Soldiers, notwithstanding their defensive armor, are often more annoyed by the round stones from the sling than by all the arrows of the enemy. Stones kill without mangling the body, and the contusion is mortal without loss of blood. It is universally known the ancients employed slingers in all their engagements. There is the greater reason for instructing all troops, without exception, in this exercise, as the sling cannot be reckoned any incumbrance, and often is of the greatest service, especially when they are obliged to engage in stony places, to defend a mountain or an eminence, or to repulse an enemy at the attack of a castle or city.

THE LOADED JAVELIN. The exercise of the loaded javelins, called martiobarbuli, must not be omitted. We formerly had two legions in Illyricum, consisting of six thousand men each, which from their extraordinary dexterity and skill in the use of these weapons were distinguished by the same appellation. They supported for a long time the weight of all the wars and distinguished themselves so remarkably that the Emperors Diocletian and Maximian on their accession honored them with the titles of Jovian and Herculean and preferred them before all the other legions. Every soldier carries five of these javelins in the hollow of his shield. And thus the legionary soldiers seem to supply the place of archers, for they wound both the men and horses of the enemy before they come within reach of the common missile weapons.

TO BE TAUGHT TO VAULT. The ancients strictly obliged both the veteran soldiers and recruits to a constant practice of vaulting. It has indeed reached our times, although little regard is paid to it at present. They had wooden horses for that purpose placed in winter under cover and in summer in the field. The young soldiers were taught to vault on them at first without arms, afterwards completely armed. And such was their attention

5

to this exercise that they were accustomed to mount and dismount on either side indifferently, with their drawn swords or lances in their hands. By assiduous practice in the leisure of peace, their cavalry was brought to such perfection of discipline that they mounted their horses in an instant even amidst the confusion of sudden and unexpected alarms.

AND TO CARRY BURDENS. To accustom soldiers to carry burdens is also an essential part of discipline. Recruits in particular should be obliged frequently to carry a weight of not less than sixty pounds (exclusive of their arms), and to march with it in the ranks. This is because on difficult expeditions they often find themselves under the necessity of carrying their provisions as well as their arms. Nor will they find this troublesome when inured to it by custom, which makes everything easy. Our troops in ancient times were a proof of this, and Virgil has remarked it in the following lines:

The Roman soldiers, bred in war's alarms,
Bending with unjust loads and heavy arms,
Cheerful their toilsome marches undergo,
And pitch their sudden camp before the foe.

THE ARMS OF THE ANCIENTS. The manner of arming the troops comes next under consideration. But the method of the ancients no longer is followed. For though after the example of the Goths, the Alans and the Huns, we have made some improvements in the arms of the cavalry, yet it is plain the infantry are entirely defenseless. From the foundation of the city till the reign of the Emperor Gratian, the foot wore cuirasses and helmets. But negligence and sloth having by degrees introduced a total relaxation of discipline, the soldiers began to think their armor too heavy, as they seldom put it on. They first requested leave from the Emperor to lay aside the cuirass and afterwards the helmet. In consequence of this, our troops in their engagements with the Goths were often overwhelmed with their showers of arrows. Nor was the necessity of obliging the infantry to resume their cuirasses and helmets discovered, notwithstanding such repeated defeats, which brought on the destruction of so many great cities.

Troops, defenseless and exposed to all the weapons of the enemy, are more disposed to fly than fight. What can be expected from a foot-archer without cuirass or helmet, who cannot hold at once his bow and shield; or from the ensigns whose bodies are naked, and who cannot at the same time carry a shield and the colors? The foot soldier finds the weight of a cuirass and even of a helmet intolerable. This is because he is so seldom exercised and rarely puts them on.

But the case would be quite different, were they even heavier than they are, if by constant practice he had been accustomed to wear them. But it seems these very men, who cannot support the weight of the ancient armor, think nothing of exposing themselves without defense to wounds and death, or, which is worse, to the shame of being made prisoners, or of betraying their country by flight; and thus to avoid an inconsiderable share of exercise and fatigue, suffer themselves ignominiously to be cut in pieces. With what propriety could the ancients call the infantry a wall, but that in some measure they resembled it by the complete armor of the legionary soldiers who had shields, helmets, cuirasses, and greaves of iron on the right leg; and the archers who had gauntlets on the left arm. These were the defensive arms of the legionary soldiers. Those who fought in the first line of their respective legions were called principes, in the second hastati, and in third triarii.

The triarii, according to their method of discipline, rested in time of action on one knee, under cover of their shields, so that in this position they might be less exposed to the darts of the enemy than if they stood upright; and also, when there was a necessity for bringing them up, that they might be fresh, in full vigor and charge with the greater impetuosity. There have been many instances of their gaining a complete victory after the entire defeat of both the principes and hastati.

The ancients had likewise a body of light infantry, slingers, and ferentarii (the light troops), who were generally posted on the wings and began the engagement. The most active and best disciplined men were selected for this service; and as their number was not very great, they easily retired in case of a repulse through the intervals of the legion, without thus occasioning the least disorder in the line.

The Pamonian leather caps worn by our soldiers were formerly introduced with a different design. The ancients obliged the men to wear them at all times so that being constantly accustomed to have the head covered they might be less sensible of the weight of the helmet.

As to the missile weapons of the infantry, they were javelins headed with a triangular sharp iron, eleven inches or a foot long, and were called piles. When once fixed in the shield it was impossible to draw them out, and when thrown with force and skill, they penetrated the cuirass without difficulty. At present they are seldom used by us, but are the principal weapon of the barbarian heavy-armed foot. They are called bebrae, and every man carries two or three of them to battle.

It must be observed that when the soldiers engage with the javelin, the left foot should be advanced, for, by this attitude the force required to throw it is considerably increased. On the contrary, when they are close enough to use their piles and swords, the right foot should be advanced, so that the body may present less aim to the enemy, and the right arm be nearer and in a more advantageous position for striking. Hence it appears that it is as necessary to provide soldiers with defensive arms of every kind as to instruct them in the use of offensive ones. For it is certain a man will fight with greater courage and confidence when he finds himself properly armed for defense.

ENTRENCHED CAMPS. Recruits are to be instructed in the manner of entrenching camps, there being no part of discipline so necessary and useful as this. For in a camp, well chosen and entrenched, the troops both day and night lie secure within their works, even though in view of the enemy. It seems to resemble a fortified city which they can build for their safety wherever they please. But this valuable art is now entirely lost, for it is long since any of our camps have been fortified either with trenches or palisades. By this neglect our forces have been often surprised by day and night by the enemy's cavalry and suffered very severe losses. The importance of this custom appears not only from the danger to which troops are perpetually exposed who encamp without such precautions, but from the distressful situation of an army that, after receiving a check in the field, finds itself without retreat and consequently at the mercy of the enemy.

A camp, especially in the neighborhood of an enemy, must be chosen with great care. Its situation should be strong by nature, and there should be plenty of wood, forage and water. If the army is to continue in it any considerable time, attention must be had to the salubrity of the place. The camp must not be commanded by any higher grounds from whence it might be insulted or annoyed by the enemy, nor must the location be liable to floods which would expose the army to great danger. The dimensions of the camps must be determined by the number of troops and quantity of baggage, that a large army may have room enough, and that a small one may not be obliged to extend itself beyond its proper ground.

The form of the camps must be determined by the site of the country, in conformity to which they must be square, triangular or oval. The Praetorian gate should either front the east or the enemy. In a temporary camp it should face the route by which the army is to march. Within this gate the tents of the first centuries or cohorts are pitched, and the dragons* and other ensigns planted.

---

* The dragon was the particular ensign of each cohort.

The Decumane gate is directly opposite to the Praetorian in the rear of the camp, and through this the soldiers are conducted to the place appointed for punishment or execution.

There are two methods of entrenching a camp. When the danger is not imminent, they carry a slight ditch round the whole circuit, only nine feet broad and seven deep. With the turf taken from this they make a kind of wall or breastwork three feet high on the inner side of the ditch. But where there is reason to be apprehensive of attempts of the enemy, the camp must be surrounded with a regular ditch twelve feet broad and nine feet deep perpendicular from the surface of the ground. A parapet is then raised on the side next the camp, of the height of four feet, with hurdles and fascines properly covered and secured by the earth taken out of the ditch. From these dimensions the interior height of the intrenchment will be found to be thirteen feet, and the breadth of the ditch twelve. On the top of the whole are planted strong palisades which the soldiers carry constantly with them for this purpose. A sufficient number of spades, pickaxes, wicker baskets and tools of all kinds are to be provided for these works.

There is no difficulty in carrying on the fortifications of a camp when no enemy is in sight. But if the enemy is near, all the cavalry and half the infantry are to be drawn up in order of battle to cover the rest of the troops at work on the entrenchments and be ready to receive the enemy if they offer to attack. The centuries are employed by turns on the work and are regularly called to the relief by a crier till the whole is completed. It is then inspected and measured by the centurions, who punish such as have been indolent or negligent. This is a very important point in the discipline of young soldiers, who when properly trained to it will be able in an emergency to fortify their camp with skill and expedition.

EVOLUTIONS. No part of drill is more essential in action than for soldiers to keep their ranks with the greatest exactness, without opening or closing too much. Troops too much crowded can never fight as they ought, and only embarrass one another. If their order is too open and loose, they give the enemy an opportunity of penetrating. Whenever this happens and they are attacked in the rear, universal disorder and confusion are inevitable. Recruits should therefore be constantly in the field, drawn up by the roll and formed at first into a single rank. They should learn to dress in a straight line and to keep an equal and just distance between man and man. They must then be ordered to double the rank, which they must perform very quickly, and instantly cover their file leaders. In the next place, they are to double again and form four deep. And then the triangle or, as it is commonly called, the wedge, a disposition found very serviceable in action. They must be taught to form the circle or orb; for well-disciplined troops, after being broken by the enemy, have thrown themselves into this position and have thereby prevented the total rout of the army. These evolutions, often practiced in the field of exercise, will be found easy in execution on actual service

MONTHLY MARCHES.   It was a constant custom among the old Romans, confirmed by the Ordinances of Augustus and Hadrian, to exercise both cavalry and infantry three times in a month by marches of a certain length. The foot were obliged to march completely armed the distance of ten miles from the camp and return, in the most exact order and with the military step which they changed and quickened on some part of the march. Their cavalry likewise, in troops and properly armed, performed the same marches and were exercised at the same time in their peculiar movement and evolutions; sometimes, as if pursuing the enemy, sometimes retreating and returning again with greater impetuosity to the charge. They made these marches not in plain and even ground only, but both cavalry and infantry were ordered into difficult and uneven places and to ascend or descend mountains, to prepare them for all kinds of accidents and familiarize them with the different maneuvers that the various situations of a country may require.

CONCLUSION.   These military maxims and instructions, invincible Emperor, as a proof of my devotion and zeal for your service, I have carefully collected from the works of all the ancient authors on the subject. My design herein is to point out the certain method of forming good and serviceable armies, which can only be accomplished by an exact imitation of the ancients in their care in the choice and discipline of their levies. Men are not degenerated in point of courage, nor are the countries that produced the Lacedaemonians, the Athenians, the Marsians, the Samnites, the Peligni and even the Romans themselves, yet exhausted. Did not the Epirots acquire in former times a great reputation in war? Did not the Macedonians and Thessalians, after conquering the Persians, penetrate even into India? And it is well known that the warlike dispositions of the Dacians, Moesians and Thracians gave rise to the fable that Mars was born among them.

To pretend to enumerate the different nations so formidable of old, all which now are subject to the Romans, would be tedious. But the security established by long peace has altered their dispositions, drawn them off from military to civil pursuits and infused into them a love of idleness and ease. Hence a relaxation of military discipline insensibly ensued, then a neglect of it, and it sunk at last into entire oblivion. Now will it appear surprising that this alteration should have happened in latter times, if we consider that the peace, which lasted about twenty years or somewhat more after the first Punic war, enervated the Romans, before everywhere victorious, by idleness and neglect of discipline to such a degree, that in the second Punic war they were not able to keep the field against Hannibal. At last, after the defeat of many consuls and the loss of many officers and armies, they were convinced that the revival of discipline was the only road to victory and thereby recovered their superiority. The necessity, therefore, of discipline cannot be too often inculcated, as well as the strict attention requisite in the choice and training of new levies. It is also certain that it is a much less expense to a state to train its own subjects to arms than to take foreigners into its pay.

PREFACE TO BOOK II

To the Emperor Valentinian

Such a continued series of victories and triumphs proved incontestably Your Majesty's full and perfect knowledge of the military discipline of the ancients. Success in any profession is the most certain mark of skill in it. By a greatness of mind above human comprehension Your Majesty condescends to seek instruction from the ancients, notwithstanding your own recent exploits surpass antiquity itself. On receiving Your Majesty's orders to continue this abridgement, not so much for your instruction as convenience, I knew not how to reconcile my devotion to Your commands with the respect due to Your Majesty. Would it not be the greatest height of presumption to pretend to mention the art of war to the Lord and Master of the world and the Conqueror of all the barbarous nations, unless it were to describe his own actions? But disobedience to the will of so great a Prince would be both highly criminal and dangerous. My obedience, therefore, made me presumptuous, from the apprehensions of appearing more so by a contrary conduct. And in this I was not a little encouraged by the late instance of Your Majesty's indulgence. My treatise on the choice and discipline of new levies met with a favorable reception from Your Majesty, and since a work succeeded so well, composed of my own accord, I can have no fears for one undertaken by your own express commands.

BOOK II

The Organization of the Legion

THE MILITARY ESTABLISHMENT. The military establishment consists of three parts, the cavalry, infantry and marine. The wings of cavalry were so called from their similitude to wings in their extension on both sides of the main body for its protection. They are now called vexillations from the kind of standards peculiar to them. The legionary horse are bodies particularly annexed to each legion, and of a different kind; and on their model were organized the cavalry called Ocreati, from the light boots they wear. The fleet consists of two divisions, the one of men of war called Liburnae, and the other of armed sloops. The cavalry are designed for plains. Fleets are employed for the protection of seas and rivers. The infantry are proper for the defense of eminences, for the garrisons of cities and are equally serviceable in plain and in uneven ground. The latter, therefore, from their facility of acting everywhere, are certainly the most useful and necessary troops to a state exclusively of the consideration of their being maintained at a less expense. The infantry are divided into two corps, the legions and auxiliaries, the latter of which are furnished by allies or confederates. The peculiar strength of the Romans always consisted in the excellent organization of their legions. They were so denominated *ab eligendo*, from the care and exactness used in the choice of the soldiers. The number of legionary troops in an army is generally much more considerable than that of the auxiliaries.

DIFFERENCE BETWEEN THE LEGIONS AND AUXILIARIES.
The Macedonians, the Greeks and the Dardanians formed
their troops into phalanxes of eight thousand men each.
The Gauls, Celtiberians and many other barbarous nations divided their armies into bodies of six thousand each.
The Romans have their legions usually six thousand
strong, sometimes more.

We shall now explain the difference between the legions
and the auxiliaries. The latter are hired corps of foreigners assembled from different parts of the Empire, made
up of different numbers, without knowledge of one another or any tie of affection. Each nation has its own
peculiar discipline, customs and manner of fighting.
Little can be expected from forces so dissimilar in every
respect, since it is one of the most essential points in military undertakings that the whole army should be put in
motion and governed by one and the same order. But it
is almost impossible for men to act in concert under such
varying and unsettled circumstances. They are, however, when properly trained and disciplined, of material
service and are always joined as light troops with the
legions in the line. And though the legions do not place
their principal dependence on them, yet they look on
them as a very considerable addition to their strength.

But the complete Roman legion, in its own peculiar
cohorts, contains within itself the heavy-armed foot, that
is: the principes, hastati, triarii, and antefignani, the light-
armed foot, consisting of the ferentarii, archers, slingers,
and balistarii, together with the legionary cavalry in-
corporated with it. These bodies, all actuated with the

same spirit, are united inseparably in their various dispositions for forming, encamping and fighting. Thus the legion is compact and perfect in all its parts and, without any foreign assistance, has always been superior to any force that could be brought against it. The Roman greatness is a proof of the excellence of their legions, for with them they always defeated whatever numbers of the enemy they thought fit, or their circumstances gave them an opportunity to engage.

CAUSES OF DECAY OF THE LEGION. The name of the legion remains indeed to this day in our armies, but its strength and substance are gone, since by the neglect of our predecessors, honors and preferments, which were formerly the recompenses of merit and long services, were to be attained only by interest and favor. Care is no longer taken to replace the soldiers, who after serving their full time, have received their discharges. The vacancies continually happening by sickness, discharges, desertion and various other casualties, if not supplied every year or even every month, must in time disable the most numerous army. Another cause of the weakness of our legions is that in them the soldiers find the duty hard, the arms heavy, the rewards distant and the discipline severe. To avoid these inconveniences, the young men enlist in the auxiliaries, where the service is less laborious and they have reason to expect more speedy recompenses.

Cato the Elder, who was often Consul and always victorious at the head of the armies, believed he should do his country more essential service by writing on military affairs, than by all his exploits in the field. For the consequences of brave actions are only temporary, while whatever is committed to writing for public good is of lasting benefit. Several others have followed his example, particularly Frontinus, whose elaborate works on this subject were so well received by the Emperor Trajan. These are the authors whose maxims and institutions I have undertaken to abridge in the most faithful and concise manner.

The expense of keeping up good or bad troops is the same; but it depends wholly on You, most August Emperor, to recover the excellent discipline of the ancients and to correct the abuses of later times. This is a reformation the advantages of which will be equally felt by ourselves and our posterity.

THE ORGANIZATION OF THE LEGION. All our writers agree that never more than two legions, besides auxiliaries, were sent under the command of each consul against the most numerous armies of the enemies. Such was the dependence on their discipline and resolution that this number was thought sufficient for any war they were engaged in. I shall therefore explain the organization of the ancient legion according to the military constitution. But if the description appear obscure or imperfect, it is not to be imputed to me, but to the difficulty of the subject itself, which is therefore to be examined with the greater attention. A prince, skilled himself in military affairs, has it in his power to make himself invincible by keeping up whatever number of well disciplined forces he thinks proper.

The recruits having thus been carefully chosen with proper attention to their persons and dispositions, and having been daily exercised for the space of four months at least, the legion is formed by the command and under the auspices of the Emperor. The military mark, which is indelible, is first imprinted on the hands of the new levies, and as their names are inserted in the roll of the legions they take the usual oath, called the military oath. They swear by God, by Christ and by the Holy Ghost; and by the Majesty of the Emperor who, after God, should be the chief object of the love and veneration of mankind. For when he has once received the title of August, his subjects are bound to pay him the most sincere devotion and homage, as the representative of God on earth. And every man, whether in a private or military station, serves God in serving him faithfully who reigns by His authority. The soldiers, therefore, swear they will obey the Emperor willingly and implicitly in all his commands, that they will never desert and will always be ready to sacrifice their lives for the Roman Empire.

The legion should consist of ten cohorts, the first of which exceeds the others both in number and quality of its soldiers, who are selected to serve in it as men of some family and education. This cohort has the care of the eagle, the chief ensign in the Roman armies and the standard of the whole legion, as well as of the images of the emperors which are always considered as sacred. It consists of eleven hundred and five foot and one hundred and thirty-two horse cuirassiers, and is distinguished by the name of the Millarian Cohort. It is the head of the legion and is always first formed on the right of the first line when the legion draws up in order of battle.

The second cohort contains five hundred and fifty-five foot and sixty-six horse, and is called the Quingentarian Cohort. The third is composed of five hundred and fifty-five foot and sixty-six horse, generally chosen men, on account of its situation in the center of the first line. The fourth consists of the same number of five hundred and fifty-five foot and sixty-six horse. The fifth has likewise five hundred and fifty-five foot and sixty-six horse, which should be some of the best men, being posted on the left flank as the first cohort is on the right. These five cohorts compose the first line.

The sixth includes five hundred and fifty-five foot and sixty-six horse, which should be the flower of the young soldiers as it draws up in the rear of the eagle and the images of the emperors, and on the right of the second line. The seventh contains five hundred and fifty-five foot and sixty-six horse. The eighth is composed of five hundred and fifty-five foot and sixty-six horse, all selected troops, as it occupies the center of the second line. The ninth has five hundred and fifty-five foot and sixty-six horse. The tenth consists of the same number of five hundred and fifty-five foot and sixty-six horse and requires good men, as it closes the left flank of the second line. These ten cohorts form the complete legions, consisting in the whole of six thousand one hundred foot and seven hundred and twenty-six horses. A legion should never be composed of a less number of men, but it is sometimes stronger by the addition of other Millarian Cohorts.

THE OFFICERS OF THE LEGION.   Having shown the ancient establishment of the legion, we shall now explain the names of the principal soldiers or, to use the proper term, the officers, and their ranks according to the present rolls of the legions.   The first tribune is appointed by the express commission and choice of the Emperor.   The second tribune rises to that rank by length of service. The tribunes are so called from their command over the soldiers, who were at first levied by Romulus out of the different tribes.   The officers who in action commanded the orders or divisions are called Ordinarii.   The Augustales were added by Augustus to the Ordinarii; and the Flaviales were appointed by Flavius Vespasian to double the number of the Augustales.   The eagle-bearers and the image-bearers are those who carry the eagles and images of the Emperors.   The Optiones are subaltern officers, so denominated from their being selected by the option of their superior officers, to do their duty as their substitutes or lieutenants in case of sickness or other accident.   The ensign-bearers carry the ensigns and are called Draconarii. The Tesserarii deliver the parole and the orders of the general to the different messes of the soldiers.   The Campignei or Antefignani are those whose duty it is to keep the proper exercises and discipline among the troops. The Metatores are ordered before the army to fix on the ground for its encampments.   The Beneficiarii are so named from their owing their promotion to the benefit or interest of the Tribunes.   The Librarii keep the legionary accounts.   The Tubicines, Cornicines, and Buccinatores derive their appellations from blowing the trumpet, cornet, and buccina. Those who, expert in their exercises, receive a double allowance of provisions, are called Armaturae Duplares, and those who have but a single portion, Simplares. The Mensores mark out the ground by measure for the tents in an encampment, and assign the troops their respective quarters in garrison. The Torquati, so denominated from the gold collars given them in reward for their bravery, had besides this honor different allowances. Those who received double were called Torquati Duplares, and those who had only single, Simplares. There were, for the same reason, Candidatii Duplares, and Candidatii Simplares. These are the principal soldiers or officers distinguished by their rank and privileges thereto annexed. The rest are called Munifices, or working soldiers, from their being obliged to every kind of military work without exception.

Formerly it was the rule that the first Princeps of the legion should be promoted regularly to the rank of Centurion of the Primiple. He not only was entrusted with the eagle but commanded four centuries, that is, four hundred men in the first line. As head of the legion he had appointments of great honor and profit. The first Hastatus had the command of two centuries or two hundred men in the second line, and is now called Ducenarius. The Princeps of the first cohort commanded a century and a half, that is, one hundred and fifty men, and kept in a great measure the general detail of the legion. The second Hastatus had likewise a century and a half, or one hundred and fifty men. The first Triarius had the command of one hundred men. Thus the ten centuries of the first cohort were commanded by five Ordinarii, who by the ancient establishment enjoyed great honors and emoluments that were annexed to this rank in order to inspire the soldiers of the legions with emulation to attain such ample and considerable rewards. They had also Centurions appointed to each century, now called Centenarii and Decani, who commanded ten men, now called heads of messes. The second cohort had five Centurions; and all the rest to the tenth inclusively the same number. In the whole legion there were fifty-five.

Lieutenants of consular dignity were formerly sent to command in the armies under the general, and their authority extended over both the legions and auxiliaries in peace and war. Instead of these officers, persons of high rank are now substituted with the title of Masters of the Forces. They are not limited to the command of two legions only, but have often a greater number. But the peculiar officer of the legion was the Praefect, who was always a count of the first order. On him the chief command devolved in the absence of the lieutenant. The Tribunes, Centurions, and all the soldiers in general were under his orders. He gave out the parole and order for the march and for the guards. And if a soldier committed a crime, by his authority the Tribune adjudged him to punishment. He had charge of the arms, horses, clothing and provisions. It was also his duty to keep both the legionary horse and foot in daily exercise and to maintain the strictest discipline. He ought to be a careful and diligent officer, as the sole charge of forming the legion to regularity and obedience depended on him and the excellence of the soldiers redounded entirely to his own honor and credit.

The Praefect of the camp, though inferior in rank to the former, had a post of no small importance. The position of the camp, the direction of the entrenchments, the inspection of the tents or huts of the soldiers and the baggage were comprehended in his province. His authority extended over the sick, and the physicians who had the care of them; and he regulated the expenses relative thereto. He had the charge of providing carriages, bat-horses and the proper tools for sawing and cutting wood, digging trenches, raising parapets, sinking wells and bringing water into the camp. He likewise had the care of furnishing the troops with wood and straw, as well as the rams, onagri, balistae and all the other engines of war under his direction. This post was always conferred on an officer of great skill, experience and long service, and who consequently was capable of instructing others in those branches of the profession in which he had distinguished himself.

THE PRAEFECT OF THE WORKMEN. The legion had a train of joiners, masons, carpenters, smiths, painters, and workmen of every kind for the construction of barracks in the winter-camps and for making or repairing the wooden towers, arms, carriages and the various sorts of machines and engines for the attack or defense of places. They had also traveling workshops in which they made shields, cuirasses, helmets, bows, arrows, javelins and offensive and defensive arms of all kinds. The ancients made it their chief care to have every thing for the service of the army within the camp. They even had a body of miners who, by working under ground and piercing the foundations of walls, according to the practice of the Beffi, penetrated into the body of a place. All these were under the direction of the officer called the praefect of the workmen.

THE TRIBUNE OF THE SOLDIERS. We have observed that the legions had ten cohorts, the first of which, called the Millarian Cohort, was composed of men selected on account of their circumstances, birth, education, person and bravery. The tribune who commanded them was likewise distinguished for his skill in his exercises, for the advantages of his person and the integrity of his manners. The other cohorts were commanded, according to the Emperor's pleasure, either by tribunes or other officers commissioned for that purpose. In former times the discipline was so strict that the tribunes or officers above-mentioned not only caused the troops under their command to be exercised daily in their presence, but were themselves so perfect in their military exercises as to set them the example. Nothing does so much honor to the abilities or application of the tribune as the appearance and discipline of the soldiers, when their apparel is neat and clean, their arms bright and in good order and when they perform their exercises and evolutions with dexterity.

CENTURIES AND ENSIGNS OF THE FOOT. The chief ensign of the whole legion is the eagle and is carried by the eagle-bearer. Each cohort has also its own peculiar ensign, the Dragon, carried by the Draconarius. The ancients, knowing the ranks were easily disordered in the confusion of action, divided the cohorts into centuries and gave each century an ensign inscribed with the number both of the cohort and century so that the men keeping it in sight might be prevented from separating from their comrades in the greatest tumults. Besides the centurions, now called centenarii, were distinguished by different crests on their helmets, to be more easily known by the soldiers of their respective centuries. These precautions prevented any mistake, as every century was guided not only by its own ensign but likewise by the peculiar form of the helmet of its commanding officers. The centuries were also subdivided into messes of ten men each who lay in the same tent and were under orders and inspection of a Decanus or head of the mess. These messes were also called Maniples from their constant custom of fighting together in the same company or division.

LEGIONARY TROOPS OF HORSE. As the divisions of the infantry are called centuries, so those of the cavalry are called troops. A troop consists of thirty-two men and is commanded by a Decurion. Every century has its ensign and every troop its standard. The centurion in the infantry is chosen for his size, strength and dexterity in throwing his missile weapons and for his skill in the use of his sword and shield; in short for his expertness in all the exercises. He is to be vigilant, temperate, active and readier to execute the orders he receives than to talk; strict in exercising and keeping up proper discipline among his soldiers, in obliging them to appear clean and well-dressed and to have their arms constantly rubbed and bright. In like manner the Decurion is to be preferred to the command of a troop for his activity and address in mounting his horse completely armed; for his skill in riding and in the use of the lance and bow; for his attention in forming his men to all the evolutions of the cavalry; and for his care in obliging them to keep their cuirasses, lances and helmets always bright and in good order. The splendor of the arms has no inconsiderable effect in striking terror into an enemy. Can that man be reckoned a good soldier who through negligence suffers his arms to be spoiled by dirt and rust?   In short, it is the duty of the Decurion to be attentive to whatever concerns the health or discipline of the men or horses in his troop.

DRAWING UP A LEGION IN ORDER OF BATTLE. We shall exemplify the manner of drawing up an army in order of battle in the instance of one legion, which may serve for any number. The cavalry are posted on the wings. The infantry begin to form on a line with the first cohort on the right. The second cohort draws up on the left of the first; the third occupies the center; the fourth is posted next; and the fifth closes the left flank. The ordinarii, the other officers and the soldiers of the first line, ranged before and round the ensigns, were called the principes. They were all heavy armed troops and had helmets, cuirasses, greaves, and shields. Their offensive weapons were large swords, called spathae, and smaller ones called semispathae together with five loaded javelins in the concavity of the shield, which they threw at the first charge. They had likewise two other javelins, the largest of which was composed of a staff five feet and a half long and a triangular head of iron nine inches long. This was formerly called the pilum, but now it is known by the name of spiculum. The soldiers were particularly exercised in the use of this weapon, because when thrown with force and skill it often penetrated the shields of the foot and the cuirasses of the horse. The other javelin was of smaller size; its triangular point was only five inches long and the staff three feet and one half. It was anciently called verriculum but now verutum.

The first line, as I said before, was composed of the principes; the hastati formed the second and were armed in the same manner. In the second line the sixth cohort was posted on the right flank, with the seventh on its left; the eighth drew up in the center; the ninth was the next; and the tenth always closed the left flank. In the rear of these two lines were the ferentarii, light infantry and the troops armed with shields, loaded javelins, swords and common missile weapons, much in the same manner as our modern soldiers. This was also the post of the archers who had helmets, cuirasses, swords, bows and arrows; of the slingers who threw stones with the common sling or with the fustibalus; and of the tragularii who annoyed the enemy with arrows from the manubalistae or arcubalistae.

In the rear of all the lines, the triarii, completely armed, were drawn up. They had shields, cuirasses, helmets, greaves, swords, daggers, loaded javelins, and two of the common missile weapons. They rested during the action on one knee, so that if the first lines were obliged to give way, they might be fresh when brought up to the charge, and thereby retrieve what was lost and recover the victory.   All the ensigns though, of the infantry, wore cuirasses of a smaller sort and covered their helmets with the shaggy skins of beasts to make themselves appear more terrible to the enemy. But the centurions had complete cuirasses, shields, and helmets of iron, the crest of which, placed transversely thereon, were ornamented with silver that they might be more easily distinguished by their respective soldiers.

The following disposition deserves the greatest attention. In the beginning of an engagement, the first and second lines remained immovable on their ground, and the trairii in their usual positions.   The light-armed troops, composed as above mentioned, advanced in the front of the line, and attacked the enemy. If they could make them give way, they pursued them; but if they were repulsed by superior bravery or numbers, they retired behind their own heavy armed infantry, which appeared like a wall of iron and renewed the action, at first with their missile weapons, then sword in hand. If they broke the enemy they never pursued them, least they should break their ranks or throw the line into confusion, and lest the enemy, taking advantage of their disorder, should return to the attack and destroy them without difficulty. The pursuit therefore was entirely left to the light-armed troops and the cavalry. By these precautions and dispositions the legion was victorious without danger, or if the contrary happened, was preserved without any considerable loss, for as it is not calculated for pursuit, it is likewise not easily thrown into disorder.

NAMES OF SOLDIERS INSCRIBED ON THEIR SHIELDS. Lest the soldiers in the confusion of battle should be separated from their comrades, every cohort had its shields painted in a manner peculiar to itself. The name of each soldier was also written on his shield, together with the number of the cohort and century to which he belonged. From this description we may compare the legion, when in proper order, to a well fortified city as containing within itself every thing requisite in war, wherever it moved. It was secure from any sudden attempt or surprise of an enemy by its expeditious method of entrenching its camp even in the open plains and it was always provided with troops and arms of every kind.

To be victorious, therefore, over our enemies in the field, we must unanimously supplicate heaven to dispose the Emperor to reform the abuses in raising our levies and to recruit our legions after the method of the ancients. The same care in choosing and instructing our young soldiers in all military exercises and drills will soon make them equal to the old Roman troops who subdued the whole world. Nor let this alteration and loss of ancient discipline in any way affect Your Majesty, since it is a happiness reserved for You alone both to restore the ancient ordinances and establish new ones for the public welfare. Every work before the attempt carries in it an appearance of difficulty; but in this case, if the levies are made by careful and experienced officers, an army may be raised, disciplined and rendered fit for service in a very short time; for the necessary expenses once provided, diligence soon effects whatever it undertakes.

RECORDS AND ACCOUNTS. Several posts in the legion requiring men of some education, the superintendents of the levies should select some recruits for their skill in writing and accounts, besides the qualification to be attended to in general, such as size, strength and proper disposition for the service. For the whole detail of the legion, including the lists of the soldiers exempted from duty on private accounts, the rosters for their tour of military duties and their pay lists, is daily entered in the legionary books and kept we may almost say, with greater exactness than the regulations of provisions or other civil matters in the registers of the police. The daily guards in time of peace, the advanced guards and outposts in time of war, which are mounted regularly by the centuries and messes in their turns, are likewise punctually kept in rolls for that purpose, with the name of each soldier whose tour is past, that no one may have injustice done him or be excused from his duty by favor.

They are also exact in entering the time and limitation of furloughs, which formerly were never granted without difficulty and only on real and urgent business. They then never suffered the soldiers to attend on any private person or to concern themselves in private occupations, thinking it absurd and improper that the Emperor's soldiers, clothed and subsisted at the public expense, should follow any other profession. Some soldiers, however, were allowed for the service of the praefects, tribunes and even of the other officers, out of the number of the accensi or such as were raised after the legion was complete. These latter are now called supernumeraries. The regular troops were obliged to carry their wood, hay, water and straw into the camp themselves. From such kind of services they were called munifices.

SOLDIER'S DEPOSITS. The institution of the ancients which obliged the soldiers to deposit half of every donative they received at the colors was wise and judicious; the intent was to preserve it for their use so that they might not squander it in extravagance or idle expense. For most men, particularly the poorer sort, soon spend whatever they can get. A reserve of this kind therefore is evidently of the greatest service to the soldiers themselves; since they are maintained at the public expense, their military stock by this method is continually increasing. The soldier who knows all his fortune is deposited at his colors, entertains no thoughts of desertion, conceives a greater affection for them and fights with greater intrepidity in their defense. He is also prompted thereto by interest, the most prevailing consideration among men. This money was contained in ten bags, one for each cohort. There was an eleventh bag also for a small contribution from the whole legion, as a common fund to defray the expense of burial of any of their deceased comrades. These collections were kept in baskets in the custody of the ensigns, chosen for their integrity and capacity, and answerable for the trust and obliged to account with every man for his own proportion.

PROMOTION IN THE LEGION. Heaven certainly inspired the Romans with the organization of the legion, so superior does it seem to human invention. Such is the arrangement and disposition of the ten cohorts that compose it, as to appear one perfect body and form one complete whole. A soldier, as he advances in rank, proceeds as it were by rotation through the different degrees of the several cohorts in such a manner that one who is promoted passes from the first cohort to the tenth, and returns again regularly through all the others with a continual increase of rank and pay to the first. Thus the centurion of the primiple, after having commanded in the different ranks of every cohort, attains that great dignity in the first with infinite advantages from the whole legion. The chief praefect of the Praetorian Guards rises by the same method of rotation to that lucrative and honorable rank. Thus the legionary horse contract an affection for the foot of their own cohorts, notwithstanding the natural antipathy existing between the two corps. And this connection establishes a reciprocal attachment and union between all the cohorts and the cavalry and infantry of the legion.

LEGIONARY MUSIC. The music of the legion consists of trumpets, cornets and buccinae. The trumpet sounds the charge and the retreat. The cornets are used only to regulate the motions of the colors; the trumpets serve when the soldiers are ordered out to any work without the colors; but in time of action, the trumpets and cornets sound together. The classicum, which is a particular sound of the buccina or horn, is appropriated to the commander-in-chief and is used in the presence of the general, or at the execution of a soldier, as a mark of its being done by his authority. The ordinary guards and outposts are always mounted and relieved by the sound of trumpet, which also directs the motions of the soldiers on working parties and on field days. The cornets sound whenever the colors are to be struck or planted. These rules must be punctually observed in all exercises and reviews so that the soldiers may be ready to obey them in action without hesitation according to the general's orders either to charge or halt, to pursue the enemy or to retire. For reason will convince us that what is necessary to be performed in the heat of action should constantly be practiced in the leisure of peace.

THE DRILLING OF THE TROOPS. The organization of the legion being thus explained, let us return to the drills. The younger soldiers and recruits went through their drills of every kind every morning and afternoon and the veterans and most expert regularly once a day. Length of service or age alone will never form a military man, for after serving many years an undisciplined soldier is still a novice in his profession. Not only those under the masters at arms, but all the soldiers in general, were formerly trained incessantly in those drills which now are only exhibited as shows in the circus for particular solemnities. By practice only can be acquired agility of body and the skill requisite to engage an enemy with advantage, especially in close fight. But the most essential point of all is to teach soldiers to keep their ranks and never abandon their colors in the most difficult evolutions. Men thus trained are never at a loss amidst the greatest confusion of numbers.

The recruits likewise are to be exercised with wooden swords at the post, to be taught to attack this imaginary antagonist on all sides and to aim at the sides, feet or head, both with the point and edge of the sword. They must be instructed how to spring forward to give the blow, to rise with a bound above the shield and then to sink down and shelter themselves under cover of it, and how to advance and retire. They must also throw their javelins at the post from a considerable distance in order to acquire a good aim and strengthen the arm.

The archers and slingers set up bundles of twigs or straw for marks, and generally strike them with arrows and with stones from the fustiablus at the distance of six hundred feet. They acquired coolness and exactness in action from familiar custom and exercise in the field. The slingers should be taught to whirl the sling but once about the head before they cast the stone. Formerly all soldiers were trained to the practice of throwing stones of a pound weight with the hand, as this was thought a readier method since it did not require a sling. The use of the common missile weapons and loaded javelins was another part of the drill strictly attended to.

To continue this drill without interruption during the winter, they erected for the cavalry porticos or riding halls covered with tiles or shingles, and if they were not to be procured, with reeds, rushes or thatch. Large open halls were likewise constructed in the same manner for the use of the infantry. By these means the troops were provided with places of drill sheltered from bad weather. But even in winter, if it did not rain or snow, they were obliged to perform their drills in the field, lest an intermission of discipline should affect both the courage and constitution of the soldier. In short, both legionary and auxiliary troops should continually be drilled in cutting wood, carrying burdens, passing ditches, swimming in the sea or in rivers, marching in the full step and even running with their arms and baggage, so that, inured to labor in peace, they may find no difficulty in war. For, as the well trained soldier is eager for action, so does the untaught fear it. In war discipline is superior to strength; but if that discipline is neglected, there is no longer any difference between the soldier and the peasant. The old maxim is certain that the very essence of an art consists in constant practice.

MACHINES AND TOOLS OF THE LEGION. The legion owes its success to its arms and machines, as well as to the number and bravery of its soldiers. In the first place every century has a balista mounted on a carriage drawn by mules and served by a mess, that is by ten men from the century to which it belongs. The larger these engines are, the greater distance they carry and with the greater force. They are used not only to defend the entrenchments of camps, but are also placed in the field in the rear of the heavy armed infantry. And such is the violence with which they throw the darts that neither the cuirasses of the horse nor shields of the foot can resist them. The number of these engines in a legion is fifty-five. Besides these are ten onagri, one for each cohort;

they are drawn ready armed on carriages by oxen; in case of an attack, they defend the works of the camp by throwing stones as the balistae do darts.

The legion carries with it a number of small boats, each hollowed out of a single piece of timber, with long cables and sometimes iron chains to fasten them together. These boats, joined and covered with planks, serve as bridges over unfordable rivers, on which both cavalry and infantry pass without danger. The legion is provided with iron hooks, called wolves, and iron scythes fixed to the ends of long poles; and with forks, spades, shovels, pickaxes, wheelbarrows and baskets for digging and transporting earth; together with hatchets, axes and saws for cutting wood. Besides which, a train of workmen attend on it furnished with all instruments necessary for the construction of tortoises, musculi, rams, vines, moving towers and other machines for the attack of places. As the enumeration of all the particulars of this sort would be too tedious, I shall only observe that the legion should carry with it wherever it moves, whatever is necessary for every kind of service so that the encampments may have all the strength and conveniences of a fortified city.

PREFACE TO BOOK III

To the Emperor Valentinian

The Athenians and Lacedaemonians were masters of Greece before the Macedonians, as history informs us. The Athenians excelled not only in war but in other arts and sciences. The Lacedaemonians made war their chief study. They are affirmed to be the first who reasoned on the events of battles and committed their observations thereon to writing with such success as to reduce the military art, before considered as totally dependent on courage or fortune, to certain rules and fixed principles. As a consequence they established schools of tactics for the instruction of youth in all the maneuvers of war. How worthy of admiration are these people for particularly applying themselves to the study of an art, without which no other art can possibly exist. The Romans followed their example, and both practiced their institutions in their armies and preserved them in their writings. These are the maxims and instructions dispersed through the works of different authors, which Your Majesty has ordered me to abridge, since the perusal of the whole would be too tedious, and the authority of only a part unsatisfactory. The effect of the Lacedaemonian skill in dispositions for general actions appears evidently in the single instance of Xantippus, who assisted the Carthaginians after the repeated ruin of their armies. And merely superior skill and conduct defeated Attilius Regulus at the head of a Roman army, till that time always victorious. Xantippus took him prisoner and thus terminated the war by a single action. Hannibal, also, before he set out on his expedition into Italy, chose a Lacedaemonian for his counsellor in military operations; and by his advice, though inferior to the Romans both in number and strength, overthrew so many consuls and such mighty legions. He, therefore, who desires peace, should prepare for war. He who aspires to victory, should spare no pains to form his soldiers. And he who hopes for success, should fight on principle, not chance. No one dares to offend or insult a power of known superiority in action.

BOOK III

Dispositions for Action

THE NUMBER WHICH SHOULD COMPOSE AN ARMY. The first book treats of the choice and exercises of new levies; the second explains the establishment of the legion and the method of discipline; and the third contains the dispositions for action. By this methodical progression, the following instructions on general actions and means of victory will be better understood and of greater use.

By an army is meant a number of troops, legions and auxiliaries, cavalry and infantry, assembled to make war. This number is limited by judges of the profession. The defeats of Xerxes, Darius, Mithridates and other monarchs who brought innumerable multitudes into the field, plainly show that the destruction of such prodigious armies is owing more to their own numbers than to the bravery of their enemies. An army too numerous is subject to many dangers and inconveniences. Its bulk makes it slow and unwieldy in its motions; and as it is obliged to march in columns of great length, it is exposed to the risk of being continually harassed and insulted by inconsiderable parties of the enemy. The incumbrance of the baggage is often an occasion of its being surprised in its passage through difficult places or over rivers. The difficulty of providing forage for such numbers of horses and other beasts of burden is very great. Besides, scarcity of provisions, which is to be carefully guarded against in all expeditions, soon ruins such large armies where the consumption is so prodigious, that notwithstanding the greatest care in filling the magazines they must begin to fail in a short time. And sometimes they unavoidably will be distressed for want of water. But, if unfortunately this immense army should be defeated, the numbers lost must necessarily be very great, and the remainder, who save themselves by flight, too much dispirited to be brought again to action.

The ancients, taught by experience, preferred discipline to numbers. In wars of lesser importance they thought one legion with auxiliaries, that is, ten thousand foot and two thousand horse, sufficient. And they often gave the command to a praeter as to a general of the second rank. When the preparations of the enemy were formidable, they sent a general of consular dignity with twenty thousand foot and four thousand horse. In our times this command was given to a count of the first order. But when there happened any dangerous insurrection supported by infinite multitudes of fierce and barbarous nations, on such emergencies they took the field with two armies under two consuls, who were charged, both singly and jointly, to take care to preserve the Republic from danger. In short, by this management, the Romans, almost continually engaged in war with different nations in different parts of the world, found themselves able to oppose them in every quarter. The excellence of their discipline made their small armies sufficient to encounter all their enemies with success. But it was an invariable rule in their armies that the number of allies or auxiliaries should never exceed that of the Roman citizens.

MEANS OF PRESERVING IT IN HEALTH. The next article is of the greatest importance: the means of preserving the health of the troops. This depends on the choice of situation and water, on the season of the year, medicine, and exercise. As to the situation, the army should never continue in the neighborhood of unwholesome marshes any length of time, or on dry plains or eminences without some sort of shade or shelter. In the summer, the troops should never encamp without tents. And their marches, in that season of the year when the heat is excessive, should begin by break of day so that they may arrive at the place of destination in good time. Otherwise they will contract diseases from the heat of the weather and the fatigue of the march. In severe winter they should never march in the night in frost and snow, or be exposed to want of wood or clothes. A soldier, starved with cold, can neither be healthy nor fit for service. The water must be wholesome and not marshy. Bad water is a kind of poison and the cause of epidemic distempers.

It is the duty of the officers of the legion, of the tribunes, and even of the commander-in-chief himself, to take care that the sick soldiers are supplied with proper diet and diligently attended by the physicians. For little can be expected from men who have both the enemy and diseases to struggle with. However, the best judges of the service have always been of the opinion that daily practice of the military exercises is much more efficacious towards the health of an army than all the art of medicine. For this reason they exercised their infantry without intermission. If it rained or snowed, they performed under cover; and in fine weather, in the field. They also were assiduous in exercising their cavalry, not only in plains, but also on uneven ground, broken and cut with ditches. The horses as well as the men were thus trained, both on the above mentioned account and to prepare them for action. Hence we may perceive the importance and necessity of a strict observance of the military exercises in an army, since health in the camp and victory in the field depend on them. If a numerous army continues long in one place in the summer or in the autumn, the waters become corrupt and the air infected. Malignant and fatal distempers proceed from this and can be avoided only by frequent changes of encampments.

CARE TO PROVIDE FORAGE AND PROVISIONS. Famine makes greater havoc in an army than the enemy, and is more terrible than the sword. Time and opportunity may help to retrieve other misfortunes, but where forage and provisions have not been carefully provided, the evil is without remedy. The main and principal point in war is to secure plenty of provisions and to destroy the enemy by famine. An exact calculation must therefore be made before the commencement of the war as to the number of troops and the expenses incident thereto, so that the provinces may in plenty of time furnish the forage, corn, and all other kinds of provisions demanded of them to be transported. They must be in more than sufficient quantity, and gathered into the strongest and most convenient cities before the opening of the campaign. If the provinces cannot raise their

quotas in kind, they must commute for them in money
to be employed in procuring all things requisite for the
service. For the possessions of the subjects cannot be
kept secure otherwise than by the defense of arms.

These precautions often become doubly necessary as
a siege is sometimes protracted beyond expectation, the
besiegers resolving to suffer themselves all the inconveniences of want sooner than raise the siege, if they have
any hopes of reducing the place by famine. Edicts should
be issued out requiring the country people to convey
their cattle, grain, wine and all kinds of provisions that
may be of service to the enemy, into garrisoned fortresses
or into the safest cities. And if they do not comply with
the order, proper officers are to appointed to compel
them to do it. The inhabitants of the province must
likewise be obliged to retire with their effects into some
fortified place before the irruption of the enemy. The
fortifications and all the machines of different kinds must
also be examined and repaired in time. For if you are
once surprised by the enemy before you are in a proper
posture of defense, you are thrown into irrecoverable
confusion, and you can no longer draw any assistance
from the neighboring places, all communication with
them being cut off. But a faithful management of the
magazines and a frugal distribution of the provisions,
with proper precautions taken at first, will insure sufficient plenty. When provisions once begin to fail, parsimony is ill-timed and comes too late.

On difficult expeditions the ancients distributed the
provisions at a fixed allowance to each man without dis-

tinction of rank; and when the emergency was past, the government accounted for the full proportions. The troops should never want wood and forage in winter or water in summer. They should have corn, wine, vinegar, and even salt, in plenty at all times. Cities and fortresses are garrisoned by such men as are least fit for the service of the field. They are provided with all sorts of arms, arrows, fustibali, slings, stones, onagri and balistae for their defense. Great caution is requisite that the unsuspecting simplicity of the inhabitants be not imposed on by the treachery or perjury of the enemy, for pretended conferences and deceitful appearance of truces have often been more fatal than force. By observing the foregoing precautions, the besieged may have it in their power to ruin the enemy by famine, if he keeps his troops together, and if he divides their, by frequent sallies and surprises.

METHODS TO PREVENT MUTINY IN AN ARMY. An army drawn together from different parts sometimes is disposed to mutiny. And the troops, though not inclined to fight, pretend to be angry at not being led against the enemy. Such seditious dispositions principally show themselves in those who have lived in their quarters in idleness and effeminacy. These men, unaccustomed to the necessary fatigue of the field, are disgusted at its severity. Their ignorance of discipline makes them afraid of action and inspires them with insolence.

There are several remedies for this evil. While the troops are yet separated and each corps continues in its respective quarters, let the tribunes, their lieutenants and the officers in general, make it their business to keep up so strict a discipline as to leave them no room to harbor any thoughts but of submission and obedience. Let them be constantly employed either in field days or in the inspection of their arms. They should not be allowed to be absent on furlough. They should be frequently called by roll and trained to be exact in the observance of every signal. Let them be exercised in the use of the bow, in throwing missile weapons and stones, both with the hand and sling, and with the wooden sword at the post; let all this be continually repeated and let them be often kept under arms till they are tired. Let them be exercised in running and leaping to facilitate the passing of ditches. And if their quarters are near the sea or a river, let them all, without exception, be obliged in the summer to have the frequent practice of swimming. Let them be accustomed to march through thickets, inclosures and broken grounds, to fell trees and cut out timber, to break ground and to defend a post against their comrades who are to endeavor to dispossess them; and in the encounter each party should use their shields to dislodge and bear down their antagonists. All the different kinds of troops thus trained and exercised in their quarters will find themselves inspired with emulation for glory and eagerness for action when they come to take the field. In short, a soldier who has proper confidence in his own skill and strength, entertains no thought of mutiny.

A general should be attentive to discover the turbulent and seditious soldiers in the army, legions or auxiliaries, cavalry or infantry. He should endeavor to procure his intelligence not from informers, but from the tribunes, their lieutenants and other officers of undoubted veracity. It would then be prudent in him to separate them from the rest under pretence of some service agreeable to them, or detach them to garrison cities or castles, but with such address that though he wants to get rid of them, they may think themselves employed by preference and favor. A multitude never broke out into open sedition at once and with unanimous consent. They are prepared and excited by some few mutineers, who hope to secure impunity for their crimes by the number of their associates. But if the height of the mutiny requires violent remedies, it will be most advisable, after the manner of the ancients, to punish the ring-leaders only in order that, though few suffer, all may be terrified by the example. But it is much more to the credit of a general to form his troops to submission and obedience by habit and discipline than to be obliged to force them to their duty by the terror of punishment.

MARCHES IN THE NEIGHBORHOOD OF THE ENEMY. It is asserted by those who have made the profession their study that an army is exposed to more danger on marches than in battles. In an engagement the men are properly armed, they see their enemies before them and come prepared to fight. But on a march the soldier is less on his guard, has not his arms always ready and is thrown into disorder by a sudden attack or ambuscade. A general, therefore, cannot be too careful and diligent in taking necessary precautions to prevent a surprise on the march and in making proper dispositions to repulse the enemy, in case of such accident, without loss.

In the first place, he should have an exact description of the country that is the seat of war, in which the distances of places specified by the number of miles, the nature of the roads, the shortest routes, by-roads, mountains and rivers, should be correctly inserted. We are told that the greatest generals have carried their precautions on this head so far that, not satisfied with the simple description of the country wherein they were engaged, they caused plans to be taken of it on the spot, that they might regulate their marches by the eye with greater safety. A general should also inform himself of all these particulars from persons of sense and reputation well acquainted with the country by examining them separately at first, and then comparing their accounts in order to come at the truth with certainty.

If any difficulty arises about the choice of roads, he should procure proper and skillful guides. He should put them under a guard and spare neither promises nor threat to induce them to be faithful. They will acquit themselves well when they know it is impossible to escape and are certain of being rewarded for their fidelity or punished for their perfidy. He must be sure of their capacity and experience, that the whole army be not brought into danger by the errors of two or three persons. For sometimes the common sort of people imagine they know what they really do not, and through ignorance promise more than they can perform.

But of all precautions the most important is to keep entirely secret which way or by what route the army is to march. For the security of an expedition depends on the concealment of all motions from the enemy. The figure of the Minotaur was anciently among the legionary ensigns, signifying that this monster, according to the fable, was concealed in the most secret recesses and windings of the labyrinth, just as the designs of a general should always be impenetrable. When the enemy has no intimation of a march, it is made with security; but as sometimes the scouts either suspect or discover the decampment, or traitors or deserters give intelligence thereof, it will be proper to mention the method of acting in case of an attack on the march.

The general, before he puts his troops in motion, should send out detachments of trusty and experienced soldiers well mounted, to reconnoiter the places through which he is to march, in front, in rear, and on the right and left, lest he should fall into ambuscades. The night is safer and more advantageous for your spies to do their business in than day, for if they are taken prisoners, you have, as it were, betrayed yourself. After this, the cavalry should march off first, then the infantry; the baggage, bat horses, servants and carriages follow in the center; and part of the best cavalry and infantry come in the rear, since it is oftener attacked on a march than the front. The flanks of the baggage, exposed to frequent ambuscades, must also be covered with a sufficient guard to secure them. But above all, the part where the enemy is most expected must be reinforced with some of the best cavalry, light infantry and foot archers.

If surrounded on all sides by the enemy, you must make dispositions to receive them wherever they come, and the soldiers should be cautioned beforehand to keep their arms in their hands, and to be ready in order to prevent the bad effects of a sudden attack. Men are frightened and thrown into disorder by sudden accidents and surprises of no consequence when foreseen. The ancients were very careful that the servants or followers of the army, if wounded or frightened by the noise of the action, might not disorder the troops while engaged, and also to prevent their either straggling or crowding one another too much, which might incommode their own men and give advantage to the enemy. They ranged the baggage, therefore, in the same manner as the regular troops under particular ensigns. They selected from among the servants the most proper and experienced and gave them the command of a number of servants and boys, not exceeding two hundred, and their ensigns directed them where to assemble the baggage. Proper intervals should always be kept between the baggage and the troops, that the latter may not be embarrassed for want of room in case of an attack during the march.

The manner and disposition of defense must be varied according to the difference of ground. In an open country you are more liable to be attacked by horse than foot. But in a woody, mountainous or marshy situation, the danger to be apprehended is from foot. Some of the divisions being apt through negligence to move too fast, and others too slow, great care is to be taken to prevent the army from being broken or from running into too great a length, as the enemy would instantly take advantage of the neglect and penetrate without difficulty.

The tribunes, their lieutenants or the masters at arms of most experience, must therefore be posted at proper distances, in order to halt those who advance too fast and quicken such as move too slow. The men at too great a distance in the front, on the appearance of an enemy, are more disposed to fly than to join their comrades. And those too far behind, destitute of assistance, fall a sacrifice to the enemy and their own despair. The enemy, it may be concluded, will either plant ambuscades or make his attack by open force, according to the advantage of the ground. Circumspection in examining every place will be a security against concealed danger; and an ambuscade, if discovered and promptly surrounded, will return the intended mischief with interest.

If the enemy prepare to fall upon you by open force in a mountainous country, detachments must be sent forward to occupy the highest eminences, so that on their arrival they may not dare to attack you under such a disadvantage of ground, your troops being posted so much above them and presenting a front ready for their reception. It is better to send men forward with hatchets and other tools in order to open ways that are narrow but safe, without regard to the labor, rather than to run any risk in the finest roads. It is necessary to be well acquainted whether the enemy usually make their attempts in the night, at break of day or in the hours of refreshment or rest; and by knowledge of their customs to guard against what we find their general practice. We must also inform ourselves whether they are strongest in infantry or cavalry; whether their cavalry is chiefly armed with lances or with bows; and whether their principal strength consists in their numbers or the excellence of their arms. All of this will enable us to take the most proper measures to distress them and for our advantage.

When we have a design in view, we must consider whether it will be most advisable to begin the march by day or by night; we must calculate the distance of the places we want to reach; and take such precautions that in summer the troops may not suffer for want of water on their march, nor be obstructed in winter by impassable morasses or torrents, as these would expose the army to great danger before it could arrive at the place of its destination. As it highly concerns us to guard against these inconveniences with prudence, so it would be inexcusible not to take advantage of an enemy that fell into them through ignorance or negligence. Our spies should be constantly abroad; we should spare no pains in tampering with their men, and give all manner of encouragement to deserters. By these means we may get intelligence of their present or future designs. And we should constantly keep in readiness some detachments of cavalry and light infantry, to fall upon them when they least expect it, either on the march, or when foraging or marauding.

PASSAGES OF RIVERS. The passages of rivers are very dangerous without great precaution. In crossing broad or rapid streams, the baggage, servants, and sometimes the most indolent soldiers are in danger of being lost. Having first sounded the ford, two lines of the best mounted cavalry are ranged at a convenient distance entirely across the river, so that the infantry and baggage may pass between them. The line above the ford breaks the violence of the stream, and the line below recovers and transports the men carried away by the current. When the river is too deep to be forded either by the cavalry or infantry, the water is drawn off, if it runs in a plain, by cutting a great number of trenches, and thus it is passed with ease.

Navigable rivers are passed by means of piles driven into the bottom and floored with planks; or in a sudden emergency by fastening together a number of empty casks and covering them with boards. The cavalry, throwing off their accoutrements, make small floats of dry reeds or rushes on which they lay their rams and cuirasses to preserve them from being wet. They themselves swim their horses across the river and draw the floats after them by a leather thong.

But the most commodious invention is that of the small boats hollowed out of one piece of timber and very light both by their make and the quality of the wood. The army always has a number of these boats upon carriages, together with a sufficient quantity of planks and iron nails. Thus with the help of cables to lash the boats together, a bridge is instantly constructed, which for the time has the solidity of a bridge of stone.

As the enemy generally endeavor to fall upon an army at the passage of a river either by surprise or ambuscade, it is necessary to secure both sides thereof by strong detachments so that the troops may not be attacked and defeated while separated by the channel of the river. But it is still safer to palisade both the posts, since this will enable you to sustain any attempt without much loss. If the bridge is wanted, not only for the present transportation of the troops but also for their return and for convoys, it will be proper to throw up works with large ditches to cover each head of the bridge, with a sufficient number of men to defend them as long as the circumstances of affairs require.

RULES FOR ENCAMPING AN ARMY.   An army on the march cannot expect always to find walled cities for quarters, and it is very imprudent and dangerous to encamp in a straggling manner without some sort of entrenchment. It is an easy matter to surprise troops while refreshing themselves or dispersed in the different occupations of the service. The darkness of night, the necessity of sleep and the dispersion of the horses at pasture afford opportunities of surprise. A good situation for a camp is not sufficient; we must choose the very best that can be found lest, having failed to occupy a more advantageous post, the enemy should get possession of it to our great detriment.

An army should not encamp in summer near bad waters or far from good ones, nor in winter in a situation without plenty of forage and wood. The camp should not be liable to sudden inundations. The avenues should not be too steep and narrow lest, if invested, the troops should find it difficult to make their retreat; nor should it be commanded by any eminences from which it may be annoyed by the enemy's weapons. After these precautions, the camp is formed square, round, triangular or oblong, according to the nature of the ground. For the form of a camp does not constitute its goodness. Those camps, however, are thought best where the length is one third more than the depth. The dimensions must be exactly computed by the engineers, so that the size of the camp may be proportioned to the number of troops. A camp which is too confined will not permit the troops to perform their movements with freedom, and one which is too extensive divides them too much.

There are three methods of entrenching a camp. The first is for the case when the army is on the march and will continue in the camp for only one night. They then throw up a slight parapet of turf and plant it with a row of palisades or caltrops* of wood. The sods are cut with iron instruments. If the earth is held strongly together by the roots of the grass, they are cut in the form of a brick a foot and one half high, a foot broad and a foot and one half long. If the earth is so loose that the turf cannot be cut in this form, they run a slight trench round the camp, five feet broad and three feet deep. The earth taken from the trench forms a parapet on the inside and this secures the army from danger. This is the second method.

But permanent camps, either for summer or winter, in the neighborhood of an enemy, are fortified with greater care and regularity. After the ground is marked out by the proper officers, each century receives a certain number of feet to entrench. They then range their shields

---

* An instrument with four points so designed that when any three of them are on the ground the fourth projects upward. These are extensively used today for antitank barriers.

and baggage in a circle about their own colors and, without other arms than their swords, open a trench nine, eleven or thirteen feet broad. Or, if they are under great apprehensions of the enemy, they enlarge it to seventeen feet (it being a general rule to observe odd numbers). Within this they construct a rampart with fascines or branches of trees well fastened together with pickets, so that the earth may be better supported. Upon this rampart they raise a parapet with battlements as in the fortifications of a city. The centurions measure the work with rods ten feet long and examine whether every one has properly completed the proportion assigned to him. The tribunes likewise inspect the work and should not leave the place till the whole is finished. And that the workmen may not be suddenly interrupted by the enemy, all the cavalry and that part of the infantry exempted by the privilege of their rank from working, remain in order of battle before the entrenchment to be ready to repel any assault.

The first thing to be done after entrenching the camp, is to plant the ensigns, held by the soldiers in the highest veneration and respect, in their proper places. After this the praetorium is prepared for the general and his lieutenants, and the tents pitched for the tribunes, who have soldiers particularly appointed for that service and to fetch their water, wood, and forage. Then the legions and auxiliaries, cavalry and infantry, have the ground distributed to them to pitch their tents according to the rank of the several corps. Four foot-soldiers of each century and four troopers of each troop are on guard every night. As it seemed impossible for a sentinel to remain a whole night on his post, the watches were divided by the hourglass into four parts, that each man might stand only three hours. All guards are mounted by the sound of trumpet and relieved by the sound of cornet. The tribunes choose proper and trusty men to visit the different posts and report to them whatever they find amiss. This is now a military office and the persons appointed to it are called officers of the rounds.

The cavalry furnish the grand guards at night and the outposts by day. They are relieved every morning and afternoon because of the fatigue of the men and horses. It is particularly incumbent upon the general to provide for the protection of the pastures and of the convoys of grain and other provisions either in camp or garrison, and to secure wood, water and forage against the incursions of the enemy. This can only be effected by posting detachments advantageously in the cities or walled castles on the roads along which the convoys advance. And if no ancient fortifications are to be met with, small forts must be built in proper situations, surrounded with large ditches, for the reception of detachments of horse and foot, so that the convoys will be effectually protected. For an enemy will hardly venture far into a country where he knows his adversary's troops are so disposed as to be ready to encompass him on all sides.

MOTIVES FOR THE PLAN OF OPERATIONS OF A CAMPAIGN. Readers of this military abridgement will perhaps be impatient for instructions relative to general engagements. But they should consider that a battle is commonly decided in two or three hours, after which no further hopes are left for the worsted army. Every plan, therefore, is to be considered, every expedient tried and every method taken before matters are brought to this last extremity. Good officers decline general engagements where the danger is common, and prefer the employment of stratagem and finesse to destroy the enemy as much as possible in detail and intimidate them without exposing our own forces.

I shall insert some necessary instructions on this head collected from the ancients. It is the duty and interest of the general frequently to assemble the most prudent and experienced officers of the different corps of the army and consult with them on the state both of his own and the enemy's forces. All overconfidence, as most pernicious in its consequences, must be banished from the deliberations. He must examine which has the superiority in numbers, whether his or the adversary's troops are best armed, which are in the best condition, best disciplined and most resolute in emergencies. The state of the cavalry of both armies must be inquired into, but more especially that of the infantry, for the main strength of an army consists of the latter. With respect to the cavalry, he must endeavor to find out in which are the greatest numbers of archers or of troopers armed with lances, which has the most cuirassiers and which the best horses. Lastly he must consider the field of battle and to judge whether the ground is more advantageous for him or his enemy. If strongest in cavalry, we should prefer plains and open ground; if superior in infantry, we should choose a situation full of enclosures, ditches, morasses and woods, and sometimes mountainous. Plenty or scarcity in either army are considerations of no small importance, for famine, according to the common proverb, is an internal enemy that makes more havoc than the sword.

But the most material article is to determine whether it is most proper to temporize or to bring the affair to a speedy decision by action. The enemy sometimes expect an expedition will soon be over; and if it is protracted to any length, his troops are either consumed by want, induced to return home by the desire of seeing their families or, having done nothing considerable in the field, disperse themselves from despair of success. Thus numbers, tired out with fatigue and disgusted with the service, desert, others betray them and many surrender themselves. Fidelity is seldom found in troops disheartened by misfortunes. And in such case an army which was numerous on taking the field insensibly dwindles away to nothing.

It is essential to know the character of the enemy and of their principal officers—whether they be rash or cautious, enterprising or timid, whether they fight on principle or from chance and whether the nations they have been engaged with were brave or cowardly.

We must know how far to depend upon the fidelity and strength of auxiliaries, how the enemy's troops and our own are affected and which appear most confident of success, a consideration of great effect in raising or depressing the courage of an army. A harangue from the general, especially if he seems under no apprehension himself, may reanimate the soldiers if dejected. Their spirits revive if any considerable advantage is gained either by stratagem or otherwise, if the fortune of the enemy begins to change or if you can contrive to beat some of their weak or poorly-armed detachments.

But you must by no means venture to lead an irresolute or diffident army to a general engagement. The difference is great whether your troops are raw or veterans, whether inured to war by recent service or for some years unemployed. For soldiers unused to fighting for a length of time must be considered in the same light as recruits. As soon as the legions, auxiliaries and cavalry are assembled from their several quarters, it is the duty of a good general to have every corps instructed separately in every part of the drill by tribunes of known capacity chosen for that purpose. He should afterwards form them into one body and train them in all the maneuvers of the line as for a general action. He must frequently drill them himself to try their skill and strength, and to see whether they perform their evolutions with proper regularity and are sufficiently attentive to the sound of the trumpets, the motions of the colors and to his own orders and signals. If deficient in any of these particulars, they must be instructed and exercised till perfect.

But though thoroughly disciplined and complete in their field exercises, in the use of the bow and javelin, and in the evolutions of the line, it is not advisable to lead them rashly or immediately to battle. A favorable opportunity must be watched for, and they must first be prepared by frequent skirmishes and slight encounters. Thus a vigilant and prudent general will carefully weigh in his council the state of his own forces and of those of the enemy, just as a civil magistrate judging between two contending parties. If he finds himself in many respects superior to his adversary, he must by no means defer bringing on an engagement. But if he knows himself inferior, he must avoid general actions and endeavor to succeed by surprises, ambuscades and stratagems. These, when skillfully managed by good generals, have often given them the victory over enemies superior both in numbers and strength.

How to Manage Raw and Undisciplined Troops. All arts and trades whatever are brought to perfection by continual practice. How much more should this maxim, true in inconsiderable matters, be observed in affairs of importance! And how much superior to all others is the art of war, by which our liberties are preserved, our dignities perpetuated and the provinces and the whole Empire itself exist. The Lacedaemonians, and after them the Romans, were so aware of this truth that to this science they sacrificed all others. And the barbarous nations even at this day think only this art worth attention, believing it includes or confers everything else. In short, it is indispensably necessary for those engaged in war not only to instruct them in the means of preserving their own lives, but how to gain the victory over their enemies.

A commander-in-chief therefore, whose power and dignity are so great and to whose fidelity and bravery the fortunes of his countrymen, the defense of their cities, the lives of the soldiers, and the glory of the state, are entrusted, should not only consult the good of the army in general, but extend his care to every private soldier in it. For when any misfortunes happen to those under his command, they are considered as public losses and imputed entirely to his misconduct. If therefore he finds his army composed of raw troops or if they have long been unaccustomed to fighting, he must carefully study the strength, the spirit, the manners of each particular legion, and of each body of auxiliaries, cavalry and infantry. He must know, if possible, the name and capacity óf every count, tribune, subaltern and soldier. He must assume the most respectable authority and maintain it by severity. He must punish all military crimes with the greatest rigor of the laws. He must have the character of being inexorable towards offenders and endeavor to give public examples thereof in different places and on different occasions.

Having once firmly established these regulations, he must watch the opportunity when the enemy, dispersed in search of plunder, think themselves in security, and attack them with detachments of tried cavalry or infantry, intermingled with young soldiers, or such as are under the military age. The veterans will acquire fresh experience and the others will be inspired with courage by the advantages such opportunities will give him. He should form ambuscades with the greatest secrecy to surprise the enemy at the passages of rivers, in the rugged passes of mountains, in defiles in woods and when embarrassed by morasses or difficult roads. He should regulate his march so as to fall upon them while taking their refreshments or sleeping, or at a time when they suspect no dangers and are dispersed, unarmed and their horses unsaddled. He should continue these kinds of encounters till his soldiers have imbibed a proper confidence in themselves. For troops that have never been in action or have not for some time been used to such spectacles, are greatly shocked at the sight of the wounded and dying; and the impressions of fear they receive dispose them rather to fly than fight.

If the enemy makes excursions or expeditions, the general should attack him after the fatigue of a long march, fall upon him unexpectedly, or harass his rear. He should detach parties to endeavor to carry off by surprise any quarters established at a distance from the hostile army for the convenience of forage or provisions. For such measures should be pursued at first as can produce no very bad effects if they should happen to miscarry, but would be of great advantage if attended with success. A prudent general will also try to sow dissention among his adversaries, for no nation, though ever so weak in itself can be completely ruined by its enemies unless its fall be facilitated by its own distraction. In civil dissensions men are so intent on the destruction of their private enemies that they are entirely regardless of the public safety.

One maxim must be remembered throughout this work: that no one should ever despair of effecting what has been already performed. It may be said that our troops for many years past have not even fortified their permanent camps with ditches, ramparts or palisades. The answer is plain. If those precautions had been taken, our armies would never have suffered by surprises of the enemy both by day and night. The Persians, after the example of the old Romans, surround their camps with ditches and, as the ground in their country is generally sandy, they always carry with them empty bags to fill with the sand taken out of the trenches and raise a parapet by piling them one on the other. All the barbarous nations range their carriages round them in a circle, a method which bears some resemblance to a fortified camp. They thus pass their nights secure from surprise.

Are we afraid of not being able to learn from others what they before have learned from us? At present all this is to be found in books only, although formerly constantly practiced. Inquiries are now no longer made about customs that have been so long neglected, because in the midst of peace, war is looked upon as an object too distant to merit consideration. But former instances will convince us that the reestablishment of ancient discipline is by no means impossible, although now so totally lost.

In former ages the art of war, often neglected and forgotten, was as often recovered from books and reestablished by the authority and attention of our generals. Our armies in Spain, when Scipio Africanus took the command, were in bad order and had often been beaten under preceding generals. He soon reformed them by severe discipline and obliged them to undergo the greatest fatigue in the different military works, reproaching them that since they would not wet their hands with the blood of their enemies, they should soil them with the mud of the trenches. In short, with these very troops he afterwards took the city of Numantia and burned it to the ground with such destruction of its inhabitants that not one escaped. In Africa an army, which under the command of Albinus had been forced to pass under the yoke, was by Metellus brought into such order and discipline, by forming it on the ancient model, that they afterwards vanquished those very enemies who had subjected them to that ignominious treatment. The Cimbri defeated the legions of Caepio, Manilus and Silanus in Gaul, but Marius collected their shattered remnants and disciplined them so effectually that he destroyed an innumerable multitude of the Cimbri, Teutones and Ambrones in one general engagement. Nevertheless it is easier to form young soldiers and inspire them with proper notions of honor than to reanimate troops who have been once disheartened.

PREPARATIONS FOR A GENERAL ENGAGEMENT. Having explained the less considerable branches of the art of war, the order of military affairs naturally leads us to the general engagement. This is a conjuncture full of uncertainty and fatal to kingdoms and nations, for in the decision of a pitched battle consists the fulness of victory. This eventuality above all others requires the exertion of all the abilities of a general, as his good conduct on such an occasion gains him greater glory, or his dangers expose him to greater danger and disgrace. This is the moment in which his talents, skill and experience show themselves in their fullest extent.

Formerly to enable the soldiers to charge with greater vigor, it was customary to order them a moderate refreshment of food before an engagement, so that their strength might be the better supported during a long conflict. When the army is to march out of a camp or city in the presence of their enemies drawn up and ready for action, great precaution must be observed lest they should be attacked as they defile from the gates and be cut to pieces in detail. Proper measures must therefore be taken so that the whole army may be clear of the gates and form in order of battle before the enemy's approach. If they are ready before you can have quitted the place, your design of marching out must either be deferred till another opportunity or at least dissembled, so that when they begin to insult you on the supposition that you dare not appear, or think of nothing but plundering or returning and no longer keep their ranks, you may sally out and fall upon them while in confusion and surprise.

Troops must never be engaged in a general action immediately after a long march, when the men are fatigued and the horses tired. The strength required for action is spent in the toil of the march. What can a soldier do who charges when out of breath? The ancients carefully avoided this inconvenience, but in later times some of our Roman generals, to say nothing more, have lost their armies by unskillfully neglecting this precaution. Two armies, one tired and spent, the other fresh and in full vigor, are by no means an equal match.

THE SENTIMENTS OF THE TROOPS SHOULD BE DETERMINED BEFORE BATTLE. It is necessary to know the sentiments of the soldiers on the day of an engagement. Their confidence or apprehensions are easily discovered by their looks, their words, their actions and their motions. No great dependence is to be placed on the eagerness of young soldiers for action, for fighting has something agreeable in the idea to those who are strangers to it. On the other hand, it would be wrong to hazard an engagement, if the old experienced soldiers testify to a disinclination to fight. A general, however, may encourage and animate his troops by proper exhortations and harangues, especially if by his account of the approaching action he can persuade them into the belief of an easy victory. With this view, he should lay before them the cowardice or unskillfulness of their enemies and remind them of any former advantages they may have gained over them. He should employ every argument capable of exciting rage, hatred and indignation against the adversaries in the minds of his soldiers.

It is natural for men in general to be affected with some sensations of fear at the beginning of an engagement, but there are without doubt some of a more timorous disposition who are disordered by the very sight of the enemy. To diminish these apprehensions before you venture on action, draw up your army frequently in order of battle in some safe situation, so that your men may be accustomed to the sight and appearance of the enemy. When opportunity offers, they should be sent to fall upon them and endeavor to put them to flight or kill some of their men. Thus they will become acquainted with their customs, arms and horses. And the objects with which we are once familiarized are no longer capable of inspiring us with terror.

CHOICE OF THE FIELD OF BATTLE.   Good generals are acutely aware that victory depends much on the nature of the field of battle. When you intend therefore to engage, endeavor to draw the chief advantage from your situation. The highest ground is reckoned the best. Weapons thrown from a height strike with greater force; and the party above their antagonists can repulse and bear them down with greater impetuosity, while they who struggle with the ascent have both the ground and the enemy to contend with. There is, however, this difference with regard to place: if you depend on your foot against the enemy's horse, you must choose a rough, unequal and mountainous situation. But if, on the contrary, you expect your cavalry to act with advantage against the enemy's infantry, your ground must indeed be higher, but plain and open, without any obstructions of woods or morasses.

ORDER OF BATTLE.   In drawing up an army in order of battle, three things are to be considered: the sun, the dust and the wind. The sun in your face dazzles the sight: if the wind is against you, it turns aside and blunts the force of your weapons, while it assists those of your adversary; and the dust driving in your front fills the eyes of your men and blinds them. Even the most unskillful endeavor to avoid these inconveniences in the moment of making their dispositions; but a prudent general should extend his views beyond the present; he should take such measures as not to be incommoded in the course of the day by different aspects of the sun or by contrary winds which often rise at a certain hour and might be detrimental during action. Our troops should be so disposed as to have these inconveniences behind them, while they are directly in the enemy's front.

PROPER DISTANCES AND INTERVALS. Having explained the general disposition of the lines, we now come to the distances and dimensions. One thousand paces contain a single rank of one thousand six hundred and fifty-six foot soldiers, each man being allowed three feet. Six ranks drawn up on the same extent of ground will require nine thousand nine hundred and ninety-six men. To form only three ranks of the same number will take up two thousand paces, but it is much better to increase the number of ranks than to make your front too extensive. We have before observed the distance between each rank should be six feet, one foot of which is taken up by the men. Thus if you form a body of ten thousand men into six ranks they will occupy thirty-six feet. in depth and a thousand paces in front. By this calculation it is easy to compute the extent of ground required for twenty or thirty thousand men to form upon. Nor can a general be mistaken when thus he knows the proportion of ground for any fixed number of men.

But if the field of battle is not spacious enough or your troops are very numerous, you may form them into nine ranks or even more, for it is more advantageous to engage in close order that to extend your line too much. An army that takes up too much ground in front and too little in depth, is quickly penetrated by the enemy's first on-set. After this there is no remedy. As to the post of the different corps in the right or left wing or in the center, it is the general rule to draw them up according to their respective ranks or to distribute them as circumstances or the dispositions of the enemy may require.

DISPOSITION OF THE CAVALRY. The line of infantry being formed, the cavalry are drawn up in the wings. The heavy horse, that is, the cuirassiers and troopers armed with lances, should join the infantry. The light cavalry, consisting of the archers and those who have no cuirasses, should be placed at a greater distance. The best and heaviest horse are to cover the flanks of the foot, and the light horse are posted as abovementioned to sur-round and disorder the enemy's wings. A general should know what part of his own cavalry is most proper to op-pose any particular squadrons or troops of the enemy. For from some causes not to be accounted for some par-ticular corps fight better against others, and those who have defeated superior enemies are often overcome by an inferior force.

If your cavalry is not equal to the enemy's it is proper, after the ancient custom, to intermingle it with light in-fantry armed with small shields and trained to this kind of service. By observing this method, even though the flower of the enemy's cavalry should attack you, they will never be able to cope with this mixed disposition. This was the only resource of the old generals to supply the defects of their cavalry, and they intermingled the men, used to running and armed for this purpose with light shields, swords and darts, among the horse, placing one of them between two troopers.

RESERVES. The method of having bodies of reserves in rear of the army, composed of choice infantry and cavalry, commanded by the supernumerary lieutenant generals, counts and tribunes, is very judicious and of great consequence towards the gaining of a battle. Some should be posted in rear of the wings and some near the center, to be ready to fly immediately to the assistance of any part of the line which is hard pressed, to prevent its being pierced, to supply the vacancies made therein during the action and thereby to keep up the courage of their fellow soldiers and check the impetuosity of the enemy. This was an invention of the Lacedaemonians, in which they were imitated by the Carthaginians. The Romans have since observed it, and indeed no better disposition can be found.

The line is solely designed to repulse, or if possible, break the enemy. If it is necessary to form the wedge or the pincers, it must be done by the supernumerary troops stationed in the rear for that purpose. If the saw is to be formed, it must also be done from the reserves, for if once you begin to draw off men from the line you throw all into confusion. If any flying platoon of the enemy should fall upon your wing or any other part of your army, and you have no supernumerary troops to oppose it or if you pretend to detach either horse or foot from your line for that service by endeavoring to protect one part, you will expose the other to greater danger. In armies not very numerous, it is much better to contract the front, and to have strong reserves. In short, you must have a reserve of good and well-armed infantry near the center to form the wedge and thereby pierce the enemy's line; and also bodies of cavalry armed with lances and cuirasses, with light infantry, near the wings, to surround the flanks of the enemy.

THE POST OF THE GENERAL AND OF THE SECOND AND THIRD IN COMMAND. The post of the commander-in-chief is generally on the right between the cavalry and infantry. For from this place he can best direct the motions of the whole army and move elements with the greatest ease wherever he finds it necessary. It is also the most convenient spot to give his orders to both horse and foot and to animate them equally by his presence. It is his duty to surround the enemy's left wing opposed to him with his reserve of horse and light infantry, and attack it in the flank and rear. The second in command is posted in the center of the infantry to encourage and support them. A reserve of good and well-armed infantry is near him and under his orders. With this reserve he either forms the wedge to pierce the enemy's line or, if they form the wedge first, prepares the pincers for its reception. The post of the third in command is on the left. He should be a careful and intrepid officer, this part of the army being difficult to manage and defective, as it were, from its situation in the line. He should therefore have a reserve of good cavalry and active infantry to enable him always to extend his left in such a manner as to prevent its being surrounded.

The war shout should not be begun till both armies have joined, for it is a mark of ignorance or cowardice to give it at a distance. The effect is much greater on the enemy when they find themselves struck at the same instant with the horror of the noise and the points of the weapons.

You must always endeavor to get the start of your enemy in drawing up in order of battle, as you will then have it in your power to make your proper dispositions without obstruction. This will increase the courage of your own troops and intimidate your adversaries. For a superiority of courage seems to be implied on the side of an army that offers battle, whereas troops begin to be fearful who see their enemies ready to attack them. You will also secure another great advantage, that of marching up in order and falling upon them while forming and still in confusion. For part of the victory consists in throwing the enemy into disorder before you engage them.

MANEUVERS IN ACTION. An able general never loses a favorable opportunity of surprising the enemy either when tired on the march, divided in the passage of a river, embarrassed in morasses, struggling with the declivities of mountains, when dispersed over the country they think themselves in security or are sleeping in their quarters. In all these cases the adversaries are surprised and destroyed before they have time to put themselves on their guard. But if they are too cautious to give you an opportunity of surprising or ensnaring them, you are then obliged to engage openly and on equal terms. This at present is foreign to the subject. However military skill is no less necessary in general actions than in carrying on war by subtlety and stratagem.

Your first care is to secure your left wing from being surrounded by the enemy's numbers or attacked in flank or rear by flying platoons, a misfortune that often happens. Nor is your right to be neglected, though less frequently in danger. There is only one remedy for this: to wheel back your wing and throw it into a circular position. By this evolution your soldiers meet the enemy on the quarter attacked and defend the rear of their comrades. But your best men should be posted on the angles of the flanks, since it is against them the enemy make their principal efforts.

There is also a method of resisting the wedge when formed by the enemy. The wedge is a disposition of a body of infantry widening gradually towards the base and terminating in a point towards the front. It pierces the enemy's line by a multitude of darts directed to one particular place. The soldiers call it the swine's head. To oppose this disposition, they make use af another called the pincers, resembling the letter V, composed of a body of men in close order. It receives the wedge, inclosing it on both sides, and thereby prevents it from penetrating the line.

The saw is another disposition formed of resolute soldiers drawn up in a straight line advanced into the front against the enemy, to repair any disorder. The platoon is a body of men separated from the line, to hover on every side and attack the enemy wherever they find opportunity. And against this is to be detached a stronger and more numerous platoon.

Above all, a general must never attempt to alter his dispositions or break his order of battle during the time of action, for such an alteration would immediately occasion disorder and confusion which the enemy would not fail to improve to their advantage.

VARIOUS FORMATIONS FOR BATTLE. An army may be drawn up for a general engagement in seven different formations. The first formation is an oblong square of a large front, of common use both in ancient and modern times, although not thought the best by various judges of the service, because an even and level plain of an extent sufficient to contain its front cannot always be found, and if there should be any irregularity or hollow in the line, it is often pierced in that part. Besides, an enemy superior in number may surround either your right or left wing, the consequence of which will be dangerous, unless you have a reserve ready to advance and sustain his attack. A general should make use of this disposition only when his forces are better and more numerous than the enemy's, it being thereby in his power to attack both the flanks and surround them on every side.

The second and best disposition is the oblique. For although your army consists of few troops, yet good and advantageously posted, it will greatly contribute to your obtaining the victory, notwithstanding the numbers and bravery of the enemy. It is as follows: as the armies are marching up to the attack, your left wing must be kept back at such a distance from the enemy's right as to be out of reach of their darts and arrows. Your right wing must advance obliquely upon the enemy's left, and begin the engagement. And you must endeavor with your best cavalry and infantry to surround the wing with which you are engaged, make it give way and fall upon the enemy in the rear. If they once give ground and the attack is properly seconded, you will undoubtedly gain the victory, while your left wing, which continued at a distance, will remain untouched. An army drawn up in this manner bears some resemblance to the letter A or a mason's level. If the enemy should be beforehand with you in this evolution, recourse must be had to the supernumerary horse and foot posted as a reserve in the rear, as I mentioned before. They must be ordered to support your left wing. This will enable you to make a vigorous resistance against the artifice of the enemy.

The third formation is like the second, but not so good, as it obliges you to begin the attack with your left wing on the enemy's right. The efforts of soldiers on the left are weak and imperfect from their exposed and defective situation in the line. I will explain this formation more clearly. Although your left wing should be much better than your right, yet it must be reinforced with some of the best horse and foot and ordered to commence the action with the enemy's right in order to disorder and surround it as expeditiously as possible. And the other part of your army, composed of the worst troops, should remain at such a distance from the enemy's left as not to be annoyed by their darts or in danger of being attacked sword in hand. In this oblique formation care must be taken to prevent the line being penetrated by the wedges of the enemy, and it is to be employed only when the enemy's right wing is weak and your greatest strength is on your left.

The fourth formation is this: as your army is marching to the attack in order of battle and you come within four or five hundred paces of the enemy, both your wings must be ordered unexpectedly to quicken their pace and advance with celerity upon them. When they find themselves attacked on both wings at the same time, the sudden surprise may so disconcert them as to give you an easy victory. But although this method, if your troops are very resolute and expert, may ruin the enemy at once, yet it is hazardous. The general who attempts it is obliged to abandon and expose his center and to divide his army into three parts. If the enemy are not routed at the first charge, they have a fair opportunity of attacking the wings which are separated from each other and the center which is destitute of assistance.

The fifth formation resembles the fourth but with this addition: the light infantry and the archers are formed before the center to cover it from the attempts of the enemy. With this precaution the general may safely follow the above mentioned method and attack the enemy's left wing with his right, and their right with his left. If he puts them to flight, he gains an immediate victory, and if he fails of success his center is in no danger, being protected by the light infantry and archers.

The sixth formation is very good and almost like the

second. It is used when the general cannot depend either on the number or courage of his troops. If made with judgment, notwithstanding his inferiority, he has often a good chance for victory. As your line approaches the enemy, advance your right wing against their left and begin the attack with your best cavalry and infantry. At the same time keep the rest of the army at a great distance from the enemy's right, extended in a direct line like a javelin. Thus if you can surround their left and attack it in flank and rear, you must inevitably defeat them. It is impossible for the enemy to draw off reinforcements from their right or from their center to sustain their left in this emergency, since the remaining part of your army is extended and at a great distance from them in the form of the letter L. It is a formation often used in an action on a march.

The seventh formation owes its advantages to the nature of the ground and will enable you to oppose an enemy with an army inferior both in numbers and goodness, provided one of your flanks can be covered either with an eminence, the sea, a river, a lake, a city, a morass or broken ground inaccessible to the enemy. The rest of the army must be formed, as usual, in a straight line and the unsecured flank must be protected by your light troops and all your cavalry. Sufficiently defended on one side by the nature of the ground and on the other by a double support of cavalry, you may then safely venture on action.

One excellent and general rule must be observed. If you intend to engage with your right wing only, it must be composed of your best troops. And the same method must be taken with respect to the left. Or if you intend to penetrate the enemy's line, the wedges which you form for that purpose before your center, must consist of the best disciplined soldiers. Victory in general is gained by a small number of men. Therefore the wisdom of a general appears in nothing more than in such choice of disposition of his men as is most consonant with reason and service.

THE FLIGHT OF AN ENEMY SHOULD NOT BE PREVENTED, BUT FACILITATED.   Generals unskilled in war think a victory incomplete unless the enemy are so straightened in their ground or so entirely surrounded by numbers as to have no possibility of escape. But in such situation, where no hopes remain, fear itself will arm an enemy and despair inspires courage. When men find they must inevitably perish, they willingly resolve to die with their comrades and with their arms in their hands. The maxim of Scipio, that a golden bridge should be made for a flying enemy, has much been commended. For when they have free room to escape they think of nothing but how to save themselves by flight, and the confusion becoming general, great numbers are cut to pieces. The pursuers can be in no danger when the vanquished have thrown away their arms for greater haste. In this case the greater the number of the flying army, the greater the slaughter. Numbers are of no signification where troops once thrown into consternation are equally terrified at the sight of the enemy as at their weapons. But on the contrary, men when shut up, although weak and few in number, become a match for the enemy from this very reflection, that they have no resource but in despair.

"The conquer'd's safety is, to hope for none."

MANNER OF CONDUCTING A RETREAT. Having gone through the various particulars relative to general actions, it remains at present to explain the manner of retreating in presence of the enemy. This is an operation, which, in the judgment of men of greatest skill and experience, is attended with the utmost hazard. A general certainly discourages his own troops and animates his enemies by retiring out of the field without fighting. Yet as this must sometimes necessarily happen, it will be proper to consider how to perform it with safety.

In the first place your men must not imagine that you retire to decline an action, but believe your retreat an artifice to draw the enemy into an ambuscade or more advantageous position where you may easier defeat them in case they follow you. For troops who perceive their general despairs of success are prone to flight. You must be cautious lest the enemy should discover your retreat and immediately fall upon you. To avoid this danger the cavalry are generally posted in the front of the infantry to conceal their motions and retreat from the enemy.

The first divisions are drawn off first, the others following in their turns. The last maintain their ground till the rest have marched off, and then file off themselves and join them in a leisurely and regular succession. Some generals have judged it best to make their retreat in the night after reconnoitering their routes, and thus gain so much ground that the enemy, not discovering their departure till daybreak, were not able to come up with them. The light infantry was also sent forward to possess the eminences under which the army might instantly retire with safety; and the enemy, in case they pursued, be exposed to the light infantry, masters of the heights, seconded by the cavalry.

A rash and inconsiderate pursuit exposes an army to the greatest danger possible, that of falling into ambuscades and the hands of troops ready for their reception. For as the temerity of an army is increased and their caution lessened by the pursuit of a flying enemy, this is the most favorable opportunity for such snares. The greater the security, the greater the danger. Troops, when unprepared, at their meals, fatigued after a march, when their horses are feeding, and in short, when they believe themselves most secure, are generally most liable to a surprise. All risks of this sort are to be carefully avoided and all opportunities taken of distressing the enemy by such methods. Neither numbers nor courage avail in misfortunes of this nature.

A general who has been defeated in a pitched battle, although skill and conduct have the greatest share in the decision, may in his defense throw the blame on fortune. But if he has suffered himself to be surprised or drawn into the snares of his enemy, he has no excuse for his fault, because he might have avoided such a misfortune by taking proper precautions and employing spies on whose intelligence he could depend.

When the enemy pursue a retreating foe, the following snare is usually laid. A small body of cavalry is ordered to pursue them on the direct road. At the same time a strong detachment is secretly sent another way to conceal itself on their route. When the cavalry have overtaken the enemy, they make some feint attacks and retire. The enemy, imagining the danger past, and that they have escaped the snare, neglect their order and march without regularity. Then the detachment sent to intercept them, seizing the opportunity, falls upon them unexpectedly and destroys them with ease.

Many generals when obliged to retreat through woods send forward parties to seize the defiles and difficult passes, to avoid ambuscades and block the roads with barricades of felled trees to secure themselves from being pursued and attacked in the rear. In short both sides have equal opportunities of surprising or laying ambuscades on the march. The army which retreats leaves troops behind for that purpose posted in convenient valleys or mountains covered with woods, and if the enemy falls into the snare, it returns immediately to their assistance. The army that pursues detaches different parties of light troops to march ahead through by-roads and intercepts the enemy, who are thus surrounded and attacked at once in front and rear. The flying army may return and fall on the enemy while asleep in the night. And the pursuing army may, even though the distance is great, surprise the adversary by forced marches. The former endeavor may be at the crossing of a river in order to destroy such part of the enemy's army as has already crossed. The pursuers hasten their march to fall upon those bodies of the enemy that have not yet crossed.

ARMED CHARIOTS AND ELEPHANTS. The armed chariots used in war by Antiochus and Mithridates at first
terrified the Romans, but they afterwards made a jest
of them. As a chariot of this sort does not always meet
with plain and level ground, the least obstruction stops
it. And if one of the horses be either killed or wounded,
it falls into the enemy's hands. The Roman soldiers
rendered them useless chiefly by the following contri-
vance: at the instant the engagement began, they strewed
the field of battle with caltrops, and the horses that drew
the chariots, running full speed on them, were infallibly
destroyed. A caltrop is a machine composed of four
spikes or points arranged so that in whatever manner it
is thrown on the ground, it rests on three and presents
the fourth upright.

Elephants by their vast size, horrible noise and the
novelty of their form are at first very terrible both to
men and horses. Pyrrhus first used them against the
Romans in Lucania. And afterwards Hannibal brought
them into the field in Africa. Antiochus in the east and
Jugurtha in Numidia had great numbers. Many expedients have been used against them. In Lucania a centurion
cut off the trunk of one with his sword. Two soldiers
armed from head to foot in a chariot drawn by two
horses, also covered with armor, attacked these beasts
with lances of great length. They were secured by their
armor from the archers on the elephants and avoided the
fury of the animals by the swiftness of their horses. Foot
soldiers completely armored, with the addition of long
iron spikes fixed on their arms, shoulders and helmets,

to prevent the elephant from seizing them with his trunk, were also employed against them.

But among the ancients, the velites usually engaged them. They were young soldiers, lightly armed, active and very expert in throwing their missile weapons on horseback. These troops kept hovering round the elephants continually and killed them with large lances and javelins. Afterwards, the soldiers, as their apprehensions decreased, attacked them in a body and, throwing their javelins together, destroyed them by the multitude of wounds. Slingers with round stones from the fustibalus and sling killed both the men who guided the elephants and the soldiers who fought in the towers on their backs. This was found by experience to be the best and safest expedient. At other times on the approach of these beasts, the soldiers opened their ranks and let them pass through. When they got into the midst of the troops, who surrounded them on all sides, they were captured with their guards unhurt.

Large balistae, drawn on carriages by two horses or mules, should be placed in the rear of the line, so that when the elephants come within reach they may be transfixed with the darts. The balistae should be larger and the heads of the darts stronger and broader than usual, so that the darts may be thrown farther, with greater force and the wounds be proportioned to the bodies of the beasts. It was proper to describe these several methods and contrivances employed against elephants, so that it may be known on occasion in what manner to oppose those prodigious animals.

RESOURCES IN CASE OF DEFEAT.   If while one part of
your army is victorious the other should be defeated,
you are by no means to despair, since even in this extremity the constancy and resolution of a general may
recover a complete victory. There are innumerable instances where the party that gave least way to despair
was esteemed the conqueror. For where losses and advantages seem nearly equal, he is reputed to have the
superiority who bears up against his misfortunes with
greatest resolution. He is therefore to be first, if possible,
to seize the spoils of the slain and to make rejoicings for
the victory. Such marks of confidence dispirit the enemy
and redouble your own courage.

Yet notwithstanding an entire defeat, all possible
remedies must be attempted, since many generals have
been fortunate enough to repair such a loss. A prudent
officer will never risk a general action without taking
such precautions as will secure him from any considerable loss in case of a defeat, for the uncertainty of war
and the nature of things may render such a misfortune
unavoidable. The neighborhood of a mountain, a fortified
post in the rear or a resolute stand made by a good body
of troops to cover the retreat, may be the means of saving the army.

An army after a defeat has sometimes rallied, returned
on the enemy, dispersed him by pursuing in order and
destroyed him without difficulty. Nor can men be in a
more dangerous situation than, when in the midst of joy
after victory, their exultation is suddenly converted into
terror. Whatever be the event, the remains of the army

must be immediately assembled, reanimated by suitable exhortations and furnished with fresh supplies of arms. New levies should immediately be made and new reinforcements provided. And it is of much the greatest consequence that proper opportunities should be taken to surprise the victorious enemies, to draw them into snares and ambuscades and by this means to recover the drooping spirits of your men. Nor will it be difficult to meet with such opportunities, as the nature of the human mind is apt to be too much elated and to act with too little caution in prosperity. If any one should imagine no resource is left after the loss of a battle, let him reflect on what has happened in similar cases and he will find that they who were victorious in the end were often unsuccessful in the beginning.

GENERAL MAXIMS. It is the nature of war that what is beneficial to you is detrimental to the enemy and what is of service to him always hurts you. It is therefore a maxim never to do, or to omit doing, anything as a consequence of his actions, but to consult invariably your own interest only. And you depart from this interest whenever you imitate such measures as he pursues for his benefit. For the same reason it would be wrong for him to follow such steps as you take for your advantage.

The more your troops have been accustomed to camp duties on frontier stations and the more carefully they have been disciplined, the less danger they will be exposed to in the field.

Men must be sufficiently tried before they are led against the enemy.

It is much better to overcome the enemy by famine, surprise or terror than by general actions, for in the latter instance fortune has often a greater share than valor.

Those designs are best which the enemy are entirely ignorant of till the moment of execution. Opportunity in war is often more to be depended on than courage.

To debauch the enemy's soldiers and encourage them when sincere in surrendering themselves, is of especial service, for an adversary is more hurt by desertion than by slaughter.

It is better to have several bodies of reserves than to extend your front too much.

A general is not easily overcome who can form a true judgment of his own and the enemy's forces.

Valor is superior to numbers.

The nature of the ground is often of more consequence than courage.

Few men are born brave; many become so through care and force of discipline.

An army is strengthened by labor and enervated by idleness.

Troops are not to be led to battle unless confident of success.

Novelty and surprise throw an enemy into consternation; but common incidents have no effect.

He who rashly pursues a flying enemy with troops in disorder, seems inclined to resign that victory which he had before obtained.

An army unsupplied with grain and other necessary provisions will be vanquished without striking a blow.

A general whose troops are superior both in number and bravery should engage in the oblong square, which is the first formation.

He who judges himself inferior should advance his right wing obliquely against the enemy's left. This is the second formation.

If your left wing is strongest, you must attack the enemy's right according to the third formation.

The general who can depend on the discipline of his men should begin the engagement by attacking both the enemy's wings at once, the fourth formation.

He whose light infantry is good should cover his center by forming them in its front and charge both the enemy's wings at once. This is the fifth formation.

He who cannot depend either on the number or courage of his troops, if obliged to engage, should begin the action with his right and endeavor to break the enemy's left, the rest of his army remaining formed in a line perpendicular to the front and extended to the rear like a javelin. This is the sixth formation.

If your forces are few and weak in comparison to the enemy, you must make use of the seventh formation and cover one of your flanks either with an eminence, a city, the sea, a river or some protection of that kind.

A general who trusts to his cavalry should choose the proper ground for them and employ them principally in the action.

He who depends on his infantry should choose a situation most proper for them and make most use of their service.

When an enemy's spy lurks in the camp, order all your soldiers in the day time to their tents, and he will instantly be apprehended.

On finding the enemy has notice of your designs, you must immediately alter your plan of operations.

Consult with many on proper measures to be taken, but communicate the plans you intend to put in execution to few, and those only of the most assured fidelity; or rather trust no one but yourself.

Punishment, and fear thereof, are necessary to keep soldiers in order in quarters; but in the field they are more influenced by hope and rewards.

Good officers never engage in general actions unless induced by opportunity or obliged by necessity.

To distress the enemy more by famine than the sword is a mark of consummate skill.

Many instructions might be given with regard to the cavalry. But as this branch of the service has been brought to perfection since the ancient writers and considerable improvements have been made in their drills and maneuvers, their arms, and the quality and management of their horses, nothing can be collected from their works. Our present mode of discipline is sufficient.

Dispositions for action must be carefully concealed from the enemy, lest they should counteract them and defeat your plans by proper expedients.

This abridgment of the most eminent military writers, invincible Emperor, contains the maxims and instructions they have left us, approved by different ages and confirmed by repeated experience. The Persians admire your skill in archery; the Huns and Alans endeavor in vain to imitate your dexterity in horsemanship; the Saracens and Indians cannot equal your activity in the hunt; and even the masters at arms pique themselves on only part of that knowledge and expertness of which you give so many instances in their own profession. How glorious it is therefore for Your Majesty with all these qualifications to unite the science of war and the art of conquest, and to convince the world that by Your conduct and courage You are equally capable of performing the duties of the soldier and the general!

My Reveries Upon the Art of War

by

Marshal Maurice de Saxe

Translated from the French by

Brig. Gen. Thomas R. Phillips

INTRODUCTION

The eldest of 354 acknowledged illegitimate children of Frederick Augustus, Elector of Saxony and King of Poland, the Prodigious Marshal, Maurice of Saxony, was born October 28, 1696. His mother was the lovely Countess Aurora von Konigsmark. Frederick Augustus was renowned for his fabulous strength, the immensity of his appetites, and his limitless lust. Maurice inherited these characteristics but combined with them a very superior intelligence.

He was tutored at his father's expense until the age of twelve, when he was placed under the tutelage of General von Schulenburg, one of the most distinguished soldiers of fortune of the time. At the same time he was commissioned an ensign in the infantry and marched on foot from Dresden to Flanders where he fought in the battle of Malplaquet under Marlborough and Prince Eugene of Savoy, being then thirteen years of age. While the slow operations of eighteenth century sieges were being carried out he found time to seduce a young girl in Tournay, by whom he had a child, thus proving himself a true son of his father.

When the peace of Utrecht was signed Maurice was 17 years old, had made four campaigns in Flanders and Pomerania, had distinguished himself for intrepidity, and commanded his own regiment of horse, which he drilled and fought with single-minded passion. He was married, much against his will, at the age of 18 to an immensely wealthy 14-year-old heiress and started distributing her immense fortune as rapidly as he knew how. It maintained his regiment of horse and his legion of mistresses. The war against the Turks provided an opportunity for his talents, and he served with Prince Eugene in the capture of Belgrade in 1717. Having squandered the immense fortune of his wife, the Court of Versailles beckoned him as the most likely place for a distinguished soldier to make a new fortune, and the year 1720 found him in Paris.

He was accepted and lionized in the degenerate society of the French capital and became a bosom friend of the Regent. In August, 1720, he was commissioned a Marechal de Camp in the French army and purchased a regiment. But his greatest successes were with the French ladies of the court. His regiment represented the serious side of his nature, and he trained this with the utmost thoroughness. Between debauches he set himself to studying tactics and fortification and reading the memoirs of great soldiers.

In Paris he became the acknowledged lover of the lovely Adrienne de Lecouvreur, the greatest tragic actress of the age and the toast of France. She was accepted in the noble society of Paris, and Voltaire was her sincere friend. Having run through his wife's fortune, his marriage was annulled.

The throne of the Duchy of Courland having become vacant in 1725, Maurice plotted to gain it. He would have to be elected by the Diet. Anna Ivanowa, niece of Peter the Great, likewise had a party favoring her.

His scheme was to marry Anna Ivanowa and combine their claims. But money was needed to make the proper show. There were plenty of women in Paris to supply it, and even Adrienne sold her jewels to help her hero to marry another woman and to gain a throne. But Russia had another scheme. This was that he should give up his claims to the Duchy of Courland, marry Elisabeth Petrovna, daughter of Peter the Great, and be satisfied with the portion she would receive.

Maurice, however, would only be contented with a kingdom of his own. He pleased the dowager duchess, Anna, much better, however, than she pleased him. And while living in her palace, supported by Adrienne de Lecouvreur's (and other women's) funds, he engaged in an intrigue with one of Anna's serving ladies. This was discovered and the outraged Duchess threw him out of her palace and out of her life. She later became Empress of Russia and was succeeded on the throne by Elizabeth Petrovna.

In the wars between 1733 and 1736, ending in the Peace of Vienna, Maurice again distinguished himself and was made a lieutenant general. Still, he was nothing but a German nobleman and a military adventurer. His fortunes commenced to improve with his acquaintance with Madame de Pompadour, mistress of King Louis XV. She recognized his greatness as a soldier and his character as a man. "Maurice de Saxe," she wrote, "does not understand anything about the delicacy of love. The only pleasure he takes in the society of women can be summed up in the word 'debauchery.' Wherever he goes he drags after him a train of street-walkers. He is only great on the field of battle."* It was probably due to her influence with King Louis XV that Maurice was retained in high rank in the French army and was given supreme command, in spite of the claims and jealousy of the princes of the blood.

In the great war of 1741, Saxe, then a lieutenant general, was sent with a division of cavalry to the aid of the Duke of Bavaria. On the invasion of Bohemia, he led the vanguard. It was by his advice and under his direction that Prague was attacked and carried. His conduct and humanity after the capture were no less conspicuous and deserving of praise than his courage and judgment had been during the assault. His troops were so uniquely disciplined, for that age, that there was no pillage. The astonished magistrates gave the victor a superb diamond in gratitude for the order he kept in the vanquished city.

The period of Maurice's glory commenced in 1745 when he was appointed a Marshal of France and placed at the head of the army with which Louis XV in person proposed to conquer the Netherlands. His difficulties were greatly augmented by presence of the King and court who came to check rather than assist operations. Notwithstanding these drawbacks, the campaigns of 1745, 46, 47, and 48 reflect the greatest credit on his military skill and sagacity. The capture of Ghent, Brussels, and Maestricht, the battles of Lafeldt, Roucous, and Fontenoy, were all splendid feats, and were due to wise planning and dispositions.

---

* Quoted by George R. Freedy, *Child of Chequer'd Fortune.*

On leaving for the campaign that resulted in the victory of Fontenoy, he was ill with dropsy and hardly able to move. He encountered Voltaire, who asked him how could he do anything in his half-dead state. Saxe answered: "It is not a question of living, but of acting." During the battle he had to be carried around the field in a wicker cart and only mounted his horse at intervals during the action. At the close of the battle he fainted from exhaustion and was immediately tapped for his dropsy.

As a reward for this victory, he was made Marshal General of the Armies of the King and given the princely castle of Chambord. Here he had his own regiment of cavalry, barracks for them, and a parade ground large enough for drill. He had his own theater and show troupe. With the exception of a visit to Frederick the Great in the summer of 1749, where he was entertained in the royal cottage of Sans-Souci in the choicest manner, Maurice passed the remainder of his days in the society of artists, men of letters, and courtesans. He still evolved various schemes to provide himself a kingdom, including the crown of Corsica, the island of Tobago, and even the founding of a Jewish kingdom in South America. Death put an end to these reveries and closed his career at Chambord, in November, 1750, in the fifty-fourth year of his age. His last words, addressed to his medical attendant, Monsieur de Senac, were: "Life, doctor, is but a dream, and I have had a fine one."

The *Reveries* were published posthumously in 1757 and were translated into the English the same year. They were quite variously appreciated. Carlyle notes that Frederick the Great gave a copy of them to the Kaiser Joseph, who kept them thenceforth on his night table, where they were found after his death, twenty-one years later, not a page read, the leaves all sticking together. Carlyle calls them "a strange military farrago, dictated, I should think, under opium."

They evince a deeper insight into tactics and leadership than any other work in Europe, since the Romans, to his time. Saxe was not merely far in advance of his age in tactical conceptions and the influence of the human heart on battles, but he was far in advance technically. He wanted breech-loading cannon and muskets. He invented his "amusette," an accompanying gun for the infantry. He wanted to reform the uniforms to make them practical rather than show clothes. He advocated company messes instead of small group cooking. He planned to break up enemy charges with specially trained groups of expert riflemen and skirmishers, who then would retire and leave the disorganized enemy an easy prey to his counterattack. His advocacy of conscription antedated all previous ideas on this matter. He rediscovered cadenced marching, lost since the time of the Romans, which was to change European armies from straggling mobs into disciplined soldiers. He was the first to object to the practice of volley fire, recognizing that accurate aim became impossible if men were forced to hold their muskets in aiming position indefinitely while awaiting the command to fire.

In the tactical field Saxe expressed his scorn for entrenchments, saying they always were taken. In their place, he would use redoubts, the eighteenth century equivalent of the modern strong point. The soldiers of the World War had to go through the same evolution, starting with entrenched lines and ending in mutually supporting strong points. He attempted to open up the formations of the day and ridiculed the results of charges in mass, which soon became confused and broke into a useless crowd who only got in each other's way. Saxe was also the first soldier of modern times to advocate implacable pursuit of defeated enemy.

A stern disciplinarian, Saxe did not overemphasize the importance of drill. "Drill is necessary to make a soldier steady and skillful, but it does not warrant exclusive attention. Among all the elements of war it even is the one that deserves the least." But marching is another matter. "The foundation of training depends on the legs and not the arms. All the mystery of maneuvers and combats is in the legs, and it is to the legs that we should apply ourselves. Whoever claims otherwise is but a fool and not only in the elements of what is called the profession of arms."

Saxe also was an innovator concerning organization. He wanted to reorganize armies after the Roman fashion, modernized, with legions and smaller units. In his time armies were divided into three or four wings regardless of size. His scheme was the progenitor of our present division organization. He also would designate organizations by number, instead of by the name of the colonel, as was the custom of the time. In support of this he argued that this would give the organization a continuing history and would result in increased esprit de corps. He also would give each man insignia to denote his regiment.

Saxe's stature is most clearly shown in his appreciation of the moral factors in war and in his conception of leadership. He states, concerning Chevalier Follard, that he errs in supposing "all men to be brave at all times, and does not realize that the courage of the troops must be reborn daily, that nothing is so variable, and that the true skill of a general consists in knowing how to guarantee it by his dispositions, his positions, and those traits of genius that characterize great captains . . . It is of all the elements of war the one that is most necessary to study. Without a knowledge of the human heart, one is dependent upon the favor of fortune, which is sometimes very inconstant." Why are panics aroused? "This is because they are faced with the unexpected and fear for their flanks and rear. In all probability they will take flight without knowing exactly why."

For the general, Saxe has high ideals. He should possess a talent for improvisation. His plans should be complete and meticulous, his orders short and simple, but on the day of battle he should be occupied with nothing but the conduct of the action. "Thus, on the day of battle, I should want the general to do nothing. Many commanding generals only spend their time on the day of battle making their troops march in a straight line, in seeing that they keep their proper distances, and in running about incessantly themselves. In short, they try to do everything and as a result, do nothing. They appear to me like men with their heads turned, who no longer see anything, and who only are able to do what they have done all their lives, which is to conduct troops methodically under the orders of a commander." What is the cause of this? "It is because few men occupy themselves with the higher problems of war. They pass their lives drilling troops and believe that this is the only branch of the military art. When they arrive at the command of armies, they are totally ignorant, and in default of knowing what should be done, they do what they know."

This translation is completely new and has been made from the text of Charles-Lavauzelle published in 1895. Certain portions of no present interest have been omitted. These include a long project for an invasion of Poland and a number of details without modern interest. The only previous translation into English was made in 1757 and is so inaccurate as to nullify frequently many of Saxe's most brilliant remarks. In particular the sentences dealing with drill, which are probably the most quoted extracts from Saxe, were so translated in the old translation as to reverse the sense of the author.

Two biographies of Saxe in English have been published recently: *The Prodigious Marshal*, by Edmund B. D'Auvergne, Dodd Mead & Co., New York, 1931, and *Child of Chequer'd Fortune*, by George R. Preedy, Hubert Jenkins, Ltd., London, 1939. Both are excellent and make fascinating reading. Neither, however, will satisfy the military reader with respect to Saxe's military operations. The best military evaluation of Saxe is contained in Liddell Hart's *Great Captains Unveiled*, in the chapter: *Marechal de Saxe—Military Prophet*. The only comprehensive studies of Saxe's campaigns are: *Les Campagnes du Marechal de Saxe*, by Captain J. Colin, Paris, 1901, and *Maurice de Saxe, Marechal de France*, by General Camon, Paris, 1934.

PREFACE

This work was not born from a desire to establish a new method of the art of war; I composed it to amuse and instruct myself.

War is a science covered with shadows in whose obscurity one cannot move with an assured step. Routine and prejudice, the natural result of ignorance, are its foundation and support.

All sciences have principles and rules; war has none. The great captains who have written of it give us none. Extreme cleverness is required even to understand them. And it is impossible to base any judgment on the relations of the historians, for they only speak of war as their imaginations paint it. As for the great captains who have written of it, they have attempted rather to be interesting than instructive, since the mechanics of war is dry and tedious. Books dealing with it have small success and their merit will not be recognized except after the passage of time. Those writing historically of war have better luck; they are sought by all the curious and kept in all libraries. That is why we have only a confused idea of the discipline of the Greeks and Romans.

Gustavus Adolphus created a method that was followed by his disciples, all of whom accomplished great things. But since his time there has been a gradual decline amongst us, which must be imputed to our having learned only his forms, without regard to principles. Hence the confusion of customs, these having been added to or detracted from according to fancy. But in reading Montecuculli, who was contemporary with Gustavus and is the only general who entered into some detail, it is very evident that we have departed already more from his methods than he did from those of the Romans. Thus there remain nothing but customs, the principles of which are unknown to us.

Chevalier Follard has been the only one who has dared to pass the bounds of these prejudices; I approve his noble courage. Nothing is so disgraceful as slavishness to custom; this is both a result of ignorance and a proof of it. But Chevalier Follard goes too far. He advances an opinion which he pronounces infallible, without reflecting that success depends upon an infinite number of circumstances which human prudence cannot foresee. He supposes all men to be brave at all times and does not realize that the courage of the troops must be reborn daily, that nothing is so variable, and that the true skill of a general consists in knowing how to guarantee it by his dispositions, his positions, and those traits of genius that characterize great captains. Perhaps he reserved discussion of this immense subject; and perhaps, also, it escaped him. Nevertheless, it is of all the elements of war the one that is most necessary to study.

The same troops, who if attacking would have been victorious, may be invariably defeated in entrenchments. Few men have accounted for it in a reasonable manner, for it lies in human hearts and one should search for it there. No one has written of this matter which is the most important, the most learned, and the most profound, of the profession of war. And without a knowledge of the human heart, one is dependent upon the favor of fortune, which sometimes is very inconstant. I shall make use of one example to reinforce my opinion.

After the French infantry had repulsed the Imperialists at the battle of Friedelingen with incomparable valor, after they had routed them several times and had pursued them through a wood and onto a plain which lay on the other side, someone cried that they were cut off— two troops had appeared (and these may have been French). All this victorious infantry fled in frightful disorganization, although no one either attacked or pursued them, repassed through the wood, and only halted on the other side of the battlefield. Marshal de Villars and the generals tried to rally them in vain. However, the battle had been won; the French cavalry had defeated that of the Imperialists, and no more of the enemy were to be seen. Nevertheless, it was those same men who at one moment had defeated the Imperial infantry with the utmost intrepidity and at another had been seized with such a panic of terror that it was almost impossible to regain their courage. Marshal de Villars himself told this to me when he was showing me the plans of his battles at Vaux-Villars. Anyone who wishes to search for similar examples will find quantities of them in the history of all nations. This one, however, is sufficient to prove the instability of the human heart and how little we should depend on it. But before enlarging too much upon the higher parts of war, it will be necessary to treat of the lesser, by which I mean the foundations of the art.

Although those who occupy themselves with details are considered to be men of limited capacity, it seems to me, nevertheless, that this part is essential, because it is the foundation of the profession, and because it is impossible to erect any edifice, or to establish any system, without first knowing the principles that support it. I shall illustrate my meaning with a comparison. A man who has a talent for architecture and can design, will draw the plan and perspective of a palace with great skill. But if he is to execute it, if he does not know how to shape his stones, to lay his foundation, the whole edifice will crash soon. It is the same with the general who does not know the principles of his art, nor how to organize his troops, for these are indispensable qualifications in all the operations of war. The prodigious success which the Romans always gained with small armies against multitudes of barbarians can be attributed to nothing but the excellent composition of their troops. Not that I would infer from this that a man of genius will not be able to succeed, even at the head of an army of Tartars. It is much easier to take men as they are than to make them as they should be; it is difficult to reconcile opinions, prejudices, and passions.

I shall commence with our system of raising troops; then I shall examine how to supply, train, and fight them.

It would be foolhardy to state that all the methods now employed are worthless, for it is a sacrilege to attack usages, albeit one less great than to propose something new. Therefore, I declare that I shall only attempt to indicate the abuses into which we have fallen.

MY REVERIES

RAISING TROOPS. Troops are raised by enlistment with a fixed term, without a fixed term, by compulsion sometimes, and most frequently by fraud.

When recruits are raised by enlistment it is unjust and inhuman not to observe the engagement. These men were free when they contracted the enlistment which binds them, and it is against all laws, human or divine, not to keep the promises made to them. What happens? The men desert. Can one, with justice, proceed against them? The good faith upon which the conditions of enlistment were founded has been violated. Unless severe measures are taken, discipline is lost; and, if severe punishments are used, one commits odious and cruel actions. There are, however, many soldiers whose term of service is ended at the commencement of a campaign. The captains who wish to have their organizations full retain them by force. This results in the grievance of which I am speaking.

Troops raised by fraud are also odious. Money is slipped secretly into the man's pocket and then he is told he is a soldier.

Troops raised by force are still worse. This is a public misfortune from which the citizens and the inhabitants can only save themselves by bribery and is founded on shameful means.

Would it not be better to prescribe by law that every man, whatever his condition in life, should be obliged to serve his prince and his country for five years. This law could not be objected to because it is natural and just that all citizens should occupy themselves with the defense of the nation. No inconvenience could result if they were chosen between the ages of twenty and thirty years. These are the years of libertinage, when youth seeks its fortune, travels the country, and is of little comfort to parents. This would not be a public calamity because one could be sure that, when five years had passed, discharge would be granted. This method of raising troops would provide an inexhaustible reservoir of fine recruits who would not be subject to desertion. In course of time, as a consequence, it would be regarded as an honor to have fulfilled one's service. But to produce this effect it is essential to make no distinctions, to be immovable on this point, and to enforce the law particularly on the nobles and the rich. Then, no one will complain. Consequently, those who have served their time will scorn those who are reluctant to obey the law, and insensibly it will become an honor to serve. The poor bourgois will be consoled by the example of the rich, and the rich will not dare complain upon seeing the noble serve. Arms is an honorable profession. How many princes have borne arms! Witness M. de Turenne. And how many officers have I seen serve in the ranks rather than live in indolence! It is thus only effeminacy that will make this law appear hard to some. But everything has a good and a bad side.

CLOTHING TROOPS. Our uniform is not only expensive but very uncomfortable; the soldier is neither shod, nor clothed, nor covered. The love of appearance prevails over attention to health, and this is one of the most important points demanding our attention. Hair is a dirty ornament for a soldier; and, once the rainy season has arrived, his head is never dry.

As for his feet, it is not to be doubted that his stockings, shoes, and feet rot together, since he has no extra pairs to change; and even if he should have, they will be of little use to him because, a moment later, he will be back in the same state. Thus the poor soldier is soon sent to the hospital. White garters spoil in washing, are good only for reviews, are inconvenient and harmful, of no real use, and very expensive.

The hat soon loses its shape and cannot resist the mistreatment of a campaign. Soon it no longer sheds rain, and as soon as the soldier lies down it falls off. The soldier, worn out with fatigue, sleeps in the rain and dew with his head uncovered and the next day has a fever.

In place of hats, I should prefer helmets. They do not weigh more than hats, are not at all uncomfortable, protect from a saber blow, and are very ornamental.

I should like to have the soldier clothed in a jacket, a little large, with a small one under it, something like a vest, and a Turkish coat with an attached hood. These coats cover a man well and do not contain more than two ells and one half of cloth. They are light and cheap.

The soldier will have his head and neck covered from the rain and wind. Lying down, he will be dry because these clothes are not tight. When wet they will dry in a moment of fair weather.

It is quite different with the present uniform. As soon as it is wet, the soldier feels it to the skin, and it must be dried on him. One need not, therefore, be astonished to see so many diseases in the army. The strongest resist the longest, but in the end they must succumb. If one adds to what I have said, the service that those who are well are obliged to do in place of the sick, the dead, the wounded, and the deserters, it is not astonishing to see battalions reduced to a hundred men at the end of a campaign. That is how the smallest things influence the greatest.

As for shoes, I would prefer the soldiers to have shoes of thin leather with low heels, instead of heavy boots. They would be perfectly shod and would march with better grace, since the low heels would force them to turn their toes out, stretch their joints, and consequently, draw in their shoulders. The shoes should be worn on the bare feet and the feet greased with tallow or fat. The fops will find this very strange, but the French veterans did this, for experience proved that they never blistered their feet, and water did not soak the shoes easily on account of the grease. On the other hand the leather did not get hard and hurt the feet.

The Germans, who make their infantry wear woolen stockings, have always had numbers of cripples from blisters, ulcers, and all sorts of diseases of the feet and legs, because wool is poisonous to the skin. Besides, these soon break through the toes, remain wet, and rot with the feet.

To keep the feet dry, wooden sandals should be added

to the footwear. This will keep the shoes from getting wet in the mud and dew and when on duty—a great nuisance and resulting in illnesses. In dry weather, for combat and for drill, they would not be used.

FEEDING TROOPS. As I would divide my troops into centuries, a sutler should be provided for each century. He should have four wagons drawn by two oxen each and should be provided with a large kettle to hold soup for the whole century. Every man would receive his portion in a wooden dish, together with boiled meat at noon and roast meat at night. It should be the officers' duty to see that they are not imposed on and have no occasion for complaint.

The profit allowed the sutlers would come from the sale of liquor, cheese, tobacco, and the skins from the cattle they killed. The sutlers should provide food for the cattle, and when the army is near forage they would be given the necessary orders to obtain it.

It might appear difficult to arrange this at first. But with a little care everyone would be satisfied. When soldiers are detached in small parties they could carry two days' supply of roast meat with them, without encumbrance. The quantity of wood, water, and kettles to make soup for a hundred men is more than would be sufficient for a thousand the way I propose, and the soup is never as good. Besides, the soldiers eat all sorts of unhealthy things, such as pork and unripe fruit, which make them ill. . The officer would only have to watch a single kitchen, that of the sutler, and an officer should always be present at each meal to see that the soldiers had no cause for complaint. On forced marches, when the baggage could not be brought up, cattle would be distributed to the troops. Wooden spits could be made and the meat roasted. This would not be inconvenient and would only last a few days. Let my method and the former one be balanced. I am persuaded that mine will be found the better.

The Turks use it and they are perfectly well nourished. One can tell their cadavers, after battles, from the German's, which are pale and emaciated. This has, at times, another advantage; the soldier's pocketbook is protected by giving them their entire pay and selling their food to them. · There are certain countries, like Poland and Germany, where cattle abound. Contributions are demanded from the inhabitants and, to enable them to sustain them, they are taken half in food and half in money. The food is sold to the soldiers; thus the pay is in continual circulation, and one has money as well as contributions, an important consideration.

Soldiers should never be given bread in the field but should be accustomed to biscuit, because it will keep for fifty years or more in depots and a soldier can easily carry a fifteen days' supply of it. It is healthy; one needs only inquire of the officers who served with the Venetians to learn the advantages of biscuit. The Russian biscuit, called Soukari, is the best of all because it does not crumble; it is square and the size of a hazelnut. Fewer wagons are needed to carry it than bread.

Soldiers at times should be accustomed to do without biscuit and should be given grain and taught to cook it on iron plates, after having ground and made it into paste with water. Marshal Turenne said something about this in his *Memoirs*. I have heard of great captains who, even when they had bread, did not allow the troops to eat it, so as to accustom them to do without it. I have made eighteen-month campaigns with troops who were habituated to do without bread without hearing complaints. I have made several others with troops who were accustomed to it, and they could not do without it. Let bread be lacking a single day and everything was lost. The result was that not a step ahead could be taken, nor any bold march.

I should not omit to mention here a custom of the Romans by which they prevented the diseases that attack armies with changes of climate. A part of their amazing success can be attributed to it. More than a third of the German armies perished upon arrival in Italy and in Hungary. In the year 1718 we entered the camp at Belgrade with 55,000 men. It is on a height, the air is healthy, the spring water good, and we had plenty of everything. On the day of battle, August 18, there were only 22,000 men under arms; all the rest were dead or unable to fight. I could produce similar instances among other nations. It is the change of climate that causes it. There were no such examples among the Romans as long as they had vinegar. But just as soon as it was lacking they were subject to the same misfortunes that our troops are at present. This is a fact to which few persons have given any attention, but which, however, is of great consequence for the conquerors and their success. As for how to use it, the Romans distributed several days' supply among their men by order, and each man poured a few drops in his drinking water. I leave to the doctors the discovery of the causes of such beneficial effects; what I report is unquestionable.

PAY. Without going into detail about the different rates of pay, I shall say only that it should be ample. It is better to have a small number of well-kept and well-disciplined troops than to have a great number who are neglected in these matters. It is not the big armies that win battles; it is the good ones. Economy can be pushed only to a certain point. It has limits beyond which it degenerates into parsimony. If your pay and allowances for officers will not support them decently, then you will only have rich men who serve for debauchery or indigent wretches devoid of spirit. For the first I have little use because they can stand neither discomfort nor the rigor of discipline. Their talk is always seditious, and they are nothing but frank libertines. As for the others, they are so depressed that one can expect no great virtue in them. Their ambition is limited because advancement hardly interests them; and worse, they prefer to remain what they are, especially when promotion is an expense.

Hope encourages men to endure and attempt everything; in depriving them of it, or in making it too distant, you deprive them of their very soul. It is essential that the captain should be better paid than the lieutenant, and so for all grades. The poor gentleman should have the moral surety of being able to succeed by his actions and his services. When all these things are taken care of you can maintain the most austere discipline among the troops. Truly, the only good officers are the poor gentlemen who have nothing but their sword and their cape, but it is essential that they should be able to live on their pay. The man who devotes himself to war should regard it as a religious order into which he enters. He should have nothing, know no other home than his troop, and should hold himself honored in his profession.

In France, a young noble considers himself badly treated by the court if a regiment is not confided to him at the age of eighteen or twenty years. This practice destroys all emulation in the rest of the officers and in the poor nobility, who are almost certain never to command a regiment, and, in consequence, to gain the more important posts whose glory is a recompense for the trouble and suffering of a laborious life that they will sacrifice if confident of a flattering and distinguished career.

I do not argue by this that no preference should be shown to some princes or others of illustrious rank, but it is essential that these marks of preference should be justified by distinguished merit.

TRAINING. Drill is necessary to make the soldier steady and skillful, although it does not warrant exclusive attention. Among all the elements of war it even is the one that deserves the least, if one excepts those which are dangerous.

The foundation of training depends on the legs and

not the arms. All the mystery of maneuvers and combats is in the legs, and it is to the legs that we should apply ourselves. Whoever claims otherwise is but a fool and not only in the elements of what is called the profession of arms.

The question whether war is a trade or a science is defined very well by Chevalier Follard. He said: "War is a trade for the ignorant and a science for the expert."

HOW TO FORM TROOPS FOR COMBAT. This is a broad subject and I propose to deal with it in a manner so different from respected custom that I shall probably expose myself to ridicule. But to lessen the danger, I shall explain the present method. This is no small affair, for I could compose a big volume on it.

I shall begin with the march, and this makes it necessary to say something that will appear highly extravagant to the ignorant. No one knows what the ancients meant by the word *tactics*. Nevertheless, many military men use this word constantly and believe that it is drill or the formation of troops for battle. Everyone has the march played without knowing how to use it. And everyone believes that the noise is a military ornament.

We should have a better opinion of the ancients and of the Romans, who are our masters and who should be. It is absurd to imagine that the warlike sounds had no other purpose than to confuse each other.

But to return to the march, about which everyone bothers themselves to death but will never reach a conclusion unless I reveal the secret. Some wish to march slowly, others would march fast; but what about the troops whom no one knows how to make march fast or slowly, as they desire, or is necessary, and who require an officer at every corner to make them turn, some like snails and others running, or to advance this column which is always trailing. It is a comedy to see even a battalion commence movement! It is like a poorly constructed machine, about to fall apart at every moment and which staggers with infinite difficulty. Do you wish to hurry the head? Before the tail knows that the head is marching fast, intervals have been formed; to fill them promptly, the tail must run; the head that follows this tail must do the same; soon everything is in disorder, with the result that you are never able to march rapidly for fear of speeding up the head of the column.

The way to remedy all these inconveniences, and many others which follow and are of greater importance, is very simple, nevertheless, because it is dictated by nature. Shall I say it, this great word which comprises all the mystery of the art and which will no doubt seem ridiculous? Have them march in cadence. There is the whole secret, and it is the military step of the Romans. That is why these musical marches were instituted, and that is why one beats the drum; it is this which no one knows and which no one has perceived. With this you can march fast or slow as you wish; the tail will not lose distance; all your soldiers will start on the same foot; the changes of direction will be made together with speed and grace; the legs of your soldiers will not get tangled up; you will not be forced to halt after each turn in order to start off on the same foot; your soldiers will not exhaust themselves a quarter as much as at present. All this may seem extraordinary. Every one has seen people dancing all night. But take a man and make him dance for a quarter of an hour only without music, and see if he can bear it. This proves that tunes have a secret power over us, that they predispose out muscles to physical exercise and lighten the exercise.

If anyone asks me what tune should be played for men to march by, I should answer, without joking, that all marches in double or triple time are suitable for it, some more, others less, depending upon whether they are more or less accented, that all the tunes played on the tamborine or fife will do, likewise, and that one needs only to choose the more suitable.

I shall be told, perhaps, that many men have no ear for music. This is false; movement to music is natural and is automatic. I have often noticed, while beating for the colors, that all the soldiers went in cadence without intention and without realizing it. Nature and instinct did it for them. I shall go further: it is impossible to perform any evolution in close order without it, and I shall prove it in the proper place.

Considering what I have said superficially, it does not appear that this cadence is of such great importance. But, in a battle to be able to augment the rapidity of march, or to diminish it, has infinite consequences. The military step of the Romans was nothing else; with it they marched twenty-four miles in five hours, the equivalent of eight leagues. Let anyone try the experiment on a body of our infantry and see if it is possible to make them do eight leagues in five hours. Among the Romans this was the principal part of their drill. From this, one can judge the attention they gave to keeping their troops in condition, as well as the importance of cadence.

What will be said if I prove that it is impossible to charge the enemy vigorously without this cadence, and that without it one reaches the enemy always with ranks opened? What a monstrous defect! I believe, how-ever, that no one has given it any attention for the past three or four hundred years.

It now becomes necessary to examine a little our method of forming battalions and of fighting. The battalions touch one another, since the infantry is all together and the cavalry also (for which, in truth, there is no common sense—but this will be covered in the proper place). The battalions, then, march ahead, and this very slowly because they are unable to do anything else. The majors cry: "Close," on which they press toward the center; insensibly the center gives way, which makes intervals between the battalions. There is no one who has had anything to do with these affairs but will agree with me. The majors' heads are turned because the general, whose head is turned also, cries after them when he sees the space between his battalions and is fearful of being taken in the flanks. He is thus obliged to call a halt, which should cost him the battle; but since the enemy is as badly disposed as he, the harm is slight. A man of intelligence would not stop to repair this con-fusion but would march straight ahead, for if the enemy moves he would be lost. What happens? Firing commences here and there, which is the height of misfortune. Finally they approach each other, and one of the two parties ordinarily takes to their heels at fifty or sixty paces, more or less. There you have what is called a charge. What is the cause of it all? Bad formations make it impossible to do better.

But I am going to suppose something impossible; I mean two battalions attacking to march toward each other without wavering, without doubling, and without breaking. Which will gain the advantage? The one that amuses itself shooting, or the one which will not have fired? The skillful soldiers tell me that it will be the one that has held its fire, and they are right. For besides being upset when he sees his opponent coming at him through the smoke, the one who has fired must halt to reload. And the one who stops while the other is marching toward him is lost.

If the previous war had lasted a little longer, indubitably everyone would have fought hand to hand. This was because the abuse of firing began to be appreciated; it causes more noise than harm, and those who depend on it are always beaten.

Powder is not as terrible as is believed. Few men, in these affairs, are killed from in front or fighting. I have seen entire salvos fail to kill four men. And I have never seen, and neither has anyone else, I believe, a single discharge do enough violence to keep the troops from continuing forward and avenging themselves with bayonet and shot at close quarters. It is then that men are killed, and it is the victorious who do the killing.

At the battle of Calcinato, M. de Reventlau, who commanded the Imperial army, had ranged his infantry on a plateau and had ordered them to allow the French infantry to approach to twenty paces, hoping to destroy them with a general discharge. His troops executed the orders exactly. The French with some difficulty climbed the hill which separated them from the Imperials and ranged themselves on the plateau opposite the enemy. They had been ordered not to fire at all. And since M. Vendome did not care to attack until he had taken a farm which was on his right, the troops remained for a considerable time looking at each other from close range. Finally they received the order to attack. The Imperials allowed them to approach to twenty or twenty-five paces, raised their arms, and fired with entire coolness and with all possible care. They were broken before the smoke had cleared. There were a great many killed by point blank fire and bayonet thrusts, and the disorder was general.

At the battle of Belgrade (August 16, 1717), I saw two battalions cut to pieces in an instant. This is how it happened. A battalion of Neuperg's and another of Lorraine's were on a hill that we called the battery. At the moment when a gust of wind dissipated the fog which kept us from distinguishing anything, I saw these troops on the crest of the hill, separated from the rest of our army. Prince Eugene, at the same time discovering a detachment of cavalry in motion on the side of the hill, asked me if I could distinguish what they were. I answered that they were thirty or forty Turks. He said: "Those men are enveloped," speaking of the two battalions. However, I could perceive no sign of their being attacked, not being able to see what was on the other side of the hill. I hastened there at a gallop. The instant I arrived behind Neuperg's colors, the two battalions raised their arms and fired a general discharge at thirty paces against the main body of the attacking Turks. The fire and the meleé were simultaneous, and the two battalions did not have time to flee for every man was cut to pieces on the spot. The only persons who escaped were M. Neuperg, who, fortunately for him, was on a horse, an ensign with his flag who clung to my horse's mane and bothered me not a little, and two or three soldiers.

At this moment Prince Eugene came up, almost alone, being attended only by his body guard, and the Turks retired for reasons unknown to me. It was here that Prince Eugene received a shot through the sleeve. Some cavalry and infantry arriving, M. Neuperg requested a detachment to collect the clothing. Sentries were posted at the four corners of the ground occupied by the dead of the two battalions, and their clothes, hats, shoes, etc., were collected in heaps. During this ceremony, I had curiosity enough to count the dead; I found only thirty-two Turks killed by the general discharge of the two battalions—which has not increased my regard for infantry fire.

It was an established maxim with the late M. de Greder, a man of reputation, and who had, for a long time, commanded my regiment of infantry in France, to make his men carry their muskets shouldered in an engagement; and, in order to be still more master of their fire, he did not even permit them to make their matches ready. Thus he marched toward the enemy, and the moment they started to fire, he threw himself sword in hand at the head of the colors, and cried, "Follow me!" This always succeeded for him. It was thus that he defeated the Frisian Guards at the battle of Fleurus (July 1, 1690).

What I have been advancing appears to me supported by reason and experience and proves that these large battalions have terrible defects; they are good only to fire, and they are organized for that alone. When fire is useless, they are worth nothing and have no recourse but to save themselves; which proves that everything from its very nature falls to its own level. Shall I tell from where I think we gained this method? It was probably taken from parades. This manner of arrangement makes a more pleasing appearance; unwittingly we have become accustomed to it, so that it was adopted in action.

Some attempt to vindicate this ignorance, or forgetfullness of good things, by apparent reason, alleging that in thus extending their front they will be able better to employ their fire; I have even known some to draw up their battalions three deep, but misfortune has been the fate of those who have done it. Otherwise, I really believe (God forgive me) they soon would have formed them two deep, and not improbably in single rank. For all my life I have heard it said that one should extend his order to out-flank the enemy. What absurdity!

But enough of this. I must first describe my method of forming regiments, legions, and the cavalry, because it is essential to base oneself on principle and on a formation for combat, which can change with the variety of situations but which will not be destroyed.

THE LEGION. The Romans vanquished all nations by their discipline; they meditated on war continually, and they always renounced old customs whenever they found better. In this respect, they differed from the Gauls, whom they defeated during several centuries without the latter thinking of correcting their errors.

Their legion was a body so formidable as to be capable of undertaking the most difficult enterprizes. "It was undoubtedly a god," says Vegetius, "that inspired the legion." I have held the same opinion for a long time, and it is this which has rendered me more aware of the defects of our own practices.

Since what I write is only a game to dissipate my boredom, I want to give full play to my imagination.

I would form my body of infantry into legions, each composed of four regiments, and every regiment of four centuries; each century would have a half-century of light-armed foot and a half-century of cavalry.

When centuries of infantry are drawn up in separate bodies, I shall call them battalions, and the cavalry, squadrons, in order to conform to our usage and aid the interchange of ideas.

The centuries, both of foot and horse, are to be composed of ten companies, every company consisting of fifteen men.

It is necessary in a monarchy to adapt the state of the troops to economy. It therefore is expedient to form them in three different establishments, which I shall call: the establishment in peace, the establishment for war, and the full establishment for war.

When the country is completely at peace the companies are to consist of one sergeant, one corporal, and five veteran soldiers. When preparations are being made for a war that is expected, an addition of five men is to be made. When war has been declared, or is about to be declared, they should consist of one sergeant, one corporal and fifteen men, which is an increase of 1600 per legion. The five veterans per company will constitute a reserve for the occasional supply of officers and noncommissioned officers, for these are always difficult to develop. In addition, among the five veterans there will always be a reserve for replacement. I do not care for newly raised regiments; sometimes they are worth nothing after ten years of war.

As for the cavalry, it should never be touched; the old troopers and the old horses are the good, and recruits of either are absolutely useless. It is a burden, it is an expense, but it is indispensable.

In regard to the infantry, as long as there are a few old heads you can do what you want with the tails; they are the greatest number, and the return of these men in peace is a noticeable benefit to the nation, without a serious diminution of the military forces.

As I am going to deal with war, I shall place my troops on a complete war establishment, so that a century of foot will consist of 184 men, and each company of seventeen.

The two half-centuries of horse and light-armed foot should not exceed ten per company, including the sergeants and corporals, because they will be recruited out of the regiments.

Any diminution of the heavy-armed forces, which compose the main body of the infantry, will be of no consequence, because the different units of the legion will still remain the same even if reduced to peace strength, that is to say, five soldiers. This will be a great advantage and a solid foundation for all your infantry, since your drills remain the same and permanent. It is inconceivable how prejudicial all such changes are. I have seen troops belonging to the same government, when assembled after a long peace, differ to such a degree in their maneuvers and formation of their regiments that one would have taken them for a collection from several distinct nations.

It is necessary, therefore, to establish one definite principle of action, and never to depart from it. No one should be ignorant of this principle because it is the foundation of the military profession. But it is impossible to assure it, unless you always maintain the same number of officers and noncommissioned officers; without that, your maneuvers will always vary.

Every heavy-armed century is to be furnished with an arm of my own invention, which I call an amusette. They carry more than four thousand paces with extreme velocity. The field-pieces used by the Germans and

Swedes with their battalions will scarcely carry a fourth of that distance.

This is also much more accurate; two men can carry it anywhere. It fires a half-pound lead ball and carries one hundred pounds with it. Going through foot paths in mountains, the rails are drawn back and two soldiers can carry the piece very easily. This arm can be used on a thousand occasions in war.

The artillery and wagons should be drawn by oxen. The wagon should be loaded with all kinds of implements necessary for building forts, such as different cordages, cranes, pullies, windlasses, saws, hatchets, shovels, mattocks, etc. These should all be marked with the number of their respective legion, so that in armies they will not be lost or mixed together.

The private soldiers should have, a piece of copper fixed on each shoulder, with the number of the legion and regiment to which they belong, respectively, on them so that they may be easily distinguished.

I would also have their right hands marked with the same numbers with a composition used by the Indians, which never wears off and will put a stop to desertion. This will be easy to introduce and will lead to innumerable good consequences. To establish it the sovereign has only to assemble his colonels and tell them that it will be of great importance in maintaining good order and preventing desertion; that they will please him if they give the example and mark themselves; that this could not be other than a mark of honor, by proving the regiment in which they have served. No one will refuse it. All the subordinate officers, ambitious to oblige their Prince, and realizing of the utility of such an institution, will gladly imitate their colonels. After this no soldier will refuse it. Marking them could even be made a ceremony. It was a practice among the Romans, but they marked with a hot iron.

For the centuries of horse, men should be chosen from the regiments to which they belong, leaving the choice of them to their centurion, but he will give preference to the old soldiers. Cavalry thus selected will never abandon their infantry and will give them confidence in a battle and be of admirable service to them, either in pursuit or covering their retreat. · But I shall speak more fully of this in another place.

The light-armed foot are in like manner to be chosen in their regiments, the centurions selecting the youngest and most active. Their arms must consist of nothing more than a very light fowling-piece and bayonet with a handle to it. This fowling-piece is to be made so as to open and receive the charge at the breech, so that it will not need to be rammed. All the equipment must be as light as possible. Their officers will be chosen in the same manner without regard to seniority. They must be drilled frequently, must practice jumping and running, but, above all, firing at a mark at three hundred paces distance. Rewards are to be posted for those who excel in all these different exercises, in order to create emulation.

A body of infantry organized according to this plan, and thoroughly trained, can march everywhere with the cavalry and, I am confident, will be capable of giving great service.

I am far from approving of grenadiers; they are the elite of our troops. Since they are employed on every important occasion, a brisk war exhausts them to such an extent that they are no longer able to furnish noncommissioned officers, who are the heart of the infantry. I would substitute veterans in place of grenadiers; they should have more pay than the simple soldiers and light foot. The light-armed forces are to be employed on all services requiring speed and activity, the veterans only on serious efforts. I believe this will result in great benefit for the military establishment. The command of the light-armed troops is always to be given to a lieutenant, who should be chosen by the colonel. But that of the veterans, being regarded as the post of honor, is to be determined by seniority. According to the present system, it is impossible to prevent the officers from succeeding to grenadier companies by seniority without affronting them to a violent degree; this always uses up the best officers you have. I have seen sieges where the companies of grenadiers had to be replaced several times. This is easily explained: grenadiers are wanted everywhere. If there are four cats to chase, it is grenadiers who are demanded, and usually they are killed without any necessity.

The heavy-armed forces are to have good muskets, five feet in length, with large bores and using a one ounce ball. These muskets also should load at the breech. They will carry over twelve hundred paces.

It is needless to be afraid of over-loading the infantry with arms; this will make them more steady. The arms of the Roman soldiers weighed over sixty pounds, and it was death to abandon them in action. It prevented any thoughts of flying and was a principle of military art with them. To these muskets I would add a bayonet with a handle, two and one-half feet long, which will serve as a sword, and oval shields or targets. These shields have many advantages; they not only cover the arms, but, when fighting in position, the troops can form a kind of parapet with them in an instant by passing them from hand to hand to the front. Two of them, one on the other, are musket proof. My opinion in regard to this piece of armor is supported by that of Montecuculli, who says that it is absolutely necessary for the infantry.

Bayonets with handles to fix within the barrel of the musket are much preferable to the others because they enable the commander to reserve his fire as long as he thinks proper. This is a matter of the utmost importance, since one cannot hope to do two different things at once. That is to say, charge, or stand and fight. In one case they must fire, in the other not at all.

Here is an example: Charles the XII, King of Sweden, wished to introduce among his troops the practice of engaging sword in hand. He had spoken of it several times, and the army knew that he favored the system. Accordingly, in a battle against the Russians, at the moment it was about to begin he hastened to his regiment of infantry, and made a fine harangue, dismounted, posted himself in the front of the colors, and led them on to the charge himself. But as soon as they came within about thirty paces of the enemy, his whole regiment fired in spite of his orders and his presence. And although he routed the Russians and obtained a complete victory, he was so piqued that he passed through the ranks, re-mounted his horse, and rode off without speaking a single word.

But to return to the formation of the battalions. I would draw them up four deep, the two front ranks being armed with muskets and the two rear with half-pikes and muskets slung over their shoulders. The half-pike is a weapon thirteen feet in length, exclusive of the iron-head, which is to be three-square, eighteen inches long, and two broad. The shaft must be of spruce, hollowed, and covered with varnished parchment. This is very strong and very light and does not whip like the pikes the infantry thinks they cannot do without. I have always heard this opinion from all experienced men; and the same reasons, neglect and indolence, which have caused the abandonment of many other excellent customs of the profession of war, are the cause of the abandonment of this one. The half-pikes were found unserviceable in some affairs that took place in Italy, where the country was very rough; since then they have been laid aside everywhere and nothing since has been thought of but to increase the quantity of firearms and to fire.

Although I have been exclaiming against firing in general, there are certain situations where it is necessary and it is well to know how. These are enclosures and rough grounds, and also against cavalry. But the method should be simple and natural. The present practice is worthless because it is impossible for the soldier to aim while his attention is distracted awaiting the command. How can all these soldiers who have been commanded to get ready to fire continue to aim until they receive the word to fire? A trifle will derange them, and, having once lost the critical instant, their fire is no longer of much use. Let no one think that this does not make a great difference; it will amount to several yards. Nothing is so easy to derange as musket fire. And besides this, and according to our method, they are kept in a constrained position.

These and many other inconveniences totally prevent the effect which small-arms should produce. But this subject demands a special article. I shall therefore return to the formation of my battalions.

In attacking infantry, the two rear ranks are to lower their pikes; in this position the pikes will extend from six to seven feet ahead of the front rank. The front ranks being sheltered in such a manner will, I am sure, aim with more confidence than if they had nothing in front of them. Besides this, the third rank can ward off blows and defend the first rank, which it will do much better, since it is covered by the first two ranks. The second rank, which is armed with muskets, can fire and defend the man in front of him in the first rank, without the latter being obliged to stoop. This avoids a serious disadvantage which is incurred in kneeling, a dangerous movement, because men who are afraid prefer this position, they cannot be made to get up when wanted, and it is always necessary to halt to kneel. According to my formation all the men are covered, each by the other, with reciprocal confidence; the front presents a forest of spears; their appearance is formidable and gives confidence to your own troops because they feel its power.

In attacking infantry, the light-armed foot are to be dispersed along the front, at the distance of a hundred, one hundred fifty, or two hundred paces in advance. They should begin firing when the enemy is about three hundred paces off, without word of command and at will, until the enemy approaches within about fifty paces. At this distance every captain is to order a retreat, taking care to retire slowly towards his regiment, keeping up his fire from time to time, until he arrives at his battalion which should be starting to move. The men should be disposed to fall into the intervals of the battalions by tens. The regiments during this time should have doubled ranks while moving forward. There should be two troops of cavalry, of thirty troopers each, thirty paces behind the regiment.

The whole moving forward with a regular and rapid step will certainly discourage the enemy. For what can they do? To attack the flanks of the centuries they must break their battalions. They neither can nor dare because the intervals are only ten paces and these are filled by the light-armed foot. In addition they are rendered still more impenetrable by the transversed pikes of the rear ranks. How can they resist, being only four deep, and having been already harassed by the light-armed infantry, when they meet fresh troops formed eight deep, with a front equal to theirs, and which come rapidly against them, disordered already by the unevenness of ranks which is unavoidable in the movement of so extensive a body? It appears highly probable that they must be defeated, and if they trust to flight they are lost without resource. For the moment they turn their backs, the light-armed foot, together with the horse posted in the rear, are to pursue, and will make dreadful havoc among them. The seventy cavalry and the seventy light-armed foot should destroy a battalion in a moment before they have had time to flee a hundred paces. During the pursuit the centuries are to stand fast, in order to receive their own troops again and to be ready to renew the charge.

I cannot avoid believing that, of all formations, this is the best for battle. Some will say that the enemy's cavalry might be thrown against my light-armed troops. No one will dare it, but so much the better if it happens. Will they not be forced to withdraw? Can they fire against seventy men scattered along the front of my regiment? It would be like firing at a handful of fleas. Ah! They will do the same thing and also will have light-armed foot. The benefit of my system is proved if it bothers them to the point where they are forced to imitate it.

I should, before I finish this article, make a concise calculation of the fire of my light-armed troops.

Let us suppose them to begin firing at the distance

of three hundred paces, which is that at which they are trained, and that they are one hundred fifty paces from me. They thus will fire during the time necessary for the enemy to march that distance, which will be from seven to eight minutes at least. My irregulars will be able to fire six times in a minute. However, I shall only say four; every one will, therefore, have fired thirty times. Consequently, every battalion will have received four or five hundred shots before the engagement can possibly commence. And from whom? From troops who have spent their life firing at a greater distance, who are not drawn up in close order, and who fire at ease without waiting for the word of command. They are not kept in that constrained attitude which is customary in the ranks, where the men crowd one another, and prevent their taking a steady aim. I contend that a single shot from one of these irregulars is worth ten from any other. And if the enemy marches in line, they will receive ten thousand musket shots per battalion before my troops attack them.

To these I add the fire of my amusettes. I have already observed that they require only two soldiers to draw and one to serve them.

Before an engagement these amusettes are to be advanced in front, along with the light-armed troops. Since they can be fired two hundred times in an hour with ease, and carry above three thousand paces, they cause great damage to the enemy when forming or after they have passed wood, defile, or village. Even when there are none of these obstacles, they will have to march in column, and then draw up in order of battle, which sometimes takes several hours. Every century is to have but one; those of both lines may be joined upon occasion, or all can be collected on a height. They should produce considerable effect because they will carry farther and are much more accurate than our cannon. Since there are four per regiment there will be sixteen to each legion. The sixteen belonging to a legion assembled in an engagement will be sufficient to silence any battery of the enemy's which bothers the cavalry or even the infantry.

With regard to my pikes, if they become useless in rough or mountainous places the soldiers have nothing more to do than to lay them aside for an hour or two. My soldiers can use their muskets which they always carry slung over their shoulders. To say that carrying them will be too great an incumbrance is an objection to which no reply is necessary. Are they not now obliged to carry their tent poles? Nothing more is required than to substitute these pikes, which are better. Their appearance above the tents will be pleasing and ornamental in a camp. Their weight, including the iron, does not exceed four pounds because they are hollow. Ordinary pikes weigh about seventeen pounds and are extremely unwieldy.

I maintain that such a body of troops will be of great service, assuming that the legionary general understands and knows what he should know. If the commander in chief of an army wants to occupy a post, to obstruct the enemy in their projects or in a hundred different situations which are found in war, he has only to order a particular legion to march. Since it is furnished with everything that can be required to fortify itself, it can soon be secure from any insult. And in the space of four or five days, it should be ready to sustain a siege and arrest an enemy's army.

This organization of the infantry appears to me the more proper, since it is well proportioned in all its parts. The acquired reputation of any single legion will both make an impression on the others and even on the enemy. Such a body will regard their reputation as a tradition and will always be moved by a desire to surpass that of any other. The exploits of an organization which is denominated by a number are not so soon forgotten as those of one which bears the name of their officers because the officers change and their actions are forgotten with them. Moreover, it is more the nature of men to be less interested in things which relate to others than about those in which they themselves are concerned. The reputation of an organization becomes personal just as soon as it is an honor to belong to it. This honor is much easier to arouse in an organization that keeps its name than one which carries some one elses, that is, its colonel's who very probably may be disliked.

Many persons do not know why all the regiments which bear the names of provinces in France have always performed so well. They give as the entire reason: "It is esprit de corps." This is far from being the real reason, as appears from what I have just been observing. Thus we see how matters of the utmost importance depend on an imperceptible point. Besides, these legions are a kind of military fatherland, where the prejudices of different nations are confounded—an important point for a monarch or for a conqueror. For wherever he finds men, he finds soldiers.

Those who imagine that the Roman legions were composed of Romans from Rome are very much deceived; they came from all the nations in the world. But their composition, their discipline, and their method of fighting were better than those of all other nations. This is why they conquered them all. Neither were they conquered in their turn until this discipline had degenerated among the Romans.

CAVALRY IN GENERAL. The cavalry should be active and mounted on horses inured to fatigue. It should be encumbered with as little baggage as possible, and, above all, should not make that common error of having fat horses. If they could see an enemy every day it would only be the better, for this would soon put them in condition to attempt anything. It is certain that the power of cavalry is not understood. Why? Because of the love we have for fat horses.

I had a regiment of German cavalry in Poland with which I marched more than fifteen hundred leagues in eighteen months. I maintain that this regiment was more fit for service at the end of this time than another supplied with fat horses. But to reach this condition they must be gradually accustomed to hardship and hardened by hunts and violent exercise. This will maintain their health and increase their endurance. Likewise, it will make cavalrymen of the troopers and give them a martial bearing. But they must be made to gallop at top speed by squadrons, reaching this point by degrees, and not be drilled gently once every three years for fear that the animals may sweat. I insist that unless they are accustomed to hard treatment they will be more subject to accidents and will never be of any service.

There should be two kinds of cavalry: cavalry and dragoons. I have no use for any others. Light cavalry and well-equipped dragoons are more useful than hussars. Of the first, which is true cavalry, although much the best, the number must be small because they are very expensive and require especial attention. Forty squadrons will suffice for an army of thirty, forty, or fifty thousand men. Their drills should be simple and in masses, free from all effort of too great speed. The essential point is to teach them to fight together and never to disperse. The supplying of main guards is the only duty they should do. Escorts, detachments, and pursuits should never be assigned to them. They should be considered like heavy artillery, which marches with the army. Consequently, they should only serve in combats and battles.

For this cavalry, selected men from five feet six to five feet seven inches tall are essential. They should be slender and without fat stomachs. Their horses should be strong and never under fifteen hands, two inches. The German horses are the best.

They should be armed from head to foot, and the front rank should have Polish lances hung by a slender strap to the pommel of the saddle. They should have good, stiff swords four feet long, with three-square blades, carbines, but no pistols, as they will only increase the weight. They need stirrups, but instead of saddles, the bows only, with a pair of panels stuffed and covered with black sheepskins, which will serve as a case and to come across the horse's chest.

As for dragoons, of which twice as many are needed, the regiments should be of the same number and similarly organized. Their horses should not be over fourteen hands high nor under thirteen hands two inches. Their drill must be full of spirit and speed. They should also know the drill of the infantry perfectly. Their arms should be the musket and the sword. Their lances should serve as pikes when they are dismounted. Their saddles and harness should be the same as that of the cavalry. The men must be small and their height from five feet to five feet one inch, not over two. They should form by squadrons three deep, the same as the cavalry, and march in the same manner.

The rear rank must be taught to vault and skirmish, rallying in the intervals between the squadrons. The front and center ranks should have their muskets slung. These dragoons should do all the service of the army, cover the camp, form escorts, furnish reconnaissance elements, and discover the enemy wherever he may be.

There in general is what concerns the cavalry. It is appropriate to enter into greater detail.

CAVALRY ARMOR. I do not know why armor has been laid aside, for nothing is either so useful or ornamental.

It may be said that the invention of gun powder abolished it. It is not that; for, in the time of Henry IV and since to the year 1667, it has been worn. Powder was introduced long before. But you will see the precious cause of its abandonment.

It is certain that a naked squadron, such as ours, will stand a poor chance opposed to one armed from head to foot (assuming the numbers are equal), for what can our men do to pierce them? Their only resource is to fire. It is a great advantage to reduce enemy cavalry to the necessity of firing.

This idea merits examination. I have invented a suit of armor, consisting of thin iron plates fixed on a strong buff-skin. This armor is not expensive, and the entire weight is not over thirty-five pounds. I have tried it; it is proof against a sword. I do not allege it to be the same against a bullet, especially one fired point-blank. But it will resist any that have not been well rammed, become loose in the barrel by the movement of the horses, or come from an oblique direction.

But leave fire at that. The fire of the cavalry is not of any importance; I have always heard it said that those who have fired were beaten. If this is true, we should try to get them to fire. The easiest method to do this is to give your cavalry armor such as I propose; that will make them safe from the sword and an enemy will be forced to fire. But what will happen if he fires? As soon as cavalry shall have received the fire, they will throw themselves on the enemy with irresistible elan, since they have nothing more to fear and wish to avenge the dangers they have just escaped. And how can those who are naked, in effect, be able to defend themselves against others who are invulnerable? If they bestir themselves I defy anyone to kill them. If there were only two such regiments in a whole army, and they had routed a few enemy squadrons, fear and terror would spread throughout because everyone would appear to be armored.

I shall be answered: "The enemy will do the same thing." This is a proof that what I propose is good, since the enemy can find no other remedy except to imitate me. But this will not occur in the following campaign. They will allow themselves to be defeated for ten years, and perhaps for a hundred, before making a change. Whether it results from pride, laziness, or stupidity, all nations change their customs reluctantly. Even good institutions are not adopted, or only after infinite time, although often every one is convinced of their utility. In spite of all this, they are abandoned frequently to follow custom and routine. And we are told coldly: " 'Tis contrary to custom."

To demonstrate what I have advanced, one need only recall the number of years during which the Gauls were always overcome by the Romans, without ever attempting to change their discipline or manner of fighting. The Turks are now in the same case; it is neither courage, numbers, nor riches which they lack, but discipline, order, and manner of combat.

At the battle of Peterwaradin, they had more than one hundred thousand men; we with only forty thousand, defeated them. At Belgrade, they had more than two hundred thousand men; we had less than thirty thousand, and they were defeated. And this will always be the case as long as they cling to customs that are injurious These examples should persuade us never to be prejudiced in any thing.

Any objections which may be made against this armor on the pretext that a shot through it will be more dangerous are false. A ball will only pierce the metal without carrying the broken pieces along with it. But even so, if the advantages of armor are weighed justly against the inconveniences, it will be found that the balance favors it infinitely. For of what consequence are a few men who die of wounds because of their armor, if battles are won and it makes the enemy inferior? If it be considered how many troopers perish by the sword, and how many are dangerously wounded by random and weak shots, accidents against which armor guarantees protection, one cannot avoid acknowledging the benefits of it.

It is nothing but indolence and relaxation of discipline that caused it to be laid aside. It is wearisome to carry a cuirass and trail a pike half a century to use it a single day. But as soon as discipline is neglected in a nation, as soon as comfort becomes an aim, it needs no inspiration to foretell that its ruin is near.

The Romans conquered all peoples by their discipline. In the measure that it became corrupted their success decreased. When the emperor Gratian permitted the legions to quit their cuirasses and helmets, because the soldiers complained that they were too heavy, all was lost. The barbarians whom they had defeated during so many centuries vanquished them in turn.

ARMS AND EQUIPMENT FOR CAVALRY. The men are to have rifled carbines, which carry much farther than any others and are more easily loaded, since ramming the charge is avoided; this is a very difficult feat on horseback. They must always be slung over their shoulders in an engagement, as well as on a march. Otherwise the troopers are never ready and do not keep ranks.

The swords should be slung the same as the carbines because in that position they will be less inconvenient and more ornamental. Their sabers should be three-square to keep them from cutting with them, a method of small effect. They are lighter and much stiffer than the flat kind. They should be four feet long, for a long sword is as necessary on horseback just as a short one is on foot. I do not care for pistols because they never are effective, they are expensive, and are a useless weight and encumbrance. The front rank are to be furnished with Polish lances. These lances extend ten feet beyond the front rank, and the horses of the enemy squadrons will be terrified at the waving of the taffetas when they are lowered. Besides, the point is not adorned. Montecuculli states in his *Memoires* that the lance is the best of all arms for the cavalry and their shock cannot be resisted. But it is essential that they be armed from head to foot.

The troopers should have a goat-skin bottle like those used in hot countries, instead of a canteen or barrel, to hold liquors in. This, with his linen, stockings, cap, a cord, and his few other necessaries, is to be put into the bottom of his sack, which will roll up with his coat and can be fastened with two straps behind him. This will reduce that monstrous load which is now carried by the cavalry.

It is necessary from time to time to inspect the baggage and force the men to throw away useless items. I have frequently done it. One can hardly imagine all the trash they carry with them year after year. The poor horse has to carry everything. It is no exaggeration to say that I have filled twenty wagons with useless rubbish which I have found in the review of a single regiment.

THE ORGANIZATION OF THE CAVALRY. The regiments of cavalry and dragoons, like those of infantry, should be composed of four centuries, each of 130 men. This will form four squadrons and the staff as in the infantry.

The squadrons of cavalry should never be reduced, nor augmented, because it takes ten years to make a cavalryman. None but veteran horses are good in war, and the cavalry should be a dependable body.

With regard to dragoons, they may be decreased or dismounted in time of peace. Provided they remain organized like infantry, they will be useful.

MARCHING, CHARGING, AND DRILLING CAVALRY. Extreme attention should be given, when marching by twos, that cavalry and dragoons do not drop into single file to pass a few bad spots on the road. If one does it, all will, with the result that instead of arriving in camp in six hours, it will take twelve. A single bad defile on a march will cause delay unless the officers give it particular attention. If there are several, it will throw a whole column into disorder. In defiles you will find some halted and others galloping to overtake the leaders. Nothing is so destructive to the cavalry as this lack of attention. It should be punished with the utmost severity. When there are holes in the road which cannot be avoided, it is much better to make a general halt and repair them than to disregard them, or else another road should be taken.

In passing through water, the horses must never be allowed to drink. A man who halts to water his horse will stop a whole army. When this happens, the officers should hasten to the spot, and, instead of fruitless reprimands and ill-timed mercy, they should instantly chastise the offender. Nothing is of such importance for the preservation of the cavalry. Otherwise the affection the men have for their horses will have them halting little or much, and then it is impossible for them to recover their ranks without galloping.

Let no one think this does not make any difference. You will reach your camp at night, when you should have arrived by noon. If this is not prevented by extraordinary care and attention, a few days' march will ruin the best cavalry.

When the cavalry are to charge, it cannot be sufficiently emphasized that they must keep together and not disperse. Their standards should be sacred. Whatever happens in combat, their duty is always to rally to them. With these principles, if you can inculcate them, your cavalry will be invincible.

In charging, they first should move off at a gentle trot for a distance of about one hundred paces and increase their speed in proportion as they advance. They should not close boot to boot until they come within about twenty or thirty paces of the enemy, and this should be done at the command from an officer: "Follow me!" It is necessary to train the cavalry to this, and this movement should be like lightening. But they must be familiarized with it by constant exercise. It is necessary to teach them, while in winter quarters, to gallop long distances in squadron formation, without breaking. A squadron that cannot charge two thousand paces at full speed without breaking is unfit for war. It is the fundamental point. When they know this, they are good, and everything else will be easy. That is everything they need to know.

The dragoons should know the same thing and, in addition, should be taught to skirmish. Their rear rank should sortie in open ranks, return, and form again with celerity. They should be trained to fire on horseback and should know all the drills of the infantry.

In time of peace, and in winter quarters in time of war, their horses should be kept in condition by violent exercise, or runs, at least three times a week. The same severe usage is also proper for the heavy cavalry at those times. It is only in the field that they must be managed carefully, to keep them in flesh and the squadrons complete and strong.

The best chance of teaching them to stand fire is when the infantry is practicing. They should advance on the fire at a walk and be kept calm, accustoming them to go closer and closer. They should never be beaten but stroked and encouraged. In the space of a month, they will be so accustomed to it that they will even put their nose on the muzzle of the muskets without any fright or surprise. Then they are all right. Nevertheless, they should not be allowed to approach too close, for if once they get burned you will not be able to bring them near again. This ordeal must be reserved for the day of battle.

CAVALRY DETACHMENTS. The country in which war is being made will determine the usefulness, as well as success, of parties. Large detachments of cavalry seldom achieve anything useful unless it is some prompt and vigorous expedition, such as intercepting a convoy, surprising a post, or supporting advanced parties of infantry which have been pushed ahead to cover your march. Then they are of immense value. Suppose that the enemy intends to attack your rear guard or your baggage; he will not dare attempt it if you send out a large detachment the day before you march. He will hesitate to place himself between the body he wants to attack and the detachment he knows certainly to have gone out, although he may not know definitely the route it took nor where it is.

Detachments of this kind should be always strong. The commanding officers should be skillful and experienced in war, for this is one of the most difficult missions to execute, at least when the objective is not fixed. Of course, when ordered to seize or surprise a post, or to intercept a convoy, they have nothing to do except to march straight ahead and attack.

If you have a good spy service you may be able to contrive ambushes in open campaign. Sometimes localities can be found that are hidden and permit unexpected attacks on bodies of troops that pass by. But this happens only rarely. Altogether, cavalry operations are exceedingly difficult, knowledge of the country is absolutely necessary, ability to comprehend the situation at a glance and an audacious spirit are everything.

Small cavalry detachments are absolutely necessary, and they should be out every day. In general they need not consist of more than fifty troopers and should always avoid a fight. Their object is to get information and take a few prisoners.

If the enemy is bold and organizes large detachments to oppose yours, he should be watched until an opportunity is found to surprise him with double his force. You will then have gained superiority in the field, and he will no longer dare to molest your small parties. You will be able to observe all his movements so that it will be impossible for him to take a step without your being informed. You will be secure and this will hinder and harass him greatly. Your foraging parties will be free from interference and he will be forced to use extreme precaution with his, because he is not master of the country, and soon will have his troops worn out.

These are duties on which dragoons may be employed. And, when they are trained, they will be infinitely superior to hussars because they are capable of the same rapidity of action and are more solid. But they need lots of practice and action. Large bodies of cavalry cannot catch them, and hussars cannot injure them. A troop of fifty dragoons has nothing to fear from a multitude of hussars. They always march at a trot and the hussars dare not follow them into the least defile.

After they have been taught by exercise and experience to know their own power, they will become so bold that they will always be harassing the main guards of the enemy. Officers will be developed in such operations, and the enemy will have nothing to oppose them with except patience.

COMBINED OPERATIONS. I am convinced every unit that is not supported is a defeated organization, and that the principles which M. de Montecuculli has given in his *Memoires* are correct. He says that infantry should always be supported by cavalry, and cavalry by infantry. Nevertheless we do not practice it. We place all our cavalry on the wings which are not supported by infantry. How are they supported? From four or five hundred paces! This destroys the assurance of the troops, for any man who has nothing behind him on which to retire or depend for aid is half beaten, and this is the reason that even the second line has sometimes given ground while the first was fighting. I have seen this many times and probably so have others. But no one seems to have sought the reason, which lies in the human heart.

It is for these reasons that I place small bodies of cavalry twenty-five or thirty paces in the rear of my infantry, and battalions in square formation in the interval between my two wings of cavalry, behind which it will be able to rally and stop the enemy cavalry.

It is certain that the second line of cavalry will never fly so long as they see the square battalions in their front, and their appearance will also reassure that of the first line. The battalions will maintain their ground because they cannot do anything else, and because they hope for prompt assistance from the cavalry, which, under the cover of their fire, will reappear in an instant wishing to retrieve the disgrace of their defeat. Besides, these battalions will cover the flanks of your infantry, which is not an unimportant consideration.

There are some who want to place small bodies of infantry between the intervals of cavalry; this is useless. The weakness of this formation will intimidate your infantry, for they feel that if the cavalry are defeated they are lost. And if the cavalry, who are also dependent on them, make a quick movement, they leave them behind and, perceiving they have lost their support, are soon in confusion. In addition, if your cavalry wing is defeated, the enemy can easily take you in the flank, and very quickly.

Others mix squadrons of cavalry with their infantry. This is of no value whatsoever, for as soon as the enemy attacks, his fire puts the cavalry in confusion, kills horses, and the cavalry gives way. This is enough to turn the heads of the infantry and make them do the same.

What are 'squadrons to do in this formation? Are they to stand fast, sword in hand, and wait the attack of the enemy's infantry, firing and advancing upon them with fixed bayonets? Or must they make the charge themselves? If they are repulsed, which will most probably be the case, they disorder their own infantry. To imagine that they will be able to find their own places again is hardly rational.

THE COLUMN. Notwithstanding the great regard I have for the Chevalier Follard, and that I think highly of his writings, I cannot agree with his opinion about the column. This idea seduced me at first; it looks dangerous to the enemy, but the execution of it reversed my opinion. It is necessary to analyze it to show its faults.

The Chevalier deceives himself in imagining that this column can be moved with ease. It is the heaviest body I know of, especially when it is twenty-four deep. If it happens that the files are once disordered, either by marching, the unevenness of the ground, or the enemy's cannon, no man alive can restore order. Thus it becomes a mass of soldiers who no longer have ranks or order, and where everything is confounded.

I have frequently been surprised that the column is not used to attack the enemy on the march. It is certain that a large army always takes up three or four times more ground on the march than is necessary to form it, even though marching in several columns. If, therefore, you get information of the enemy's route and the hour at which he is to begin his march, although he is at the distance of six leagues from you, you will always arrive in time to intercept him, for his head usually arrives in the new camp before his rear has left the old. It is impossible to form troops scattered over such a distance without making large intervals and dreadful confusion. I have often seen such a movement made without the enemy having thought of profiting by the occasion. And I thought they must have been bewitched.

This subject would furnish a useful chapter, for many diverse situations produce such marches. And in how many places may not one attack without risking anything? How frequently an army is separated on its march by bad roads, rivers, difficult passes? And how many such situations will enable you to surprise some part of it? How often do opportunities present themselves of separating it, so as to be able, although inferior, to attack one part with advantage and, at the same time, by the proper placement of a small number of troops, prevent its being relieved by the other? But all these circumstances are as various and intermediate as the situations which produce them, and nothing more is required than to keep well-informed, to acquire a knowledge of the country, and to dare. You risk nothing, for as these affairs are never decisive for you, they can be for the enemy. The heads of your columns attack as they arrive, and they are supported by the troops that follow them. This results from the formation itself. And you attack regiments which have no support.

But I find I have wandered from the first principles of the military art and that it is not yet time to commence on such higher subjects.

SMALL ARMS. Fire should not be used against infantry where they can envelop you or you can envelop them. But where you are separated from an enemy by hedges, ditches, rivers, hollows, and such obstacles, then it is necessary to know how to aim and execute such terrible fire that it cannot be resisted.

I recommend the breech-loading musket. It can be loaded quicker, carries farther, is more accurate, and the effect is greater. In the excitement of battle, soldiers will not be able to put cartridges in the barrel without opening them. This often happens now and makes the muskets useless. They will not be able to insert two charges because the chamber will not hold them. Consequently, muskets will not burst as they often do.

To dislodge the enemy from a position on the other side of a river, from hedges, ditches, and such other places where the use of small arms is necessary, I would designate an officer or noncommissioned officer to every two files. He should advance the leader of the first a pace forward and show him where he is to direct his fire, allowing him to fire at will, that is, when he has found a target. The soldier behind him will then pass his gun forward, and the others in the same manner. The file leader will thus fire four shots in succession. It would be unusual if the second or third shot does not reach its mark. The commanding officer is close by him, watches his aim, directs him where to fire, and exhorts him not to hurry. This man is not hindered, nor crowded, nor hastened by the word of command. No one presses him; he can fire at ease and aim as long as he wishes, and he can fire four times in succession.

This file having fired, the officer withdraws it and advances the second which performs in the same fashion.

Then he returns the first which has had ample time to load. This can be repeated for several hours.

This fire is the most deadly of all, and I do not think any other can resist it. It would silence that by platoons or ranks, and even if they all were Caesars I would defy them to hold for a quarter of an hour. For with my guns one can fire six rounds a minute with ease. Call it four to allow for shifting guns; every musket will have fired sixty shots in a quarter of an hour, and consequently the file leaders of a regiment of five hundred men will have fired thirty thousand, not considering the light-armed forces. In an hour this will amount to 120,000 shots, and including the fire of the light-armed troops, 140,000, all better aimed than ordinary fire.

COLORS OR STANDARDS. The general or commander-in-chief of an army should have a standard to be carried ahead of him as a mark of his rank. This also has a purpose. Anyone searching for him will know instantly where to find him, especially in battle, and the troops seeing the standard will know that the general is observing them.

Since nothing is more useful than colors or standards in action, they should be given particular attention. In the first place, they should all be of different colors so that the legions, regiments, and even centuries to which they belong may be readily distinguished in combat. The soldiers of each century should make it an article of faith never to abandon their standard. It should be sacred to them; it should be respected; and every type of ceremony should be used to make them respected and precious. This is an essential point, for after troops are once attached to them you can count on all sorts of successes; resolution and courage will be the natural consequences of it; and if, in desperate affairs, some determined man seizes a standard, he will render the whole century as brave as himself because it will follow him.

If the standards are distinguished by their different colors, the actions of every century will be conspicuous. This will create the greatest emulation because both officers and soldiers will know that they are seen and that their countenance, conduct, and behaviour are not ignored by the rest of the army. For example, the first standard of a regiment that has fled will be seen, distinguished, and recognized by the generals and all the troops. The first century that shall have forced a pass, carried an entrenchment, or made a vigorous charge, will be easily distinguished, deserve praise, and gain the applause of the whole army. The men as well as officers will tell of it; in the field and in garrison their exploits will be the constant subject of conversation. The desire to imitate brave actions will be aroused by praise. And these trifles will diffuse a spirit of emulation among the troops which affects both officers and soldiers and in time will make them invincible.

The number of every century should be distinguished by the color of its standard. Every standard should have a white quarter near the staff to hold the number of the legion marked in Roman numerals. Thus the designs and colors of the standards will distinguish the centuries of every legion, and the numerals, the legions themselves.

ARTILLERY AND TRANSPORT. I never would have an army composed of more than ten legions, eight regiments of cavalry, and sixteen of dragoons. This would amount to thirty-four thousand foot and twelve thousand horse, a total of forty-six thousand men. With such an army, one of a hundred thousand can be stopped if the general is clever and knows how to choose his camps. A greater army is only an embarrassment. I do not say that reserves are unnecessary, but only that the acting part of an army ought not to exceed such a number.

M. de Turenne was always victorious with armies infinitely inferior in numbers to those of his enemies because he moved more easily and knew how to select positions such that he could not be attacked while still always keeping near the enemy.

It is sometimes impossible to find a piece of ground in a whole province that will contain a hundred thousand men in order of battle. Thus the enemy is almost always forced to divide, in which case I can attack one of the parts; if I defeat it, I thereby intimidate the other and soon gain superiority. In short, I am convinced that the advantages which large armies have in numbers are more than lost in the encumbrance, the diversity of operations under the jarring conduct of different commanders, the deficiency of provisions, and many other inconveniences which are inseparable from them. But this is not the subject that I am discussing here, and it is only the question of proper proportions that led to this digression.

Sixteen pounders are equally as useful as twenty-four pounders to batter a breach and are much less difficult to transport. Fifty of them, together with twelve mortars and ammunition in proportion, will be sufficient for such an army as I have been describing. Boats, with all the tackle to make a bridge, twelve hinged bridges for the passage of canals and small rivers, together with the necessary equipment, also are required.

For the rest of the transport and food supplies of the army, I prefer wagons made of wood, without any iron work in them. These are used by the Russians, and also we see them coming from Franche-Comté to Paris. They can travel from one end of the world to the other without damaging the roads. One man can drive four with ease. Each is drawn by two oxen. Ten of our wagons do more harm to a road than a thousand of these.

If we would only consider the disadvantages caused by our present method of transport, we should see the utility and benefit of adopting this. How many times is food totally lacking because the wagons have not been able to get up? How often is the baggage and artillery left behind, and the army forced to make a sudden halt? A little rainy weather and a hundred or two wagons are enough to destroy a good road and make it impassable; it is repaired and a hundred more wagons make it worse than it was before; put fascines on it and in no time they will be cut to pieces by the wheels which carry such a heavy weight on two points only.

All the wagons of the army should be drawn by oxen, both because of their even pace and their economy. They can be pastured anywhere and, if there is any shortage of them, more can be obtained from the depot. In addition, they require little harness. Wherever the army halts they pasture and feed themselves.

A single man can handle four wagons, each drawn by two oxen. It would require twelve or fifteen horses to haul as much as these eight oxen. The latter do not consume the forage they haul because they are sent out to pasture while the wagoners are cutting and loading it.

If one of the oxen is injured, it is killed and eaten and another one is purchased. All of these reasons induce me to prefer oxen to horses for transport. Each one, however, should be branded so that everyone can distinguish his own in the pasture.

MILITARY DISCIPLINE. After the organization of troops, military discipline is the first matter that presents itself. It is the soul of armies. If it is not established with wisdom and maintained with unshakable resolution you will have no soldiers. Regiments and armies will be only contemptible, armed mobs, more dangerous to their own country than to the enemy.

It is a false idea that discipline, subordination, and slavish obedience debase courage. It has always been noted that it is with those armies in which the severest discipline is enforced that the greatest deeds are performed.

Many generals believe that they have done everything as soon as they have issued orders, and they order a great deal because they find many abuses. This is a false principle; proceeding in this fashion, they will never reestablish discipline in an army in which it has been lost or weakened. Few orders are best, but they should be followed up with care; negligence should be punished with-

out partiality and without distinction of rank or birth;
otherwise, you will make yourself hated. One can be
exact and just, and be loved at the same time as feared.
Severity must be accompanied with kindness, but this
should not have the appearance of pretense, but of goodness.

Whippings need not be severe. The more moderate
they are the more quickly will abuses be remedied, since
all the world will join in ending them.

We have a pernicious custom in France of always
punishing with death. A soldier caught pillaging is hung.
The result is that no one arrests him because they do not
want to cause the death of a poor devil who is only try-
ing to live. If, instead, he were only turned over to the
guard to be put in chains and condemned to bread and
water for one, two, or three months, or put to work at
any of the labors that always have to be done in an army,
and then were sent to his regiment before a battle or
when the general wished, everyone would agree with this
punishment and the officers of the patrols would arrest
them by hundreds. Soon there would be no pillaging because everyone would join in putting it under control.

At present only the unlucky are arrested. The guard
and all the world, when they see them, turn the other
way. The general complains because of the outrages
committed; finally the provost marshal arrests one and
he is hung. And the soldiers say that it is only the unlucky that loses. Does this conserve discipline? No, it
only causes the death of a few men without reforming
the evil.

Ah, it may be said, officers also allow them to pass their posts unnoticed. There is a remedy for this abuse. It is only necessary to question soldiers that the provost marshal has captured, make them admit what posts they have passed, and send the officers in charge of them to prison for the rest of the campaign. This soon will make them vigilant, attentive, and inexorable; but, when it is a question of the death of the man, there are few officers who will not risk two or three months in prison.

There are some things of great importance for discipline to which no attention is given and which officers ridicule. They even treat those as pedants who attempt to enforce them. The French, for example, ridicule the custom of the Germans of not touching dead horses. Nevertheless, it is very prudent and very wise if not carried too far. Its purpose, in armies, is to prevent soldiers from eating the carcass which, besides its uncleanliness, is very unhealthy. This does not prevent them, during sieges and in case of necessity, from killing their horses and eating them. Let us judge if the infamy that is now attached to this regulation is useful or otherwise.

The Germans are reproached for whipping; it is an established military punishment among them. If a German officer strikes or otherwise abuses a soldier, he is dismissed on the complaint of the soldier. The officer is obliged to give him satisfaction in a duel, if the soldier demands it, when he is no longer under his command, without dishonoring the officer. This obligation prevails through all the military ranks, and there are often instances of generals giving satisfaction at the point of a sword to simple officers after they have left the service. They are unable to refuse the challenge without dishonoring themselves.

The French do not hesitate to strike a soldier with their hand, but they fear to use whipping as punishment because false ideals of personal rights have destroyed its use. Nevertheless, this type of punishment is often needed, and promptly, and is neither injurious nor dishonorable. Let us compare these different customs and judge which is best for the service and which is most consistent with personal honor.

It is the same with the discipline of officers. The French reproach the Germans with their provosts and their chains; the latter retort by exclaiming against the prisons and ropes of the French. German officers are never confined in prison, where they may be thrown in with thieves or men about to be hanged. They have a provost in every regiment; it is always an old sergeant who is given this post as a reward for his services. With respect to chains, I have never seen them used unless a criminal affair was involved. I have seen French tied with ropes. Let one balance these methods again, and it will serve to demonstrate the absurdity of condemning customs before the causes have been examined.

After having explained my ideas about infantry and cavalry, on methods of fighting and on discipline, which are, so to speak, the base and the fundamentals of the military art, I shall now proceed to the sublime parts. Perhaps few will understand me, but I write for experts and to instruct myself from their criticisms. They should not be offended by the assurance with which I deliver my opinions. They should correct them; that is the fruit I expect from this work.

THE DEFENSE OF PLACES. I am always astonished that no one objects to the abuse of fortifying cities. These words may seem extraordinary, and I shall justify them. First examine the utility of fortresses. They cover a country, oblige the enemy to attack them or march around them, one can retire into them with troops and place them in security, they protect supplies, and, during the winter, troops, artillery, ammunition, etc., are kept in security.

If these considerations are examined, it will be found that fortresses are most advantageous when they are erected at the junction of two rivers. To invest them, when so placed, it is necessary to divide an army into three parts; the defender may defeat one of these three corps before the other two come to its aid. Before being invested, such a fortress always has two open sides, nor can the enemy completely surround the fortress in a day. He will need equipment for three bridges, and these often are hazards in themselves, due to storms and floods in the campaign season.

Besides this, in holding such a post and controlling the rivers, one is master of the country. Their course can be diverted if necessary, and they permit easy supply, formation of depots, and transport of munitions and all the other stores required in war.

Lacking rivers, places can be found fortified by nature so strongly that it is almost impossible to surround them, and which can be attacked only in spots. Small expense will make them impregnable. Others can be provided with locks and protected by extensive inundations. Everyone will admit that such situations can be found, and that, by aiding nature with art, they can be made impregnable. Nature is infinitely stronger than the works of man; why not profit from it?

Few cities have been founded for these purposes. Commerce has caused their growth, and their location was chosen by hazard. In the course of time they have grown and the inhabitants have surrounded them with walls for defense against the incursions of common enemies and for protection from internal disturbances in which nations are involved. All this was dictated by reason. The citizens fortified them for their own preservation, and they have defended them.

But what could be the inducement for rulers to fortify them? It could have some appearance of reason when Christianity lived in the midst of barbarism, when one city enslaved another, and when countries were devastated. But now that war is made with more moderation, what is there to fear? A town surrounded with a strong wall and capable of holding three or four hundred men, besides the inhabitants, together with some artillery, will be as secure as if the garrison consisted of as many thousands. For I maintain that these troops will not defend themselves longer than the four hundred and that the terms of surrender of the citizens will not be better.

But besides, what use will the enemy make of it after he has taken it? Will he fortify it? I think not. Thus he will be content with a contribution and will march on; perhaps he will not even besiege it because he will not be able to keep it. He will never hazard leaving a small garrison in it, and still less will he leave a large one because it will not be secure.

A still stronger reason persuades me that fortified cities are hard to defend. Suppose you have stored food supplies for three months for the garrison; after it is besieged you find that they last only eight days because you have not counted on twenty, thirty, or forty thousand mouths that must be fed. These are the peasants from the country who take refuge in the city and augment the number of the citizens. The wealth of a prince would not be able to establish such magazines in all the cities that might be attacked, and to renew them every year. And if he had the philosopher's stone, still he could not do it without creating a famine in the country.

I imagine some one will say: "I should expel the citizens who are unable to provide their own provisions." This would be a worse desolation than the enemy could cause, for how many are there in the cities who do not live from day to day? Besides, can you be sure that you will be besieged? And if you are, will the enemy tranquilly allow this multitude to withdraw? He will drive them back into the city. What will the governor do? Will he allow these unfortunates to die from hunger? Could he justify this conduct to his ruler? What can he do then? He will be forced to supply them with provisions and surrender in eight or fifteen days.

Suppose the garrison of a city consist of five thousand

men and that there are forty thousand mouths besides that. The magazine is established for three months. But the forty-five thousand will eat in one day the supplies that would have lasted the five thousand for nine days. Thus the city cannot hold for more than eleven or twelve days. Even grant that it will last twenty days; in this case it will not even need to be attacked. It is obliged to surrender, and all the millions that have been spent in fortifying it are a useless expense.

It seems to me that what I have said should demonstrate the irremediable defects of fortified cities, and that it is more advantageous for a ruler to establish his strong points in localities aided by nature, and situated to cover the country, than to fortify cities at immense expense or to augment their fortifications. It is necessary, on the contrary, after having constructed others, to destroy the fortifications of cities down to the walls. At least no thought should be given to fortifying them further or of using the money to construct fortifications for such purposes.

Notwithstanding that what I have advanced is founded on reason, I expect hardly a single person to concur, so absolute is custom and such is its power over us. A fortified place, located as I have proposed, could hold out several months or even years, provided it can be supplied, because it is not encumbered with the civil population.

The sieges in Brabant would not have been carried on with such rapid success if the governors had not calculated the duration of their defense by that of their provisions. On this account they were as impatient as the

enemy to have a breach made so that they could surrender honorably. In spite of this goodwill, I have seen
several governors obliged to surrender without having
had the honor of marching out through the breach.

I shall not write extensively on the manner of defending fortified places, since I do not intend in this work
to deal with all the phases of war in detail. My intention
simply is to expose such of my ideas as seem new to me.

I have noticed, in sieges, that the covered ways are
crowded at night with men and a great fire of small arms
is constantly made from them, but that it does little damage. This is worth nothing because it fatigues the troops
to excess. The soldier who has been firing all night is
worn out. His musket is out of order, and he passes part
of the next day cleaning and repairing it and making
cartridges. This deprives him of the rest that he should
take, a matter of infinite consequence and which results,
if great attention is not given it, in illness and a general
disgust which even goodwill cannot resist.

However, it is towards the end of a siege when the
most vigor should be shown, for it is then a question of
skill. The more vigor you display the more the enemy
will be discouraged. It is then that sickness spreads in
his camp, that forage and provisions run short, and that
everything seems to concur to his ruin, adding to the
despondency of his officers and soldiers. If, added to
this, they feel that your resistance is becoming stronger
than it was, and that it augments in the measure in which
they expected it to diminish, they will be at a loss and
give themselves up wholly to despair. That is why the

best troops should be reserved for sudden blows; they should not be allowed even to stick their noses over the ramparts and, especially, should be relieved from guard duty at night. As soon as they have completed their assignment, they should be returned to their quarters, their dug-outs, or wherever they are lodged.

With regard to the fire from the covered way or from the ramparts on the workmen at night, it amounts to little more than noise.

It is much better to place some barbette batteries, toward the end of the day, either in the covered way or upon the ramparts, align them with chalk so that they are pointed in the directions desired, and fire on that line during the night. They can be withdrawn at daybreak. This fire is more deadly than small arms because it pierces fascines and gabions and the wounds it causes are mortal, since the balls are as big as walnuts. These balls will scour the breadth of the trenches and will ricochet and roll far beyond the range of musketry. Enemy cannon cannot silence them during the night, and they will kill workmen and enemy cannoneers like flies.

Twelve pieces emplaced in this fashion will require only thirty-six soldiers and twelve cannoneers, and I am confident they will do more damage than a thousand men firing all night from the covered way. During all this time your troops are at rest and the next morning are in condition to make raids or work.

It may be objected that this will use lots of powder, but soldiers firing small arms would use more. If too much is being used it is only necessary to emplace a smaller number of pieces. It will always give you an advantage; your troops will be less fatigued and consequently freer from illness. Nothing causes so much sickness as night duties.

REFLECTIONS UPON WAR IN GENERAL.* Many persons believe that it is advantageous to take the field early. They are right when it is a question of seizing an important post; otherwise, it seems to me that there is no need to hasten and that one should remain in winter quarters longer than usual. What difference does it make if the enemy lays a few sieges? He will weaken himself by doing it, and, if you attack towards autumn with well-disciplined and well-ordered army, you will ruin him.

I have always noticed that a single campaign reduces an army by a third, at least, and sometimes by a half, and that the cavalry especially is in such a pitiable state by the end of October that they are no longer able to keep the field. I would prefer to continue in quarters until then, harass the enemy with detachments, and, towards the end of a good siege, fall on him with all my forces. I believe that I would have a good bargain and that he soon would think of withdrawing, although this might not be easy for him when opposed to troops that are well led and complete. He probably would be forced to abandon his baggage, cannon, part of his cavalry, together with all his wagons. This loss will not facilitate his going in the field so early next year. Perhaps he even

---

* I am taking matters as they occur to me. Thus, no one should be surprised if I quit the chapter on fortification to revert to it later. It is because I considered this digression necessary here, before entering more particularly into the details of each subject.

might not dare to reappear. It is the affair of a month. And then one returns to winter quarters in good order, while the enemy is ruined. At this time of the year the barns are full, it is dry everywhere, and there is little sickness.

One can even turn in another direction and subsist all winter in the enemy's country. Winter need not be feared for troops so much as is commonly believed. I have made several winter campaigns in frightful climates; the men and horses kept well. There are no illnesses to fear, fevers are not prevalent as in summer, and the horses are in good condition.

There are situations which will permit you to place your troops in security in cantonments and with abundant food. The problem is to create these conditions. An experienced general does not live at the expense of his sovereign; on the contrary he will raise contributions for the subsistence of his army and for the ensuing campaign. Being well-lodged and warm, with an abundance of everything, the soldiers are contented and happy, and live at ease. In order to accomplish this it is necessary to know how to collect provisions and money from afar without fatiguing the troops. Large detachments are in danger of being attacked and cut off. They do not produce much and wear out the troops. To obviate this, the best way is to send circular letters to those places from which contributions are required, threatening them that parties will be sent out at a definite time to set fire to the houses of those who do not have quittances for the tax imposed. The tax should be moderate.

Following this, intelligent officers should be selected and assigned a certain number of villages to visit. They should be sent with detachments of twenty-five or thirty men and should be ordered to march only at night. The men should be ordered to refrain from pillage on pain of death. When they have arrived in the locality and it is time to determine if the villages have paid, they should send a sergeant with two men to the chief magistrate of the village to see if he has procured the quittance. If he has not, the leader of the detachment should show himself with his troops, set fire to a single house, and threaten to return and burn more. He should neither pillage, nor take the sum demanded, nor a larger one, but march away again.

All these detachments should be assembled at the same rendezvous before they are dismissed. There they should be searched and those who are found to have stolen the slightest thing should be hung without mercy. If, on the contrary, they have faithfully followed the orders given to them they should be rewarded. By such means, this method of raising contributions will become familiar to the troops, and the country a hundred leagues around will bring in food and money in abundance. The troops will not be exhausted, since twenty detachments a month can carry out the duty. These detachments will not be betrayed, whatever demand the enemy may make. And since it is a calamity that they feel and that they are unable to see until its effect are felt, their terror is increased, and no one sleeps in repose unless he has paid, regardless of any prohibitions the enemy may order.

A large body engaged in exacting contributions covers little of the country and causes trouble wherever it is. The inhabitants hide their goods and their cattle. In this state little is collected because they know the troops cannot remain long; they expect help—oftentimes they have gone for it themselves—with the result that the troops retire in haste without having accomplished much, and some are always lost. Even when things go best, the commander of the detachment, from fear or prudence, makes the best compromise he can with the inhabitants and only brings back worn-out troops in bad condition, some food, and little money. Such is the success that contributions ordinarily have. In place of this, in the fashion I propose, everything goes well and of itself.

Since only so much a month is required to be paid, the inhabitants will aid each other. They are able to furnish just so much more because they are not bothered by the presence of troops, because they have time, and because they do not see any recourse except to be burned out if they do not satisfy the demands. Finally, an immense extent of country is covered. The more distant inhabitants sell their supplies to bring in money, and those closer in bring in provisions. They should always be allowed to choose.

These detachments must be very unfortunate, or badly conducted, to be discovered. For a detachment of twenty-five men can cross a whole kingdom without being captured. They march off when they are discovered, and an army cannot take them.

The last war proved the truth of what I maintain. In

1710 I was attacked by a party of French between Brussels and Malines. Three days later another detachment of fifty men entered Alost, which is five leagues from Brussels, at noon and carried off my baggage. At this time there were 1500 men at the gate of the town waiting for their billets which were being assigned at the city hall. I was almost captured myself. It was dangerous to go by boat from Brussels to Antwerp without a passport because it was stopped two or three times every day. No one dared to walk in the suburbs of Brussels, Antwerp, Louvain, or Malines, without a passport. Nevertheless, the Allies were masters of all Flanders. Lille, Tournai, Mons, Douai, Ghent, Bruges, Ostend, and all the barrier towns were in their hands. There were 140,000 troops in these garrisons, and it was the middle of winter. Nevertheless, French partisans were everywhere.

This proves completely the possibility of what I advocate and convinces me that its success will be infallible.

How to Construct Forts. We excell the Romans in the art of fortification, but we have not reached perfection. I am not particularly wise, but the great reputations of Vauban and Coehorm do not overwhelm me. They have fortified places at enormous expense and have not made them any stronger. The speed with which they have been captured proves it.

We have modern engineers, hardly known, who have profited from their faults and surpass them infinitely. But they only hold a mean between the defects of those gentlemen and the point of perfection toward which we should strive.

I have made the plan and the profiles of an octagon fort and have calculated the time in which 4800 men could construct it. The entire work could be built in 111¾ hours or, at ten hours a day, in eleven days and one and three-quarter hours. Although these calculations are correct, they should not be depended on practically. I made them only to obtain an approximation of practicability of my plan. If the estimate of time is doubled or tripled, no mistake can be made and the difference is not very great.

The best method of employing workmen is by dividing them into four reliefs of three hours each. Then work is continuous and all the troops are employed without being worn out, and work vigorously, since a soldier who works only three hours a day cannot be overworked. The work should be accompanied by the beat of the drum in cadence. Lysander with a detachment of three thousand Spartans destroyed the port of Piraeus in Athens to the sound of the flute in six hours. We still have some remnants of this custom, and it is only a few years since galley slaves at Marseilles worked in cadence to the sound of the timbrel.

For terraced works, the earth should be shoveled from step to step, or from stage to stage. Wheelbarrows are expensive and hard to push up a slope; the gentle ramps that they require lengthen the distance they must be wheeled considerably.

A soldier can easily throw his shovel of earth from a depth of from nine to twelve feet. When this is impracticable the earth must be removed in baskets. In this case the workers are divided into two groups; one digs and loads and the other carries. The pioneers, in digging, must leave steps on which to rest the baskets while they are being filled. The baskets are emptied at the places marked. All this should be done in cadence to the sound of some instrument.

It is absolutely necessary to accustom soldiers to labor. If we examine Roman history we shall find that Republic looked on ease and indolence as the most formidable enemies. The consuls prepared their legions for battle by rendering them indefatigable. Rather than have them idle, they employed them on unnecessary works. Continual exercise makes good soldiers because it qualifies them for military duties; by being habituated to pain, they insensibly learn to despise danger. The transition from fatigue to rest enervates them. They compare one state with another, and idleness, that predominant passion of mankind, gains ascendancy over them. They then murmur at every trifling inconvenience, and their souls soften in their emasculated bodies.

MOUNTAIN WARFARE. Those who wage war in mountains should never pass through defiles without first making themselves masters of the heights; this will prevent ambushes and they can pass in security. Otherwise there is great risk of destruction or of being forced to turn about, not without great loss. And sometimes everyone perishes without a chance of saving themselves. If the passes and the heights already are occupied, it is necessary to pretend to force them to draw the attention of the enemy, while you search for a route at some other place. This disconcerts the enemy, for he has not counted on it. He does not know what disposition to make because he fears for himself and often he abandons everything. However rough and impracticable mountains may appear, passages can be found by searching for them. Men who live in the mountains do not know them themselves because they are never obliged to seek them, and the inhabitants never should be believed for they only know their country by tradition. I have often proved the ignorance and imposture of their recitals. In such a case, it is necessary to search and see for oneself or use men who are not frightened by difficulties. You will almost always find passes when you search for them; and the enemy, who is unaware of them himself, does not know what to do and flees because he has only counted on ordinary things, which in this case are the customary roads.

WAR IN BROKEN COUNTRY. Since the enemy, in this kind of country, is as much embarrassed as anyone can be, there is little to be feared. These are affairs of detail that decide nothing and where the more determined carries the day. There is but one thing to observe, which is to have your rear open so as to be able to send out detachments and to retire in case of need. In broken country, skill in locating artillery is of great importance. Since the enemy does not dare leave the posts he occupies, he can be fired on at will. If he abandons them, the retreat is not always successful and sometimes he can be attacked. Altogether, these affairs are never decisive and should be governed by the situation; rules of conduct cannot be prescribed. However, one should never neglect, as a course of conduct, to send out detachments in front and on the flanks of the march. These detachments of a hundred men should be supported by a second, and the second by a third, to make the cover of the main body secure.

A detachment of six hundred men can stop a whole army because, along roads bordered with hedges and ditches such as one finds in Italy and in all fertile and wet countries, they can present the same extent of front. The smallest house becomes a fortification and causes an obstinate combat. This allows time to reconnoiter and make dispositions, for in this type of country one cannot be too cautious in preventing surprises.

An audacious partisan with three or four hundred men will cause you frightful disorder and will even attack an army. If he cuts off the baggage at the beginning of darkness, he will be able to carry away a large part of it without risking much because he retreats between two obstacles and closes the gap behind him. In case he is hard pressed he marches beside the wagons and at the first house he finds he throws you back on your haunches. While this is going on the baggage he has taken from you is moving on.

If he uses this stratagem on your cavalry he will cause you frightful disorder. It is for this reason that advanced parties should cover all the avenues of your march. And they must not be too weak, for it is not a question of being informed but of fighting to the death. Otherwise, ruin and disgrace may be your fate if you are opposed by an enemy general of understanding. He will have no difficulty in finding men in his army ready to undertake any enterprise and who see possibilities as they really are.

RIVER CROSSINGS. It is far from being as easy as one might think to prevent the enemy from crossing a river. He can do it more easily when he is advancing to attack you than when he is retreating in front of you. In the first of these cases he presents his head to you and supports it with good dispositions and strong artillery fire. In the second he exposes his rear, which is not always so easy to withdraw, especially if he is being pressed. In addition, dispositions are not taken with such care and are not executed with such attention for a withdrawal as for an attack, and everyone becomes negligent in the latter from a sort of timidity which results in a half defeat before the action starts. It would be difficult to furnish a good reason for this; it should be sought for in the natural failings of the human heart.

There is still another sort of river crossing, in which a flank is presented to the enemy. Before the battle of Turin, Prince Eugene crossed three rivers in this fashion in two days in the presence of the Duke of Orleans. The terrain between the two armies was flat, and it was a good occasion to fight, even with inferior numbers. Nothing was done, however, and the siege of Turin had to be abandoned.

In such a case, if the siege is not raised opportunely to march against the enemy, the one who is bringing help always has the advantage because the fight is never a general one for him, while it is for the one attacked. This is because the former has all his troops assembled between two rivers, his flanks are secure, and he is disposed in great depth. The latter, who is investing the fortress, is dispersed and can only guard his communications across the rivers with a small number of troops. If they are defeated the entire circle is shattered, their lines are exposed on the flanks, and they soon are routed. Hesitation in such situations brings disaster. Sometimes, also, the enemy will show himself only to alarm the besiegers and to induce them to quit their posts so that he can throw help into the fortress. It is a part of the skill of the general to distinguish the true from the false.

The surest method for the besiegers is to assemble a sufficient number of troops to oppose the enemy and to leave the remainder in the lines so that they can move and attack anything that attempts to enter the fortress. But they cannot stand with arms crossed, as if bewitched, and watch an enemy cross a river before them, with his flanks exposed, unmolested. It is only necessary to choose which flank to fall on, and it appears that very little resistance will be met.

At the battle of Denain, Marshal de Villars would have been lost if Prince Eugene had marched against him; he had exposed his flank and crossed a river in his presence. The Prince could never imagine that the Marshal would make any such attempt in his presence, and this was what deceived him. Marshal de Villars had masked his march very skillfully. Prince Eugene watched him and examined his dispositions until 11:00 o'clock, without comprehending. All the troops were under arms; he had only to march straight ahead and the French army was lost because its flank was exposed and a large part had already crossed the Escaut. At 11:00 o'clock Prince Eugene said: "I think we might as well go to dinner," and recalled the troops. He was hardly at table when Lord Albemarle sent word that the head of the French army had appeared on the other side of the river and acted as if they were preparing to attack. There was still time to march and cut off a third of the French army. But Prince Eugene only ordered a few brigades on his right to march to the entrenchments of Denain, which were four leagues off. He then went with all speed to reconnoiter in person, being still unable to believe that it was the head of the French army. At length he discovered his error and saw them forming for attack. Instantly he gave up the entrenchment as lost.

I have been told (for I was not there) that he examined the enemy for a moment and chewed his glove in vexation. Whatever his feelings, he instantly gave orders to withdraw the cavalry that was in that post.

The effects produced by this affair are hardly credible. It made a difference of more than a hundred battalions in the relative strength of the two armies. Prince Eugene was obliged to place garrisons in all the adjacent cities. The Marshal, perceiving that the Allies were no longer able to carry on a siege after they had lost all their magazines, withdrew about fifty battalions from the neighboring garrisons. This strengthened his army to such a degree, in comparison to the decreased strength of the Allies, that Prince Eugene no longer dared remain in the field and was forced to move all his cannon into Quesnoy, where they were afterwards captured.

With regard to forcing a passage across rivers, I believe it is hardly possible to prevent it. A river crossing ordinarily is supported by such massive artillery fire that it is impossible to prevent an advanced force from crossing, entrenching, and throwing up works to cover the bridgehead. There is nothing to be done about it during daylight, but during darkness this work can be attacked. If the attack should take place at the time the enemy has begun his crossing, everything will be thrown into confusion. Those who have crossed over will be lost, while the rest will be turned back. But this operation must be made with a large force. If the night is allowed to pass without action, you will find that the entire hostile army has crossed. Then it is no longer an affair of detachments but a general engagement, a hazard which the political situation does not always warrant.

There are a large number of stratagems and ruses for the passage of rivers which each employs depending upon whether he is more or less skillful or ingenious.

Since I am dealing with affairs of detail, I should not omit how to decoy horses. There are few partisans who understand it. The decoy is a diverting stratagem to capture the enemy's horses in a foraging party or from the pasture. You must be disguised on horseback among the foragers or the pasturers on the side toward which you propose to fly. You commence by firing a few shots. Those detailed to drive up the rear answer from the other extremity of the pasture or foraging ground.

Then they gallop toward the side fixed for the flight, shouting and firing all the way. All the horses will start to run from this side, whether they are harnessed or picketed, and will throw their riders. No matter how great their number they can be led several leagues in this manner. They should be directed into a locality bordered by hedges or ditches where they can be stopped without noise and captured at will. This is a good trick to play on the enemy and will distress him not a little. I have seen it done; but, as all things are forgotten, no one thinks of this now.

The day of the battle of Denain, when it was over, the cavalry dismounted. The Marshal de Villars, passing along the lines, gay as always, speaking to the soldiers of a regiment on the right, said to them: "Well, my lads, we have taken them." Some of them started to shout: "Long live the King!" and threw their hats in the air. The rest of the line took it up and started shouting, throwing their hats in the air and firing, the cavalry joining in the acclamation. This frightened the horses so that they broke loose from the men and ran away. If there had been four men in front of them, they could have led them to the enemy. This accident caused considerable damage and disorder; there were a number of men wounded and a quantity of arms lost.

DIFFERENT SITUATIONS. Not all the situations of nature are combined as if they were planned. There are very few that are. Almost all have their features and a skillful general will profit from them. I am speaking of ravines, depressed roads, chains of lakes, and an infinity of other terrain features, all of which aid marvelously in ruses when God has had the grace to give some common sense to a man. Sometimes these things which change the situation in question so greatly are overlooked until they are forced on your attention. Then it is too late, and you see yourself reduced to being ridiculous.

It is the nature of the French to attack. When a general is unwilling to depend on the exact discipline of the troops and the great order required in pitched battles, he has only to create the occasions to fight in detail and arrange for brigade attacks. And assuredly these occasions can be found. The courage and elan which animate this nation have never been contradicted, and, since Julius Caesar (he states it himself in his *Commentaries*), I know of no example in which they have failed to make a dent in what was presented to them. Their first shock is terrible. It is only necessary to know how to renew it by skillful dispositions, and this is the business of the general.

Nothing facilitates this so much as redoubts. You can always send fresh troops to them to counterattack the enemy when he attacks. Nothing causes the enemy so much distraction, nor renders him so fearful. For while he attacks he is always afraid of being taken in the flank. On the other hand, your troops, feeling that their retreat is assured and that the enemy will not dare follow them beyond the redoubts, attack with better spirit. It is on such occasion that you can reap the greatest advantages from their vigor and impetuousness, so well-known and feared among all nations and at all times. But to put them behind entrenchments is to deprive them of the means of conquering; they then are only ordinary men.

What would have been the result at Malplaquet if Marshal de Villars had taken the larger part of his army and attacked half of that of the Allies, who had had the kindness to dispose themselves so that they were separated by woods and were unable to communicate with each other? The flanks and rear of the French army would have been secure.

There is more skill than one might think in making poor dispositions intentionally, but one must be able to change them into good ones in an instant. Nothing is more disconcerting to the enemy—he has counted on a certain thing, has disposed himself accordingly, and, at the instant of attacking, it has changed. I repeat: nothing confuses him so greatly and leads him into more serious faults. If he does not change his dispositions he will be defeated, and if he changes them in the presence of the enemy he still will be defeated. Human spirit cannot meet it.

LINES AND ENTRENCHMENTS. I do not care for either the one or the other of these works. When I hear talk of lines I always think I am hearing talk of the walls of China. The good ones are those that nature has made, and the good entrenchments are good dispositions and brave soldiers. I practically never have heard of entrenchments having been assaulted that were not carried. I have stated the reasons in other places. If you are inferior in numbers to the enemy, you will not be able to hold in entrenchments when they are attacked with all his forces in two or three different places at once. If you are equal with him the same will be the case. Why then go to the trouble of constructing them? They are only good for circumvallations and to prevent the enemy from throwing help into a besieged place.

The enemy's certainty that you will never dare leave them renders him audacious. He feints in your front and takes chances with flank movements that he would not dare if you were not entrenched. This boldness is infused into officers and soldiers equally. Man always fears the consequences of danger more than danger itself. I could give a multitude of examples. Suppose that a column attacks an entrenchment and that the head reaches the edge of the ditch: if a handful of men appeared a hundred paces outside the entrenchment it is certain that the head of the column would halt or would not be followed by the rear elements. Why? The reason must be found in the human heart. Let ten men get footing on the entrenchment and all who are behind it will fly and entire battalions will abandon it. They no sooner see a troop of cavalry a half league from them than they give themselves up to flight.

When one is obliged to defend entrenchments, one should post all the battalions directly behind the parapet because, if once the enemy sets foot upon that, those in the rear will think of nothing but to save themselves. This is because of the consternation in men when something happens that they have not expected. This is a general rule in war and decides all battles and all actions. It comes from the human heart and is what induced me to compose this work. I do not believe that anyone yet has attempted to find there the reasons for the poor success of armies.

Thus when you have stationed your troops behind a parapet, they hope, by their fire, to prevent the enemy from passing the ditch and mounting it. If this happens, in spite of the fire, they give themselves up for lost, lose their heads, and fly. It would be much better to post a single rank there, armed with pikes, whose business will be to push the assailant back as fast as they attempt to mount. And certainly they will execute this duty because it is what they expect and will be prepared for. If with this, you post infantry formed according to my method into centuries at a distance of thirty paces from the entrenchment, these troops will see that they are placed there to charge the enemy as fast as he enters and attempts to form. They will not be astonished to see the enemy enter, because they expect it, and will charge vigorously. If, instead, they had been placed on the parapet, they would have fled. That is how a trifle changes everything in war and how human weaknesses cannot be managed except by allowing for them.

If the enemy endeavors to occupy the berm of the entrenchment, as happens frequently, to dislodge you from the sill, you can await him with your pikes and throw him, man by man, into the ditch as fast as they uncover themselves. And finally, if the enemy enters the entrenchment and commences to form, you charge him in detail by century. The centuries will not be surprised to see the enemy enter because they expect it and will charge vigorously because that is what they have proposed to themselves. That is all that can be said concerning the defense of entrenchments.

In major engagements one should always have different reserves to move to the point where one sees the enemy direct the most men, a matter that is not always easy to accomplish. If the enemy is skillful, you will see nothing. Thus it is necessary to place reserves as advantageously as possible, either inside or outside the entrenchments, according to terrain. You need not fear being attacked in places where the ground is level for any considerable distance, since the enemy will not want to uncover his real purpose by exposing the main body of his force. In such places he will only have a battalion in depth. But whenever there happens to be a hill, valley, or least thing to cover his approach, there you may expect him to make all his efforts because he will hope to conceal his maneuver and numbers.

If you are able to contrive some passages in your entrenchments for a party or two to sally out at the moment when the head of some one of the enemy's columns reaches the brink of the ditch, it will be stopped infallibly, even though they may have forced the entrenchment and some have entered it. This is because they are faced with the unexpected and fear for their flanks and rear. In all probability they will take to flight without exactly knowing why.

Here are two examples which support my ideas. Caesar, wishing to relieve Amiens when it was besieged by the Gauls, arrived with his army, which was only seven thousand strong, along the banks of a stream where he entrenched himself with such haste that the barbarians, convinced that Caesar feared them, attacked the entrenchments. The Roman general had no intention of defending them. On the contrary, while the barbarians were filling up the ditch and gaining the parapet, he sallied out with his cohorts and surprised them so that they fled without a single one making the slightest attempt to defend himself.

At the siege of Alesia by the Romans, the Gauls, although infinitely superior in numbers, marched to attack them in their lines. Caesar, instead of defending them, gave orders to his troops to make a sally and fall on the enemy on one side, while he attacked them on the other. In this he succeeded so well that the Gauls were routed with considerable loss, exclusive of twenty thousand men and their general who were taken prisoners.

If one considers the manner in which I arrange my troops (checkerboard), it is easy to understand that they can maneuver more easily than in line. It is also much easier to charge in detail than in massed lines. For this order of battle is much stronger than all the others and is not subject to any confusion, which cannot be said of the formation by battalions. What good are several battalions drawn up four deep, one behind the other? They are unwieldy, a trifle embarrasses them, the ground, the doubling, or any other such circumstance. And if the first is repulsed, it falls in disorder on the second and throws it in confusion. But suppose that the second does not break; nevertheless it will require a long period of time before it can attack because the first, which is not broken, must be allowed to move clear of its front. And unless the enemy is so complaisant as to wait with arms folded during this time, he will certainly drive the first battalion back on the second, and the second on the third. For after having repulsed the first, he has nothing to do but to advance forward briskly. If there were thirty, one in rear of the other, he would throw them all into confusion. Yet this is what is called attacking in column by battalions! What wretchedness!

My formation is decidedly different. For even if the first battalion should be driven back, the one which follows it can charge instantly, thus returning blow for blow. I am formed eight deep and have no fear of confusion; my charge is violent and my march rapid; I do not fear confusion and I shall always outflank the enemy, although equal in numbers. The enemy's battalions cannot remedy this fault because they do not know how to extend. Nothing certainly can be more wretched and absurd than the formations with which we fight, and I cannot conceive why the generals have not thought of changing it.

What I propose is not a novelty. It is the Roman formation. With this formation they vanquished all the nations on earth.* The Greeks were very skillful in the art of war and well disciplined. But their large phalanx was never able to contend with the small bodies of the Romans disposed in this formation. Thus Polybius gives

---

* I shall be told: "But the Romans did not have powder." It is true, but their enemies had missile weapons which had almost the same effect.

preference to the Roman formation. What could our battalions, which have neither body nor spirit, do against this same formation? No matter how the centuries are posted—in a plain or in rough ground—make them sally out of a narrow pass or any other place, and you will see with what surprising speed they will form. They can be ordered to run at full speed to seize a defile, hedge, or height, and by the time the standards have arrived they will be aligned and formed. This is impossible with our battalions; for to form as they should, they need ground made to order and considerable time to make several movements. And all this is pitiful to see and often has given me a nightmare.

I had not read Polybius throughout in 1732 when I wrote this work on war, and it was not until this year, 1740, that I had completed him. Here is what I found on the Grecian phalanx and on the Roman formation for combat. I am flattered to have thought like this contemporary of Scipio, Hannibal, and Philip, who during several of the wars of these great men was in different armies and had distinguished commands for several years. Such an illustrious author can only justify my ideas. I leave to the readers of this work to judge if I thought like him. It is Polybius who speaks:

"Having left an assurance with my readers, in the sixth book of this work, that I would choose some proper time to compare the arms and orders of battle of the Macedonians and the Romans, and to show in what respects they severally have the advantage, or are inferior to each other, I shall here take the occasion which the action now described has offered, and shall endeavor to discharge my promise.

"For as the order of battle of the Macedonian armies was found, in the experience of former ages, to be superior to that of the Asiatics and the Greeks, and the Roman order of battle in the same manner surpassed that of the Africans and all the western parts of Europe; and as, in later time, these two orders have been often set in opposition to each other, it must be useful, as well as interesting, to trace out the differences between them and to explain the advantages that turned the victory to the side of the Romans in these engagements. From such a view, instead of having recourse to chance and blindly applauding, like men of superficial understanding, the good fortune of the conquerors, we shall be able to remark with certainty the true causes of their success, and to ground our admiration upon the principles of sound sense and reason.

"With regard to the battles that were fought by Hannibal and the victories which he obtained against the Romans, there is no need, on this occasion, to enter into a long discussion of them. For it was not his arms, nor his order of battle, which rendered that general superior to the Romans, but his dexterity alone and his admirable skill. In the accounts that were given by us of those engagements, we have very clearly shown that this was the cause of his success. And this remark is still more strongly confirmed, in the first place, by the final issue of the war. For, as soon as the Romans had obtained a general whose ability was equal to that of Hannibal, they immediately became the conquerors. Add to this that Hannibal himself rejected the armor which he first had used and, having furnished the African troops with the arms that were taken from the Romans in the first battle, used afterwards no other. In the same manner, also, Pyrrhus employed not only the arms, but the troops of Italy, and ranged in alternate order a company of those troops and a cohort disposed in the manner of the phalanx in all his battles with the Romans. And yet, even with the advantage of this precaution, he was never able to obtain any clear or decisive victory against them. It was necessary to premise these observations for the sake of preventing any objection that might be made to the truth of what we shall hereafter say. Let us now return to the comparison that was proposed.

"It is easy to demonstrate by many reasons that while the phalanx retains its proper form and full power of action, no force is able to stand against it in front or support the violence of its attack. When the ranks are closed in order to engage, each soldier, as he stands with his arms, occupies a space of three feet. The spears in their ancient form were seventeen cubits long (a cubit is eighteen inches), but for the sake of rendering them more commodious in action they have since been reduced to fourteen. Of these, four cubits are contained between the part which the soldier grasps in his hands, and the lower end of the spear behind, which serves as a counterpoise to the part that is extended before him; and the length of this last part from the body of the soldier when the spear is pushed forwards with both hands against the enemy is, in consequence, ten cubits. From hence it follows that when the phalanx is closed in its proper form, and every soldier pressed within the necessary distance with respect to the man that is before him, and on his side, the spears of the fifth rank are extended to the length of two cubits, and those of the second, third, and fourth, to a still greater length beyond the foremost rank.

"It is manifest, then, that several spears, differing each from the other in the length of two cubits, are extended before every man in the foremost rank. And when it is considered, likewise, that the phalanx is formed by sixteen in depth, it will be easy to conceive what must be the weight and violence of the entire body and how great the force of its attack. In the ranks that are behind the fifth the spears cannot reach so far as to be employed against the enemy. In these ranks, therefore, the soldiers, instead of extending their spears forwards, rest them upon the shoulders of the men that are before them, with their points slanting upwards; and in this manner they form a kind of rampart which covers their heads and secures them against those darts which may be carried in their flight beyond the first ranks and fall upon those that are behind. But when the whole body advances to charge the enemy even these hindmost ranks are of no small use and moment; for, as they press continually upon those that are before them, they add, by their weight alone, great force to the attack and deprive the foremost ranks of the power of drawing themselves backward or retreating. Such then is the disposition of the phalanx with regard both to the whole and to the several parts. Let us now consider the arms and the order of battle of the Romans, so that we may see by the comparison in what respect they are different from those of the Macedonians.

"To each of the Roman soldiers as he stands in arms is allotted the same space of three feet; but as every soldier, in time of action, is constantly in motion, being forced to shift his shield continually so that he may cover any part of his body against which a stroke is aimed and to vary the position of his sword, so as either to push or make a falling stroke, there must be also a distance of three feet, the least that can be allowed for performing these motions with advantage, between each soldier and the man that stands next to him, both on his side and behind him.

"Therefore, in charging against the phalanx each Roman soldier has two Macedonians opposite him and also has ten spears which he is forced to encounter. But it is not possible for a single man to cut down these spears with his sword before they can take effect against him. Nor is it easy, on the other hand, to force his way through them. For the men that are behind add no weight to the pressure nor any strength to the swords of those that are in the foremost rank.

"It will be easy, therefore, to conceive that while the phalanx retains its proper position and strength no troops, as I have before observed, can support the attack of it in front. To what cause, then, is it to be ascribed that the Roman armies are victorious and those defeated that employ the phalanx? The cause is this: in war, the times and places of action are various and indefinite, but there is only one time and place, one fixed and determinate manner of action that is suited to the phalanx. In the case of a general action, if an enemy be forced to encounter with the phalanx in the very time and place which the latter requires, it is probable in the highest degree that the phalanx always must obtain the victory. But, if it be possible to avoid an engagement in such circumstances, and indeed it is easy to do it, there is nothing to be dreaded from this order of battle.

"It is well known, and an acknowledged truth, that the phalanx requires a ground that is plain and naked and free from obstacles of every kind such as trenches, breaks, obliquities, the brows of hills, or the channels of rivers, and that any of these are sufficient to impede it and to dissolve the order in which it was formed. On the other hand again, it must readily be allowed that if it be not altogether impossible, it is at least extremely rare to find a ground containing twenty stadia or more in its extent and free from all these obstacles. But let it, however, be supposed that such a ground may perhaps be found. If the enemy, instead of coming down on it, should lead their army through the country, plundering the cities and ravaging the lands, of what use then will be the phalanx? As long as it remains in this convenient post, it not only has no power to succor its friends, but cannot even preserve itself from ruin. For the troops that are masters of the whole country, without resistance, will easily cut off all supplies from it. And if, on the other hand, it should relinquish its own proper ground and endeavor to engage in action, the advantage is then so great against it, that it soon becomes an easy prey to the enemy.

"But further let it be supposed that the enemy will come down into this plain; yet if he does not bring his whole army at once to receive the attack of the phalanx, or if in the instant of the charge he withdraws a little from the action, it is easy to determine what will be the consequence from the present practice of the Romans. For now our discourse is not based on bare reasoning only, but from facts which have lately happened. When the Romans attack the phalanx in front they never employ all their forces so as to make their line equal to that of the enemy, but lead on only a part of their troops and keep the rest of the army in reserve. Now whether the troops of the phalanx break the line that is opposed to them, or whether they are broken themselves, the formation peculiar to the phalanx is alike dissolved. If they pursue the fugitives, or if, on the other hand, they retreat and are pursued, in either case they are separated from the rest of their own body. And thus there is left some space which the reserve of the Roman army takes care to seize and then charges the remaining part of the phalanx. But the charge is not made against the front, but in flank or in rear. Since it is easy then to avoid the conditions that are favorable to the phalanx and since those, on the contrary, that are disadvantageous to it can never be avoided, it is certain that this difference alone must carry with it a decisive weight in time of action.

"To this it may be added that the troops of the phalanx also are, like others, forced to march and to camp in every kind of place, to be the first to seize the advantageous posts, to invest the enemy, and to engage in sudden actions without knowing that an enemy was near. These things all happen in war and either tend greatly to promote or sometimes wholly determine the victory. But at all such times the Macedonian order of battle either cannot be employed or is employed in a manner that is altogether useless. For the troops of the phalanx lose all their strength when they engage in separate companies or man with man.

"The Roman order, on the contrary, is ne.er attended even on such occasions with any disadvantage. Among the Romans every single soldier, when he is on. armed and ready for service, is alike fitted to engage in any time or place, or on any appearance of the enemy, and preserves always the same power and the same capacity in action whether in separate companies or man to man. As the parts, therefore, in the Roman order of battle are so much better contrived for use than those in the other, so the success in action must also be greater in the one than the other. If I have been long in examining this subject, it was because many of the Greeks, at the time when the Macedonians were defeated, regarded that event as a thing surpassing all belief, and because many others also may hereafter wish to know for what reasons and in what particular respects the order of the phalanx is excelled by the arms and the order of battle of the Romans."

THE ATTACK OF ENTRENCHMENTS. When an entrenchment is to be attacked an attempt should be made to extend the lines as much as possible. This will make the enemy fearful everywhere so that he will not withdraw troops from any point to reinforce that which you intend to attack, even after he discovers it. This makes many of his troops useless. To effect this, all the battalions which are used only to deceive the enemy should be drawn up four deep and march in line. The rest of the maneuver and the preparations for the real assault should take place behind them. This is what is called masking the attack. This part of the military art depends on the imagination; a general can embroider it as much as he pleases. Everything is good, since the certitude that he will not be attacked permits him to do whatever he thinks apropos. He can make use of ravines, valleys, hedges, and a thousand other things.

In charging by centuries there need be no fear of confusion. Each centurion will consider it a matter of honor for his color, and among them it is impossible that there will not be some who will seek to risk their lives to distinguish themselves. This is because, according to my system, the behavior of every century becomes conspicuous by the distinction of their color.

In approaching the entrenchment. the light-armed troops should be advanced to draw the enemy's fire. They should be supported by other troops. Finally, after the firing has commenced, the centuries should come up and charge. If they are repulsed, others should replace them before the first engaged have time to flee, and force and numbers will surmount all obstacles. The centuries which have been drawn up four deep should arrive at the same time, provided you have forced the entrenchment in several places at once. The enemy battalions which are between the two forces and who see the line advance will fly, and the line will gain the parapet. After that the troops can be reformed and the enemy, during this time, will retire because he will imagine that he has done everything possible.

There is still another method of attacking entrenchments, entirely different from this, and which is equally as good. But it must be favored by the terrain, and the terrain must be known perfectly.

When there are ravines or hollows near the entrenchments where troops can be concealed during the march without discovery by the enemy, several columns, with large intervals between them, should be marched towards him. He will give all his attention to these columns, dispose his troops to meet them, and strip his entrenchments. When the columns attack, all the enemy will move toward them, and the troops who have remained concealed can appear suddenly and attack the parts of the entrenchments that have been abandoned. Seeing this, the troops that have been opposing the attacks of the columns will be surprised and lose their heads, since they had not expected this event. They then will leave the attack, under pretext of running to defend the entrenchment, but actually from the terror that overcomes them. Thus you will be able to enter the entrenchment at the points of the true and false attacks at the same time.

Of all the varieties of war, the defense of entrenchments seems to me to be the most difficult. And although
I have indicated the methods that seem best to me of the
different manners of defense, I do not have much faith
in the best. As far as I am concerned, I do not believe
in constructing them. Redoubts are my favorite works,
and I shall speak of them next.

REDOUBTS. It behooves me to justify by facts the high
opinion that I have of redoubts.

The arms of Charles XII, King of Sweden, had always
been victorious before the battle of Pultowa. Their superiority over those of the Russians is almost incredible.
It was not unusual for ten or twelve thousand Swedes to
force entrenchments defended by fifty, sixty, or even
eighty thousand Russians, and cut them to pieces. The
Swedes never inquired about the number of the Russians,
but only where they were.

Czar Peter, the greatest man of his age, bore the poor
success of this war with a patience equal to his genius
and did not stop fighting in order to give his troops experience.

In the course of his adversities, the King of Sweden
laid siege to Pultowa. The Czar held a council of war
at which various opinions were expressed. Some were
for surrounding the King of Sweden with the Russian
army and for throwing up a large entrenchment to force
him to surrender. Other generals were for burning all
the country within a hundred leagues to reduce him by
famine. This advice was not, in my opinion, at all bad,
and the Czar inclined toward it. Other generals said

that this expedient could always be adopted, but that they first should hazard a battle, since Pultowa and its garrison were in danger of being captured by the invincible determination of the King of Sweden. Here he would find a large depot and all the supplies to subsist him to cross the desert it was proposed to create around him.

This resolution was adopted. Then the Czar addressed them and said: "Since we have decided to fight the King of Sweden, we should agree on the method and choose the best. The Swedes are impetuous, well disciplined, trained, and skillful. Our troops do not lack in resolution, but they do not have these advantages. It is necessary, therefore, to counteract the Swedish superiority. They often have forced our entrenchments, and in the open our troops have always been defeated by the skill and facility with which they maneuver. Hence it is necessary to break up their maneuver and render it futile. To accomplish this, I should march toward the Swedish army, throw up several redoubts with deep ditches along the front of our infantry, garrison them with infantry and protect them with palisades and brush. This will only require a few hours labor, and we shall await the enemy behind these redoubts. He will have to raise the siege to attack us. When he has lost a lot of men and is weakened and in disorder, we shall attack. There can be no doubt that he will raise the siege and come to attack us as soon as he sees us approaching him. It is necessary, therefore, to arrange our march so that we will reach his vicinity toward the end of the day, so that he will withhold his attack until morning. During the night we will raise the redoubts."

Thus spoke the sovereign of the Russias, and all the council approved his dispositions. The orders were given for the march, the tools, the cannon, the fascines, the palisades, etc. Late in the afternoon, July 8, 1709, the Czar arrived in the vicinity of the King of Sweden.

The King of Sweden, although wounded, informed his generals that he intended to attack the Russian army in the morning. They made the necessary dispositions, drew up the troops, and marched a little before daybreak.

The Czar had thrown up seven redoubts in his front. They were constructed with care, and each was manned with two battalions of infantry. They were supplied with everything needed for their defense. All the Russian infantry was behind them, and the cavalry was on the wings. Thus it was impossible to reach the Russian infantry without taking the redoubts, since they could not be left intact in the rear and it was impossible to pass between them without being destroyed by their fire. Neither the King of Sweden, nor his generals, were aware of these dispositions until they ran into them. But, since the machine had been put in motion, it was now impossible to stop it. The two wings of the Swedish cavalry routed that of the Russians and pursued them too far. The center was stopped by the redoubts. The Swedes attacked them and were resisted obstinately.

Every soldier knows the difficulty of taking a good redoubt. It requires a special formation with several battalions and fifteen or twenty companies of grenadiers, in order to attack on several sides at the same time, and even then success is uncertain. Nevertheless the Swedes carried three of these and were repulsed with great loss at the others. It was inevitable that all the Swedish infantry was thrown into disorder in attacking the redoubts, while that of the Russians, drawn up in order at the distance of two hundred paces, watched the scene in tranquility.

The King and the Swedish generals saw the danger in which they were involved, but the inaction of the Russians gave them some hope that they might be able to withdraw. It was absolutely impossible to do it in good order since everything was disorganized, attacks were being made uselessly, or men stood and were killed. To retire was the only step that could be taken. The troops that had taken the redoubts were withdrawn and the rest followed.

There was no way to form within range of the fire of the redoubts and, consequently, everyone was withdrawn, disorganized and intermingled. In the meantime the Czar called his generals and asked their advice. M. Allart, one of the juniors, without giving anyone else a chance to say a word, spoke to his master as follows: "If Your Majesty does not attack the Swedes instantly, there will be no time afterwards." Without delay the whole line moved forward in good order, pikes high, in the intervals between the redoubts, which were left garrisoned to protect the retreat in case it became necessary.

The Swedes had hardly halted to reform and restore

order when they saw the Russians at their heels. They
again became disorganized and the confusion was general. Nevertheless they did not fly. They even made
a brave effort to turn as if to charge. But order, which
is the soul of battle, was lacking, and they were dispersed
without resistance.

The Russians, being unaccustomed to conquer, did
not dare follow them, and the Swedes withdrew without interference to Boristhene, where they all were later
taken prisoner. That is how to render fortune favorable
by skillful dispositions.

If the Russians, who at this time were inexperienced
and discouraged by a series of misfortunes, were able to
conquer with these dispositions, what success may not
be expected from them with a brave and spirited nation
whose instinct is to attack? For, although one is on the
defensive, all the advantages of attacking are conserved.
The enemy is charged with brigades that are advanced
in the measure that the enemy attacks some one of the
redoubts.

The charge is frequently renewed and always with
fresh troops. They await the order with impatience and
attack vigorously because they are seen and supported,
and especially because they know their retreat is secure.
Panic, which sometimes seizes armies, need not be feared,
and you make yourself master of the favorable moment
which is capable of deciding the combat. By that I mean
the time at which the enemy is in disorder. What an
advantage to be able to await this moment with assurance!

The Russians did not profit from all the advantages that their dispositions afforded them. They calmly allowed three of their redoubts to be taken before their face, without attempting to aid them. This would discourage the defenders of the others, intimidate their own troops, and augment the audacity of the Swedes. One may, therefore, venture to say that it was the dispositions alone which conquered the Swedes in this action, without the Russian troops having contributed greatly to the victory.

These redoubts are also the more advantageous in that they require but little time for their construction and are useful in an infinity of situations. A single one is frequently sufficient to stop a whole army in a terrain corridor. They can be used to prevent your being harassed on a critical march, to support one of your wings, to divide a piece of ground, to occupy a large space when there are not enough troops to support a flank on a wood, a marsh, a river, etc.

SPIES AND GUIDES. Too much attention cannot be paid to spies and guides. Montecuculli says that they are like eyes and are equally necessary to a general. He is right. Too much money cannot be spent to get good ones. These men should be chosen in the country where the war is being fought. They should be intelligent, cunning, and discreet. They should be placed everywhere, among the officers, the generals, the sutlers, and especially among purveyors of provisions, because their stores, magazines, and other preparations furnish the best intelligence concerning the real designs of the enemy.

Spies should not know one another. There should be several ranks of them. Some should associate with soldiers; others should follow the army under the guise of peddlers. These should know one of their companions of first rank from whom they receive anything that is to be conveyed to the general who pays them. This detail should be committed to one who is faithful and intelligent. He should report his activities every day, and it should be certain that he is incorruptible.

SIGNS. There are particular signs in war that must be studied and by which judgments can be formed with some certainty. The knowledge you have of the enemy and his customs will contribute a great deal to this. And there are signs common to all nations.

During a siege, for example, you discover towards the horizon and on the heights, as evening approaches, unorganized and idle groups of men looking at the city; this is a sure sign that a considerable attack is being prepared. This is because attacks are made with elements of different corps and thus are known to the whole army. Those who are not to take part in the attack gather on the heights to watch it at their ease.

When your camp is near that of the enemy and you hear much firing in it, you may expect an engagement the day following because the men are discharging and cleaning their arms.

When you are in the presence of the enemy under arms and you see the soldiers changing shirts, it is certain that you are going to be attacked, because they put on all their shirts, one over the other, in order not to lose any.

If there is any extensive movement in the enemy's army, this can be judged from several leagues by the dust which is never raised except for several reasons. The dust caused by foraging columns is not the same as that of columns on the march, but you should be able to distinguish the difference.

You also can judge the direction of the enemy's movement by the reflection of the sun on his arms. If the rays are perpendicular, he marches towards you; if they are varied and infrequent, he retreats; if they slant from right to left, he is moving towards the left; if, in the contrary, they slant from left to right, his march is to the right. If there is a great amount of dust in his camp, not raised by foraging parties, he is sending off his sutlers and baggage, and you can be certain that he will march soon. This will give you time to make your dispositions to attack him on the march. You should know if it is practicable for him to march in your direction, whether that is his intention, and what way it is most probable that he will march. This can be judged from his position, his supplies, his depots, the terrain and, in short, his conduct in general.

Sometimes he places his ovens on his right or on his left. If you know the time and the quantity of his baking and if you are covered by a small stream, you can make a flank movement with your whole army. If he imitates you, as sometimes he is forced to do, you can return suddenly and attack the ovens with ten or twelve thousand men. The expedition should be accomplished before he is aware of it because you always have several hours advantage of him, exclusive of the time that may elapse between his receipt of intelligence and the confirmation of it. He will undoubtedly wait before he puts his army in motion, so that in all probability he will receive information of the attack of his depot before he has given orders for the march.

There are an infinite number of such stratagems in war that can be employed with little risk. Their consequences are often as great as those of a complete victory. They may force the enemy to attack you at a disadvantage or even to retreat shamefully with a superior army. And you will have risked little or nothing.

THE GENERAL COMMANDING. I have formed a picture of a general commanding which is not chimerical—I have seen such men.

The first of all qualities is COURAGE. Without this the others are of little value, since they cannot be used. The second is INTELLIGENCE, which must be strong and fertile in expedients. The third is HEALTH.

He should possess a talent for sudden and appropriate improvisation. He should be able to penetrate the minds of other men, while remaining impenetrable himself. He should be endowed with the capacity of being prepared for everything, with activity accompanied by judgment, with skill to make a proper decision on all occasions, and with exactness of discernment.

He should have a good disposition free from caprice and be a stranger to hatred. He should punish without mercy, especially those who are dearest to him, but never from anger. He should always be grieved when he is forced to execute the military rules and should have the example of Manlius constantly before his eyes. He should discard the idea that it is he who punishes and should persuade himself and others that he only administers the military laws. With these qualities, he will be loved, he will be feared, and, without doubt, obeyed.

The functions of a general are infinite. He must know how to subsist his army and how to husband it; how to place it so that he will not be forced to fight except when he chooses; how to form his troops in an infinity of different dispositions; how to profit from that favorable moment which occurs in all battles and which decides their success. All these things are of immense importance and are as varied as the situations and dispositions which produce them.

In order to see all these things the general should be occupied with nothing else on the day of battle. The inspection of the terrain and the disposition of his troops should be prompt, like the flight of an eagle. This done, his orders should be short and simple, as for instance: "The first line will attack and the second will be in support."

The generals under his command must be incompetent indeed if they do not know how to execute this order and to perform the proper maneuvers with their respective divisions. Thus the commander in chief will not be forced to occupy himself with it nor be embarrassed with details. For if he attempts to be a battle sergeant and be everywhere himself, he will resemble the fly in the fable that thought he was driving the coach.

Thus, on the day of battle, I should want the general to do nothing. His observations will be better for it, his judgment will be more sane, and he will be in better state to profit from the situations in which the enemy finds himself during the engagement. And when he sees an occasion, he should unleash his energies, hasten to the critical point at top speed, seize the first troops available, advance them rapidly, and lead them in person. These are the strokes that decide battles and gain victories. The important thing is to see the opportunity and to know how to use it.

Prince Eugene possessed this quality, which is the greatest in the art of war and which is the test of the most elevated genius. I have applied myself to the study of this great man and on this point can venture to say that I understand him.

Many commanding generals only spend their time on the day of battle in making their troops march in a straight line, in seeing that they keep their proper distances, in answering questions which their aides de camp come to ask, in sending them hither and thither, and in running about incessantly themselves. In short, they try to do everything and, as a result, do nothing. They appear to me like men with their heads turned, who no longer see anything and who only are able to do what they have done all their lives, which is to conduct troops methodically under the orders of a commander. How does this happen? It is because very few men occupy themselves with the higher problems of war. They pass their lives drilling troops and believe that this is the only branch of the military act. When they arrive at the command of armies they are totally ignorant, and, in default of knowing what should be done, they do what they know.

One of the branches of the art of war, that is to say drill and the method of fighting, is methodical; the other is intellectual. For the conduct of the latter it is essential that ordinary men should not be chosen.

Unless a man is born with talent for war, he will never be other than a mediocre general. It is the same with all talents; in painting, or in music, or in poetry, talent must be inherent for excellence. All sublime arts are alike in this respect. That is why we see so few outstanding men in a science. Centuries pass without producing one. Application rectifies ideas but does not furnish a soul, for that is the work of nature.

I have seen very good colonels become very bad generals. I have known others who were great takers of villages, excellent for maneuvers within an army, but who, outside of that, were not even able to lead a thousand men in war, who lost their heads completely and were unable to make any decision.

If such a man arrives at the command of an army, he will seek to save himself by his dispositions, because he has no other resources. In attempting to make them understood better he will confuse the spirit of his whole army with multitudinous messages. Since the least circumstances changes everything in war, he will want to change his arrangements, will throw everything in horrible confusion, and infallibly will be defeated.

One should, once for all, establish standard combat procedures which the troops, as well as the general who leads them, know. These are general rules, such as: preserving proper distances on the march; when charging to charge vigorously; to fill up intervals in the first line from the second. No written instructions are required for this; it is the A-B-C of the troops and nothing is simpler. And the generals should not give all their attention to these matters as most of them do.

But what the general should do, is to observe the attitude of the enemy, the movements he makes, or where he directs his troops. He should endeavor, by a feint at one point, to draw his troops from another, to confuse him, to seize every opportunity, and to know how to deliver the death thrust at the proper place. But, to be capable of all this, he should preserve an unfettered mind and not occupy himself with trifles.

I do not favor pitched battles, especially at the beginning of a war, and I am convinced that a skillful general could make war all his life without being forced into one.

Nothing so reduces the enemy to absurdity as this method; nothing advances affairs better. Frequent small engagements will dissipate the enemy until he is forced to hide from you.

I do not mean to say by this that when an opportunity occurs to crush the enemy that he should not be attacked, nor that advantage should not be taken of his mistakes. But I do mean that war can be made without leaving anything to chance. And this is the highest point of perfection and skill in a general. But when a battle is joined under favorable circumstances, one should know how to profit from victory and, above all, should not be contented to have won the field of battle in accordance with the present commendable custom.

The words of the proverb: "A bridge of gold should be made for the enemy," is followed religiously. This is false. On the contrary, the pursuit should be pushed to the limit. And the retreat which had appeared such a satisfactory solution will be turned into a route. A detachment of ten thousand men can destroy an army of one hundred thousand in flight. Nothing inspires so much terror or occasions so much damage, for everything is lost. Substantial efforts are required to restore the defeated army, and in addition you are rid of the enemy for a good time. But many generals do not worry about finishing the war so soon.

If I wished to cite examples to support my opinion I could find an infinite number. I shall mention but one.

As the French army, at the battle of Ramillies, was retreating in good order on a narrow plateau, bordered on both sides with deep ravines, the Allied cavalry followed it at a slow pace as if they were marching for exercise. And the French army also withdrew gently, twenty or more deep at times, on account of the narrowness of the ground. An English squadron approached two battalions of French and commenced to fire. These two battalions, believing that they were going to be attacked, faced about and fired a general discharge on the squadron. What happened? All the

French troops gave way at the noise of the discharge. The cavalry fled at a gallop and the infantry threw itself into the two ravines in horrible confusion, so that in an instant the ground was clear and no one was to be seen.

Can anyone boast to me, after that, of the good order of retreats and the prudence of those who build à "bridge of gold" for the enemy after they have been defeated in battle. I should say that they serve their master badly.

This is not to say that it is necessary to give yourself up totally to the pursuit and follow the enemy with all your forces. A corps should be ordered to push as long as the day lasts and to follow in good order. Once the enemy has taken flight they can be chased with bladders. But if the officer you have ordered in pursuit prides himself upon the regularity of his formation and the precautions of his march, that is to say if he maneuvers like the army which he follows should, there is no use in having sent him. He must attack, push, and pursue without cease. All maneuvers are good then; it is only precautions that are worthless.

To THE READERS. I wrote this book in thirteen nights. I was sick; thus it very probably shows the fever I had. This should supply my excuses for the irregularity of the arrangement, as well as for the inelegance of the style. I wrote militarily and to dissipate my boredom. Done in the month of December, 1732.

The Instruction of Frederick The Great for His Generals 1747

TRANSLATED

by

BRIG. GEN. THOMAS R. PHILLIPS

INTRODUCTION

Frederick the Great, King of Prussia, was the founder of modern Germany. When he became King of Prussia it was a small state, in two parts, and of minor importance among the great powers of Europe. During his reign the population increased from 2,240,000 to 6,000,000, and the territory was increased by nearly thirty thousand square miles. Singlehanded he fought all the great powers of Europe in the Seven Years War and successfully defended the national territory. Although he gained no new lands during this war his success against the overwhelming coalition of his enemies made him the greatest man of his time and the soldier whom all other soldiers in Europe were to imitate. Frederick's upbuilding of Prussia determined whether the many small German states eventually were to group themselves around Prussia or around Austria. The expansion of Prussia was continued by Bismarck and now has been completed by Chancellor Hitler, making one great nation of all the people of the German race.

Frederick the Great was born January 24, 1712. His father, Frederick William, brought him up with extreme rigor in the hope that he would become a hardy soldier and "acquire thrift and frugality." To his father's intense disgust he showed no interest in military affairs and devoted all his time to literature and music. He was so harshly treated by his father that he resolved to escape to England and take refuge there. He was helped by two friends, Lieutenant Katte and Lieutenant Keith. The plan was discovered, and the Crown Prince was arrested, deprived of his rank, tried by court-martial and imprisoned in the fortress of Kustrin. Lt. Keith escaped, but Lt. Katte was captured, tried, and sentenced to life imprisonment. The King changed the sentence to death, and Frederick was forced to watch his friend beheaded.

While still restricted he was put to work in the auditing office of the war department checking invoices, payrolls, etc. He was allowed to appear in uniform a year later. He became King May 31, 1740, on the death of his father. He seized Silesia from Austria and gained a victory at Mollwitz, April 10, 1741. At this battle he fled from the field under the impression that it had been lost as a result of a furious charge of Austrian cavalry—a mistake which gave rise to a false reputation for lack of personal courage.

He gained a second victory at Caslau on May 17, 1742, the war ending in the peace of Breslau and the cession of Silesia by Austria. He captured Prague in 1744, but was forced to retreat. In 1745 he won a series of victories and concluded the peace of Dresden, which for a second time assured him possession of Silesia.

Between this time and the commencement of the Seven Years War in 1756, he devoted himself to building up his kingdom. He restored the Academy of Sciences, encouraged agriculture, extended the canal system, drained and dyked the marshes of Oderbruch, encouraged manufacture, and increased his army to 160,000 men. He worked arduously all his life, rising habitually at four or five o'clock in the morning and working until midnight. He was economical in the conduct of his personal and state affairs and was scorned and lampooned for this at the time. His economy was not understood in that age of glittering and useless royalty.

The Seven Years War ended with the status quo established, but it was, in effect, a great victory. From this time on he devoted his energies to reconstitution of the devastated kingdom. Taxes were remitted for a time to the provinces that had suffered most. Army horses were distributed among the farmers, and treasury funds were used to rebuild devastated cities. When he died August 17, 1786, he left an army of 200,000 men and 70,000,000 thalers in the treasury.

Frederick the Great was a liberal, allowing freedom of press and speech, and permitting books and cartoons deriding and lampooning him. Riding along the Jäger Strasse one day he saw a crowd of people. "See what it is," he said to his groom. "They have something posted up about your majesty," said the groom, returning. Riding forward, Frederick saw a caricature of himself: "The King in very melancholy guise," (Preuss as translated by Carlyle), "seated on a stool, a coffee mill between his knees, diligently grinding with one hand, and with the other picking up any bean that might have fallen. "Hang it lower,' said the King, beckoning his groom with a wave of his finger; 'lower that they may not hurt their necks about it.' " The crowd cheered him and followed him with shouts as he rode slowly away.

He was greatly interested in the administration of justice and called himself "l'avocat du pauvre." It has been a fashion among recent writers to judge Frederick the Great harshly on the grounds of his diplomatic duplicity and the severity of his punishments in the army. This is probably unjust. He was successful in the game of deception that all monarchs played in his time. He, like all the rest of them, was intent on adding to his domain. Punishment was severe in the Prussian army, but so was it in all other armies. In the French army pillaging and desertion were punishable by death, whereas in the Prussian army flogging was the prescribed punishment for these crimes. Flogging was given up in the French revolutionary army, but it continued longer in the English army than it did in Germany. It was not until 813 that flogging was abolished in the American army.

Saxe gained his successes in battles of position; he did not live long enough to take advantage of the mobility which his cadence gave to armies. Frederick was to take advantage of the new mobility of masses like Napoleon did later. He was the greatest in this respect before Napoleon. He regularly marched his armies at a rate of twenty kilometers a day during periods of two, three, and four weeks.

Armies, in his time, were more numerous but not so well composed as formerly. Increases in numbers broke the relationship between men and their commanders. Lines were thinner and fronts were extended, reducing control. This was the state in which Frederick found

European tactics. At the same time his army was more perfect in details, the work of his father, and he spent more time on strategy. Prussian soldiers, through constant drill, were able to load and fire their muskets twice as rapidly as their opponents. This had the same effect as if they were closer to their adversaries when they fired. At the same time, they charged much more rapidly than the enemy and thus gained a further advantage in avoiding the enemy's fire. Until his enemies learned from him, these advantages helped greatly in his victories.

Frederick's tactics were based on mobility. This was especially favorable to him because the heavy, slow battalions of his enemies did not have it. In his early years Frederick agreed with Saxe in his belief about the uselessness of fire in the attack. Initially, and renewed from year to year, he gave the order for the soldiers to carry their guns on their shoulders in the attack and to fire the least possible. But in 1758, he commences to write that "to attack the enemy without procuring oneself the advantage of superior, or at least equal fire, is to wish to fight against an armed troop with clubs, and this is impossible." Ten years later, in his *Military Testament*, he wrote: "Battles are won by superiority of fire." A decisive word, remarks Captain J. Colin, which marks a new era of combat.

Frederick was a sincere admirer of Saxe in his lifetime and his true testamentary executor. Frederick II breathes only the offensive, the offensive always, in every situation, in the whole of the operations as well as on the field of battle, even in the presence of a superior enemy.

"With such ardor," writes Capt. Colin, "how does he operate when he makes contact with the adversary? Not an immediate battle, but a long, drawn out jockeying for position. This was a characteristic of operations from ancient times until Frederick. Far from the enemy they forced the pace, but as soon as they approached they beat about, using days, weeks, and months to decide to fight. Either side could refuse battle because they could get away while the other was arranging his lines." Frederick carried the operations of ancient war to the highest degree of perfection they ever attained.

Among the innovations to be attributed to Frederick are: the division of armies so that they could march in a number of columns with less fatigue; the use of flank marches; the oblique order, a practical method of envelopment with the armies of his time; the lightening of the cavalry; increased mobility of artillery and the development of horse artillery; increase in the number of howitzers.

It has been one of the misfortunes of armies that Frederick's great reputation led to slavish imitation of the forms of the Prussian military system. Young officers from England and France attended the reviews at Potsdam and thought all the secrets of Frederick's success lay in Prussian drill, Prussian uniforms, and the shine and polish tradition. They were unable to distinguish the symbol from the substance in the Prussian army. Drill was mistaken for the art of war although Frederick never so interpreted it. He "laughed in his sleeve," says Napoleon, "at the parades of Potsdam, when he perceived young officers, French, English, and Austrian, so infatuated with the maneuver of the oblique order, which was fit for nothing except to gain a few adjutant-majors a reputation."*

Napoleon ranked Frederick the Great along with Caesar, Hannibal, Turenne, and Prince Eugene. What distinguished him above all other generals, Napoleon thought, was his extraordinary audacity. Frederick's fame was quickly eclipsed by that of Napoleon himself. The result has been that his battles have not been truly appreciated nor is there even in English any good analytical account of them. Guibert, in his *Essai General de Tactique,* was an admitted expounder of Frederick the Great's methods, just as Jomini later was to be of Napoleon's. Guibert influenced Napoleon profoundly. The introduction of a permanent divisional organization into the French army by the Duke of Broglie in 1759 made possible the new advances in mobility and rapid deployment of which Napoleon was to take such great advantage.

The Instruction of Frederick the Great for his Generals was written in 1747 following a period of illness. It is a remarkable book for a Prince, aged 35. It was revised in 1748 under the title of *General Principles of War.* One copy of it was sent to his successor to the throne in 1748 with a request enclosed that it should be shown to no one. In January, 1753, an edition of fifty copies was printed and sent to a list of officers whom the King considered models. A cabinet order enjoined

---

* Quoted by Col. E. M. Lloyd, *A Review of the History of Infantry.*

each recipient on his oath not to take it with him in the field and to take care that on his death it would be handed over to the King again well sealed.

General Czettertiz was captured by the Austrians in a small affair February 21, 1760. On him was found Frederick's secret manuscript. It was duly prized, reprinted in German in 1761 and translated back into French and printed in France the same year. It was translated into English in 1762 under the title, *Military Instructions by the King of Prussia*. It was reprinted and edited by Scharnhorst in Germany in 1794 for instruction purposes. It appeared again in the collected works of Frederick the Great in 1856 and in the military writings of Frederick the Great edited by General von Taysen in 1891.

The present text is translated from the Instruction of 1747, published for the first time in Berlin in 1936, on the one hundred and fiftieth anniversary of the death of Frederick the Great. This edition has been very carefully edited by Dr. Richard Fester and contains the original French text and a German translation. The present translation, made with permission of the German publisher, E. S. Mittler & Sohn, marks the first appearance of the Instruction of 1747 in English.

The Instruction of Frederick The Great for His Generals, 1747

PRUSSIAN TROOPS, THEIR DEFICIENCIES AND THEIR ADVANTAGES. The discipline and the organization of Prussian troops demand more care and more application from those who command them than is demanded from a general in any other service.

If our discipline aids the most audacious enterprises, the composition of our troops requires attentions and precautions that sometimes are very troublesome. Our regiments are composed half of citizens and half of mercenaries. The latter, not attached to the state by any bonds of interest, become deserters at the first occasion. And since the numbers of troops is of great importance in war, the general should never lose sight of the importance of preventing desertion.

He can prevent it:

(1) By being careful to avoid camping too close to large woods;

(2) By having the soldiers visited frequently in their camps;

(3) By keeping them busy;

(4) By forming carefully a chain of guards around the camp so that no one can pass between them;

(5) By ordering patrols of hussars to watch the flanks and rear of the army;

(6) By examining, when desertion occurs in a regiment or in a company, whether it is not the fault of the captain, if the soldiers have received the pay and com-

forts which the King provides for them, or if the officer is guilty of some embezzlement;

(7) By observing strictly the orders that soldiers shall be led in ranks by an officer when they go to bathe or forage;

(8) By avoiding night marches unless they are required by the exigencies of war;

(9) By careful observance of order on marches with strict prohibition against a soldier leaving the ranks or his squad, by placing officers at the debouches of defiles or where roads traverse the route of march, and by having hussars patrol the flanks;

(10) By not withdrawing guards from villages until the whole army is under arms and ready to commence the march;

(11) By hiding carefully from the soldiers the movements we are forced to make to the rear or by endowing retreats with some specious reason which flatters the greed of the soldier;

(12) By preventing pillage, which is the source of the greatest disorders.

THE CAPABILITIES OF PRUSSIAN TROOPS AND THEIR PARTICULAR MERIT. The greatest force of the Prussian army resides in their wonderful regularity, which long custom has made a habit, in exact obedience, and in the bravery of the troops.

The discipline of these troops, now evolved into habit, has such effect that in the greatest confusion of an action and the most evident perils their disorder still is more orderly than the good order of their enemies. Consequently, small confusions are redressed in a moment and all evolutions are made promptly. A general of other troops could be surprised in circumstances in which he would not be if commanding Prussians, since he will find resources in the speed with which they form and maneuver in the presence of the enemy.

Prussians' discipline renders these troops capable of executing the most difficult maneuvers, such as traversing a wood in battle without losing their files or distances, advancing in close order at double time, forming with promptness, reversing their direction suddenly to fall on the flank of the enemy, gaining an advantage by a forced march, and finally in surpassing the enemy in constancy and fortitude.

Obedience to the officers and subordination is so exact that no one ever questions an order, hours are observed exactly, and however little a general knows how to make himself obeyed, he is always sure to be. No one ever reasons about the possibility of an enterprise, and, finally, its accomplishment is never despaired of.

The Prussians are superior to their enemies in constancy since the officers, who have no other profession nor other fortune to hope from except their arms, animate themselves with an ambition and a gallantry beyond all test, because the soldier has confidence in himself, and because he makes it a point of honor never to give way. Many have been seen to fight even when wounded since the organization in general, proud of its past brave engagements, considers that any soldier who has shown the least cowardice in action affronts it.

PROJECTS OF CAMPAIGN. We cannot have any enemies except our neighbors, that is Austrians, whom I place at the head of them all, the Saxons, the most envious of our expansion, and the Russians, who can become our declared enemies as a consequence of the rivalry they have conceived since we have labored to relieve Sweden. from their tyranny.

One should know one's enemies, their alliances, their resources, and the nature of their country in order to plan a campaign. One should know what to expect of one's friends, what resources one has oneself, and see the future effects to determine what one has to fear or hope from political maneuvers. Since all these cases can be complicated and since it is impossible to foresee all the combinations that the caprice of fortune may give birth to, I shall enclose my precepts in some general maxims.

One should not embarrass oneself in the project of campaign with the number of the enemy, provided they do not exceed you more than a third. That is to say, with 75,000 men you can attack 100,000 in all security and even promise yourself to defeat them. Extravagant projects of campaign are worthless; I call extravagant those which require you to make penetrations, or those which reduce you to a too rigid defensive. Penetrations are worthless because in pushing too far into the enemy's country you weaken yourself, your communications become very difficult to maintain on account of their length, and in order to make assured conquests it is necessary always to proceed within the rules: to advance, to establish yourself solidly, to advance again, to establish yourself the same, and always to prepare to have within reach of your army your resources and your requirements.

Projects of absolute defensive are not practicable because while wishing to close yourself in strong camps the enemy will envelop you, deprive you of your sustenance from the rear, and oblige you to lose ground while disheartening your troops. Thus, I prefer to this conduct the temerity of the offensive with the hazard of losing the battle since this will not be more fatal than your retreat and your timid defensive. In the one you lose ground by withdrawing and soldiers by desertion and you have no hope; in the other you do not risk more and, if you are fortunate, you can hope for the most brilliant success.

The projects of campaign that I propose for the offensive and the defensive according to my method are the following:

For the offensive I require a general to examine the enemy's frontier; after having weighed carefully the favorable and difficult factors in the different points of attack, he determines the locality through which he will advance. To make this more clear I am going to apply it to Saxony, Bohemia, and Moravia.

To attack Saxony, I would assemble my army in the vicinity of Halle. The first thing to think about then will be the question of subsistance; without supplies no army is brave, and a great general who is hungry is not a hero for long. The handling of food supplies should be entrusted to a man of integrity—capable, intelligent and discreet; it is essential to collect as much grain as it is thought will be consumed during a campaign, to protect the city where the food depot is established with a good garrison and secure it from any surprise, and even take precautions so that the enemy cannot have it set on fire by spies or hired agents. This done, it is necessary to provide for the wagon trains. First you should take with you a large enough provision of grain to last for three weeks. This done, if the enemy is in the field, it is necessary to find out where he is and get rid of him. Following this, the seige of Wittenburg becomes indispensable; this makes you master of the Elbe and gives you communication with your country and covers it at the same time. From there it is necessary to march to the capital, which will fall of itself, expel the enemy from the country, and collect some winter magazines. The troops should not be dispersed too much. Your succeeding projects will depend on the circumstances of the time.

Projects of campaign against Bohemia should be made only after much meditation. Examine the frontier! You will see four considerable passages, one beside the Lusace, the other which leads to Trautenau, the third to Braunau, the fourth by the Comte of Glatz, Rückers, and Reinerz to Königgrätz. The one closest to the Lusace is of. no value because you have no strong point in your rear, because you enter the kingdom in the corner of a difficult and mountainous country, where, if the enemy happens to be there, he will have a wonderful chance to wage a war of ruses and chicanery against you.

The road to Trautenau is almost equally bad. If the enemy is found at Schatzlar, he will make your operation difficult, and perhaps impracticable,. because of the advantage the terrain gives him and the heights which dominate all this country.

The road through Braunau is the best of all because you have Schweidnitz behind you. This is and will be made a good fortress because from there to Braunau it is only four miles and because, in spite of the difficulty of the roads, it is, nevertheless, the best of all those leading into Bohemia. I prefer this to the routes of Glatz and Reinerz because in entering by Braunau you cover all of Lower Silesia, the replenishment of the depots can be made with facility from Schweidnitz, while at Glatz this is very difficult because of the length of transport and the difficult roads. For you should always in Silesia regard the Oder as the nourishing mother for the magazines. It is closer than Schweidnitz and if there were only this reason, it should be regarded as decisive.

After having chosen this point of attack it is necessary to consider the security of the depots and the country. For this purpose we cannot dispense sending a body of 6000 or 7000 men to the border of Neisse to oppose continually the incursion of the Hungarians and to cover the country in such a manner that the convoys from the interior of Lower Silesia, which furnish and refill the depot at Schweidnitz, can arrive there in security. This Upper Silesian córps has three points of support. One is Neisse, and for all operations beyond the Oder, Cosel and Brieg can serve for a retreat and depots.

As for the nature of your operations it is very difficult to determine them without knowing the circumstances in which you will find yourself. I daresay, always with certitude and from experience, that Bohemia will never be taken by making war there. In order to capture it permanently from the house of Austria it is necessary for an allied army to go along the Danube, while ours traverses Moravia, and for the two armies to arrive at the same time against Vienna, while a small body of troops cleans up Bohemia and draws contributions from it.

If you make war on the Queen of Hungary alone without having a marked superiority over her, your projects of campaign can only be a mass defensive, clothed with the externals and appearances of the offensive. The campaign will be used to penetrate into Bohemia. You will take Königgrätz and even Pardubitz there, if you wish; but with these two cities you will have gained nothing because they are too poor to place depots there in security, because there is no tenable city nor navigable river in this country. As a consequence there is no way to sustain yourself there during the winter without risking the troops, unless some allies furnish you the means, as happened to us during the winter of 1741 and '42. Besides, the difficulties of the convoys in wooded country, where they necessarily have to traverse the gorges of the mountains, always render your operation questionable and exposed by the slightest capture of your convoys by the enemy's light troops. Thus the campaign in Bohemia with equal forces against the Queen of Hungary will reduce itself to making part of your army subsist at her expense, after which your principal care should be to forage and exhaust all the outskirts of Bohemia which border on Silesia, so that the enemy will not be able to put large bodies in winter quarters there. These large bodies of troops would disturb you in Silesia, and your troops would have no repose.

I would form an entirely different project of campaign against Moravia. It can only be attacked by the road from Troppau to Sternberg, or by the Prerau route. The Sternberg road is the closest, most convenient to Neisse, and, as a consequence, the more suitable. I am always assuming in these offensive projects that the forces are approximately equal. In this case it is necessary to leave a body of 7000 or 8000 men on the border of Braunau to oppose to the incursions that the hussars would be able to make from Bohemia into Silesia. If this corps found itself in contact with too formidable an enemy, there is a sure retreat at Schweidnitz. I am obliged still to make a second detachment in the vicinity of Jablunka, even more necessary than the first. The success of my whole project is founded on the solidity of the conduct of the officer who will command it. This officer should defend the entry into Silesia against the Hungarians, and here is why his defensive is important. If some clever and pillaging troops penetrate Upper Silesia, the security of no convoy can any longer be counted on, and, just as the first campaign proposed in Moravia depends on subsisting on the Silesian depots, it follows that the convoys which are to follow the army should be able to do so with complete security.

As for magazines, I would establish my principal accumulation at Neisse, and I would advance a depot for two months' supply of grain at Troppeau. I would repair the walls, raise earthworks where needed, and pallisade the places which require it. From there I would march on Olmütz; I would fortify Sternberg in the same way to assure the passage of my convoys; then I would attack the enemy wherever I found him; I would take thirty 12-pounder cannon, twenty-five howitzers, and six 24-pounder pieces of light seige artillery, which will suffice to conduct the seige. The place will hold at least twelve days with open trenches. I would have my provisions advance there from Troppeau. I would have the breaches repaired; then I would advance on the enemy who will have withdrawn from the vicinity of Brünn.

It is then that it is necessary to employ ruses to draw him away from that place, to draw him on to the plains, in order to fight or finally to make ready to form the second seige. The fortress could hold eight days; if the enemy is in the vicinity, it will be necessary to build a strong entrenchment, to amass food there from Olmütz for three weeks, and to take the place. The city will not be able to resist a long time; the chateau may be able to hold you for twelve days. This requires that the magazines follow, and as soon as you establish them at Brünn, as soon as the place is supplied, you can advance on Znaim and Nikolsbourg, which will throw the enemies back into Austria if they are thoroughly defeated and if they have not received help by this time. Even though they have left the field, the country is too favorable for them to expect that they will not send their light troops back on your two flanks, that is in the Trebitsch Mountains on your right and in the mountains near Hradisch on your left.

I am now coming to what I call the defensive which turns into the offensive.

The greatest secret of war and the masterpiece of a skillful general is to starve his enemy. Hunger exhausts men more surely than courage, and you will succeed with less risk than by fighting. But since it is very rare that a war is ended by the capture of a depot and matters are only decided by great battles, it is necessary to employ all these means to attain this object. I shall content myself in exposing two projects of the defensive according to this method—one for Lower Silesia, the other for the Electorate of Brandebourg.

I would defend Lower Silesia against the Austrians if they intended to attack through Bohemia in the following fashion. I would establish my principal magazine at Schweidnitz, which I would garrison with five battalions and three squadrons of hussars. I would establish a small depot at the Chateau of Liegnitz, to be prepared to follow the enemy if he went along the mountains. I would place seven battalions at Glatz with three or four regiments of hussars. The more of them that are there the better it will be. All the attention of the governor of Glatz should be directed on convoys and the depot of the enemy. If he strikes a good blow in that direction their projected offensive is ruined for a whole campaign.

On my part I would encamp the army at Schönberg, and I would throw up trenches so as to appear timorous. If the enemy goes along the mountains, I would follow him, always taking up strong camps but open, nevertheless, on the flanks and in the rear, if I were able. It would be necessary to fall either on his advance guard or on his rear guard and cut him off from it. Such a check is capable of reducing him to the defensive. If he acts as if he wished to attack me, he should find so many disadvantages in his situation that the desire will leave him. If he wished to envelop me, it would be necessary to let him pass and to place myself behind him, upon which I would cut him off from his supplies. I would be able to choose ground of advantage to my troops and oblige him to fight in the locality that pleased me, and if I defeat him he will have no retreat and his entire army is lost. And I risk nothing seeing him break into the country because my magazines are protected by my fortresses and he will be unable to capture them by a sudden blow.

I would make a project of defensive campaign for Brandebourg in the following manner.

I would assemble my army not far from Brandebourg. The enemy could only form two plans to penetrate the country. The more solid would be that of following the course of the Elbe; but since they would find Magdebourg, which is a fortress hard to digest, in their road, they would not think of this plan too readily. Their plan would be, without doubt, to assemble their forces around Wittenberg and to march straight on Berlin. In this case I would approach from the direction of Teltow, having my magazines at Brandebourg and Spandau. If the enemy had his supplies following in wagons, I would send all my light troops through the forest of Beelitz which extends into Saxony, and from there they would fall on the rear of the enemy and capture his convoys. The hussars would have a sure retreat in these great forests where they know the trails and through which they could always return to my army. This defensive could only be made with vigor. It is essential to gain the rear of the enemy, or to surprise them in their camp, or to cut them from their country by a forced march. I would not advise anyone to place himself behind the Havel and the Spree; the country would soon be lost by this.

I shall limit myself to the two examples that I have cited. It is always necessary to form projects of campaign, as I have said, on estimates of the weather, and as this is always changing one cannot imitate in one season what has been good in another. I shall only add to these maxims that a general in all his projects should not think so much about what he wishes to do as about what his enemy will do; that he should never underestimate this enemy, but he should put himself in his place to appreciate difficulties and hinderances the enemy could interpose; that he will be deranged at the slightest event if he has not foreseen everything and if he has not invented the means with which to surmount the obstacles.

SUBSISTENCE AND COMMISSARY. Understand that the foundation of an army is the belly. It is necessary to procure nourishment for the soldier wherever you assemble him and wherever you wish to conduct him. This is the primary duty of a general.

I divide the problem of subsistence into two parts, of which one deals with the place and manner of assembling supplies and the other with the means of rendering these magazines mobile and making them follow the army. The first rule is always to place magazines and fortified places behind the localities where you are assembling the army. In Silesia our principal magazine has always been at Breslau. By placing your principal magazine at the head of your army, you risk being cut off from it by the first misfortune, and then you would be without resources; whereas, if your supplies were distributed by echelons the loss of one of these parts would not lead to that of the whole. In the defense of the Electorate, one of your magazines should be at Spandau, the other at Magdebourg. The latter could serve for the offensive, and it is in relation to Saxony much like the depot of Schweidnitz to Bohemia, and Neisse to Moravia. The first attention that should be given magazines is to choose the chief commissaries carefully. If they are dishonest men, the sovereign can lose prodigiously from theft; under any circumstances they should be watched carefully.

There are two methods of assembling magazines; one is to collect the grain in the country and credit the contributions of the peasants and gentlemen against their regular tax. It is not necessary to have recourse to the other expedient—that of contractors—except when this one is physically impossible. These men plunder pitilessly and make their own law by the exorbitant prices they place on food.

I add again to these maxims that it is always necessary to form large magazines in good time, because considerable time is required to amass them and sometimes the weather makes the roads bad, or rivers useless, or wagons impracticable. Besides the caissons attached to the regiments, the commissary should have enough caissons to carry meal to subsist your army for a three weeks' period. These caissons should be drawn by horses. Experience has demonstrated to us that oxen are of no use. Inspectors are required for the horses and the caissons. The care that they should have for their preservation is of the more consequence, for if they break down without your being able to replace them, your whole project will be halted. It is necessary for the general to keep his eye on all this.

Whenever an army operates along a river, subsistence becomes easier. The great generals, when they were able, have always reflected on this fact as being of great advantage. The Elbe gives us this advantage against the Saxons; but, if you wish to act in Bohemia or in Moravia, you can only count on your caissons. Sometimes three or four magazines are formed in file, from which you subsist, but as soon as you wish to progress into the enemy country, the magazine at Schweidnitz, for example, is fortified, while that at Breslau is obliged to refill in proportion as supplies are drawn from the first. The caissons which follow the army are filled from this one. Then you are assured of supplies for four weeks. In addition to the caissons, the field commissary carries with it its iron ovens. A large number are necessary in order to have plenty of bread, for it is impossible to do without this. If you undertake an expedition, bread should be on hand for ten days ahead and biscuits for five. Biscuits are excellent in case of need, but in place of eating them like bread, our soldiers break them up and make soup of them, which is not sufficient for their nourishment.

I shall be asked: but if you advance, for example, into Bohemia with all this meal, where will you store it? I answer that this only can be done at Pardubitz, which is the only locality at all reasonable. If not, it will have to be in a city from which your army is supported and where you have your ovens. And upon advancing from there this ambulating magazine always follows the army. I have had hand mills made for each company. These can be useful because wheat can be found everywhere and the soldiers can grind it. They then deliver the meal to the commissary who returns it to them converted into bread. This is a resource in necessity that experience should show whether more or less use should be made of it. But, I may be told, what will you do when you have lived four weeks in the enemy's country; then your meal will be eaten. Before reaching that point I would return my caissons to the nearest depot and have them filled and conducted to the army.

This is the place to speak of convoys.

The number of troops required to escort convoys increases or diminishes according to circumstances, the distance or the nearness of the enemy, the strength of his light troops, and the localities where he posts them. I have always made infantry the principal element of my convoys. This infantry is given some cannon and one hundred, two hundred or more hussars, simply to scout and notify the escort of the places where the enemy is. The cities where the escort rests should be garrisoned with troops and in the same way, if there is some village located on difficult terrain, such as a mountain gorge, it should be occupied to facilitate the passage. The general also takes the precaution of putting out a detachment forward which covers the march of the convoy toward the most exposed flank. I cover the duties of the minor officers in my *Institutions Militaires*.

BEER, BRANDY, AND SUTLERS. When an invasion of enemy territory is planned, all the beer and brandy possible to furnish the army should be brewed on the frontier. And within the enemy territory all the breweries that are found near the encampment are put to work. It is necessary to protect the sutlers, especially in enemy country, and send them out to pillage with the foragers in all the territory where the peasants have deserted their harvests. Under such circumstances the inhabitants do not furnish anything to the camp, and the sutlers have to pillage and supply it. In the camp itself, prices of everything are established with equity so that the soldier is not surfeited and the sutler is able to live.

I shall add another two words to this subject. We have always furnished bread free to the poor soldier because, in making war in territory that the enemy had made into deserts, it was only just to relieve him. In addition he has been furnished two pounds of meat a week, from herds of cattle with us which followed the troops. This provision was supplied at the same time that the caissons came to camp.

GREEN AND DRY FORAGE. I treat the question of forages here, since it has an affinity with magazines and the commissariat. Dry forage is collected in magazines. It consists of oats, barley, hay and straw which is cut. The oats should be dry and not sunburned, or they will give the strangles to the horses. Cut straw, according to many cavalry officers, bloats the horses without giving them any nourishment. These magazines serve to hinder the enemy in the field and forestall winter expeditions; however, it is difficult to move very far with the enormous baggage that the nourishment of men and animals at the same time demands.

During the first campaign in Silesia the horses were fed with dry forage, but we had the Oder which carried the provisions up to Ohlau, from where we were but a short distance. When it is desired to make a winter expedition, hay for five days is sent out and each cavalryman is given oats for the same period to carry on his horse. Any time that it is desired to attack Bohemia or Moravia, it is necessary to wait until green forage is growing in the country, or the risk is run of making the campaign without cavalry. Green forage can be seized in the field and the dry can be taken later in the season in the villages where the peasants have harvested their crops.

This is done by large foraging parties escorted by cavalry and infantry with numbers proportioned to those the enemy is able to oppose to us. Foragers are ordered out either by wings or by the entire army. They assemble by wing toward the flank where they wish to forage, and from the whole army, either in its front or rear. A foraging party is composed of the escort of cavalry foragers, those of the infantry, and some of the army wagons. If foraging is being done in level country, the hussars march at the head and move uncovered. They are followed with some squadrons and battalions mingled with the foragers, with a battalion between them of foragers from the infantry, and some cavalrymen and grenadiers who form the enclosure, followed by a rear guard of hussars. The foragers should be armed with their sword and a carbine.

When you arrive on the field which you have had reconnoitered and which you wish to forage, you first form your chain, that is to say you garrison the villages, if there are any, with infantry, placing the cavalry squadrons between them; if there are no villages, the cavalry should be mingled with the infantry, which always carries its cannon with it. You retain a reserve of cavalry which you hold in the center, so as to be able to use it on any flank that the enemy wishes to make his greatest effort to penetrate. This disposition having been made, the ground is divided up and foraging is commenced. On such an occasion the hussars need only to skirmish to keep away the enemy. Care should be taken that the foraging is well done and the bundles are large. When everything is completed, the foragers return to camp with some escort. When almost everyone has left, you reassemble the escort and, forming the rear guard, follow the rest.

Foraging parties in villages are made about the same way with the difference that the infantry of the escort garrisons the enclosures of the village, or defiles in the road, and the cavalry is placed on the wings, on the flanks, or sometimes in the rear of the village in accordance with the demands of the terrain. The most difficult of all foraging is in wooded and mountainous country. Then the advance guard and rear guard come from the infantry. Foraging parties are formed according to the occasion. If you wish to remain in a camp and the enemy is in your vicinity, your foraging between his army and yours is living at his expense; following this you forage a league around, taking the most distant forage first, always approaching your camp and conserving the nearest to the last. If you only encamp for a few days you will forage what is easiest to bring in.

ENCAMPMENTS. The art of choosing his camp well is, according to my opinion, one of the primary studies that a general should make because of its importance and the influence that the camp has on many happenings which are related to it. For those who are interested in the details of the encampments of regiments I refer to my *Institutions Militaires*. In this work I am concerning myself only with the larger aspects of war and the functions of the general. Camps are of different natures, and they are not perfect except to the extent that they approach the intentions proposed for them. There are camps to cover a country, offensive camps, defensive camps, entrenched camps for armies making sieges, foraging camps, rest camps, and concentration camps. The camps which cover a country should be well chosen, primarily with knowledge of the country, which is the basis of projects of war, just as the checkerboard is indispensable to those who want to play chess.

I am first going to tell about three camps which equally cover a country. There is one near Neustadt in Upper Silesia. You leave the city and river of Hotzenplotz in front of you and, by raising two redoubts on the wings of your army, you cover all of Lower Silesia. This is the place where the camp should be, but, after having marked the place, the skill of the general decides the manner in which he occupies its ground. The first rule that I give is always to occupy the heights; the second, that if you have a river or a stream in front of the camp, not to move more than half a rifle shot's distance from it. Tallard and the Elector of Bavaria were defeated at Höchstadt for having neglected this rule. The third: to place your camp in such a fashion that if the enemy passes on your right or on your left, the terrain will give you an equal advantage. Bends in rivers, marshes, or precipices will serve for this. The fourth: having your front and flanks well supported, your rear should be free; that is to say that there are no defiles and that you are able to make a march to the rear in several columns without embarrassment. In these unassailable sorts of camps you are able to garrison the villages with infantry. It is necessary that you have laid out in advance two other camps on your flank so that everything will be prepared and that you can act first in every eventuality. There is a camp between the cities of Neisse and Ottmachau just like this. Those who have a military eye for the terrain and knowledge of war will see it without me designating it more precisely.

On the borders of Bohemia there is a similar camp at Liebau. Two roads meet there. The enemy cannot turn you except by way of Braunau. The city of Liebau should be on your left. If you are there simply to cover the country, it is necessary to raise redoubts at varying distances in front of the infantry and to accommodate yourself to the ground. The fortified city of Schweidnitz and the Schweidnitzer Wasser which flows there will also furnish you with camps for the defensive and from which your skill can gain a great advantage.

The Electorate is more difficult, not to say impossible, to cover. It is a large front which is too long to be defended; in placing yourself near Berlin you abandon all the rest; in a word this country cannot be defended except by battles.

Camps for the offensives are open in front, but the wings should always be covered by marshes, or streams, or woods, or precipices. I do not speak of villages at all, since in our locality they are almost all of wood and there is no way to defend them. However, in all camps, villages which are within a quarter of a mile from the front and flanks of the camp are garrisoned so that enemy detachments cannot sneak into them and approach the army too closely, and to be secure against surprise. However, they are almost never garrisoned during fights, as I shall explain in its proper place. It should be observed that your camp should always be withdrawn about three hundred paces from the true field of battle that you choose, so that in case of surprise when there will not be time to strike the tents, your two lines will have room to form and maneuver.

There are some rules to observe for entrenched camps surrounding besieged villages. First, the entrenchment should not be made too large and of such a nature that it cannot be garrisoned in a continuous line by your infantry. The terrain should be used carefully. Marshes, streams, or abatis which can narrow the extent of ground to be held should be put to profit. The least heights should be occupied to avoid having your entrenchments dominated. Ditches should be as deep as possible. The entrenchments should be flanked with redans and redoubts. The weakest localities should be fortified with foxholes, or by some works, and even by fougasses. Food and provisions for the entire length of the seige should be massed in the camp. When the city is taken the entrenchments should be filled up.

Camps for the defensive are similar in many respects to those of the first type of which I have spoken. I should add that usually they are chosen either on high ground, such as that at Marschowitz, or behind defiles, or in the bend of some river, like that of the Prince of Lorraine, in 1745, near Königgrätz, or near fortified places, like that of Monsieur de Neipperg after the battle of Mollwitz. But it is not sufficient just to have found the camp; it is necessary that you should have two or three in your head that you can occupy in your rear in case the enemy turns you. Of all the countries I know, Bohemia is the most favorable for strong camps. You even are often obliged to use them when you are looking for others. I should add to this something that I cannot repeat often enough—which is to warn that when you place yourself in a strong camp you do not enclose yourself in a cul de sac. Thus I call a post unassailable when you cannot leave it except through defiles; for, if the enemy is clever and vigilant, he will seize the defiles, and in this case you will be taken without fighting. I cannot sufficiently repeat that your camp should, in consequence, always be open at the rear.

Foraging camps are sometimes close and sometimes distant from the enemy. I shall speak only of the first, the others demanding less application. Either foraging camps should be extremely strong, naturally, or they must be fortified because the enemy is able to attack you suddenly, while your foragers are absent, and profit from your weakness to cut you off. If you have no other purpose than to forage on enemy country, it must carefully be hidden from him; this is done by false demonstrations of which I shall speak in their place. This article is only concerned with the precautions to be taken so as not to be surprised while your forces are divided up to forage. To accomplish this it is necessary to choose infantry posts, place infantry in the first line, raise redoubts where the ground requires it, and make abatis where there are woods, much as we did in the camp at

Chlum and like the Prince of Lorraine in his strong camp at Königgrätz.

After these first precautions have been taken it is necessary to conceal the days and places where you are going to forage. One or two days after arrival in camp, the environs to a distance of a mile and a half should be reconnoitered under the pretext of waging guerrilla war. Guiding yourself on the information you receive, have all the different foraging parties ready but do not issue the orders until late in the evening to the officer who is to execute them, send out a large number of small parties to obtain information of the movements of the enemy, and regulate yourself by that. Foraging is done in greater security when it is carried on during the same day and at the same time as that of the enemy.

Rest camps are those where there is nothing to be done and where the *demarches* of the enemy are awaited, or where one waits for spring to commence operations. The most tranquil are those which have rivers or marshes in front of them, and the most convenient are those which are closest to the magazines. Such was our camp at Strehlen.

The duty of the general in these sorts of camps is to restore his army and personally to oversee order and discipline. The cavalry and infantry should be visited often and examined to determine if the first is well nourished and if these two corps are complete. The energy of the general can often find means to recruit troops. A man with his heart in his profession imagines and finds resources where the worthless and lazy despair, for—I repeat it again—numbers are an essential point in war, and a general who loves his honor and his reputation will always take extreme care to conserve and recruit his troop. Likewise, the troops should be exercised frequently, cavalry as well as infantry, and the general should often be present to praise the ones, to criticize the others, and to see with his own eyes that the orders which are found in my *Institutions Militaires* are observed exactly. The camp guards should be visited to see if they are vigilant, if the officer is attentive, or if he is negligent, to be extremely strict so that the mounted sentries will not allow anyone to enter the camp without examining and announcing him, and to prevent desertion by all the means that I have indicated previously.

The army, divided into separate brigades, moves into a concentration camp that has been laid out under the orders of four or more lieutenant generals. Often they are allowed to camp in separate bodies to facilitate subsistence but close enough, however, to come together within a few hours. But this sort of camp is never adopted close to the enemy, where one runs risks like the King of England at Dettingen. He camped by corps and marched in the same fashion when suddenly he found the French army on his road without expecting it. In all the camps that you will make, the water should be close and good and there should be enough wood nearby so that the soldiers can cook their porridge. In addition, to be secure against surprise by numbers of light troops in which the enemy is ordinarily superior to us, we have adopted the usage of the Romans of making light entrenchments all around our camp, as can be found in my *Institutions Militaires*. We have even found that this light entrenchment prevents desertion.

MEASURES OF SECURITY TAKEN FOR THE PROTECTION OF THE CAMP. Infantry pickets surround the camp, front and rear, as is prescribed in my regulations. A light entrenchment is made surrounding the camps in which it is expected to remain. The villages on the wings or a quarter of a mile in front are garrisoned with battalions of grenadiers, and sometimes battalions are placed in the posts which are beyond the extremity of the wings, where there are either bridges or causeways to pass, to cover the camp and to guarantee it against the enterprises of light troops. The cavalry camp guards are placed toward the front and according to the situation; since they are only posted to warn of the enemy, large bodies are not used, at least unless you are close to the enemy army and nothing separates you. With an army of 40,000 men we have had but 300 troopers on guard and sometimes fewer, but other precautions are taken which are more effective than these grand guards to prevent surprise. I have given the regulations for placing them in my *Institutions Militaires*.

Detachments are pushed out in front or on the flanks of the army toward the enemy. This sort of detachment should be composed of cavalry, infantry, and plenty of hussars. By this mixture of arms they sustain each other on all types of terrain. Such a corps, composed of two or three thousand hussars, one thousand cavalry, and

fifteen hundred or two thousand grenadiers, is advanced
a half or three-quarters of a mile ahead of the army. One
of the most skillful and vigilant generals is chosen to be
given this command. He should camp in a locality where
he will have a defile or a small wood, of which he is the
master, in front of him. In this case he lines the other
side of the wood toward the enemy with his mounted
sentinels and camps his corps on this side of it. He
should have patrols continually on the road, and mes-
sengers should be detached from them day and night to
keep him informed of what is happening and to send
notice to the general. If you see that numbers of the
enemy's light troops attempt to cut the communication
with your advance guard, you may conclude from this
that the enemy is on the point of executing some enterprise, either on this corps or on the army. Be on guard
in this case and send a large detachment strong enough
to force its way and give you notice of what is happening.

Even though a detachment or advance guard covers
the camp, neither more nor less, have your hussars send
out patrols on your wings and rear so that nothing will
be neglected. I should add to these regulations that no
general can be permitted to lodge in a village that is not
situated within the camp itself.

KNOWLEDGE OF THE COUNTRY AND COUP D'OEIL.
Knowledge of the country is to a general what a rifle
is to an infantryman and what the rules of arithmetic are
to a geometrician. If he does not know the country he
will do nothing but make gross mistakes. Without this
knowledge his projects, be they otherwise admirable,

become ridiculous and often impracticable. Therefore study the country where you are going to act! When it is desired to apply oneself to this essential part of war, the most detailed and exact maps of the country that can be found are taken and examined and re-examined frequently. If it is not in time of war, the places are visited, camps are chosen, roads are examined, the mayors of the villages, the butchers, and the farmers are talked to. One becomes familiar with the footpaths, the depth of the woods, their nature, the depth of the rivers, the practicable marshes and those which are not, and one observes in this study to distinguish carefully between the conditions of the marshes and the streams in the different seasons of the year. It cannot be said that a stream is impracticable in the month of August because it had been in the month of April. The road is chosen to be taken on such or such a march, the number of columns in which the march can be made, and all the strong camping places found on the route are examined to see if they can be used.

In reconnoitering these camps, they are examined to determine if the exits are numerous and easy, if they can be fortified by damming the streams and about what effect can be expected from this, if abatis can be made, and how large a number are required for this work to complete it in a certain time. Following this, the plans open to the enemy are considered, the marches he might make and the camps he might occupy are examined, and an estimate is made if he could be attacked during his march or in his camp, if he could be turned, and all the movements that could be made against him are studied. The larger cities and the better cemeteries on the outskirts are reconnoitered to estimate likewise to what extent they could serve the one who occupies them.

This sort of knowledge can be obtained promptly in the plains but requires more skill and research in mountainous country where one of your first cares is to place your camp so that it will not be dominated but will be dominant over all the surrounding ground. The difficulty of procuring this advantage will perplex you, for you will be hindered in obtaining water, which must necessarily be close to camp, and you dare not place your troops in a locality more distant from your road than they should be.

To make this clearer I shall explain myself with some examples. Assume that you wish to form a project of campaign against Moravia. You examine carefully the best map that you can find, and you see the principal highways which lead into this country, one from Glatz through Mittelwalde, Landskrom, Littau, and Olmütz; a second through Hof, Bentz, Freudenthal, Sternberg, and Olmütz; the third through Hultschin, Ostrau, Fulnek, Weisskirchen, Prerau, and Olmütz. Then these different routes should be ridden over, and the defiles and the posts from which the enemy could profit and the means to evade his opposition, the number of columns with which you will be able to march, and whether certain passages are not excessively bad, should be noted especially. It is necessary to learn if there is no other way by which you can avoid an obstacle that appears invincible. Make a detour and judge, if, by taking it with the army, the enemy would be able to prevail against this movement, or if you would be able by this means to place him in an embarrassing position. When you reconnoiter these three routes and have examined the locale with all your attention, it is necessary to see Olmütz.

I assume that you have a map of it and that you will always estimate your projects, and what the enemy may be able to do, in this fashion. But in such reasoning it is essential to be objective and it is dangerous to delude oneself. To accomplish this put yourself in the place of your enemy, and all the hindrances which you will have imagined and which he will not make for you, when war comes, will be just so many things that will facilitate your operations. Good dancers often go through their steps in sabots, and they become more agile when they are in pumps. An examination of this nature needs to be made with reflection. As much time should be allotted to it as the matter requires; when this is done in a neighboring country, it is necessary to hide your secret intention with the most specious pretexts that you are able to invent.

COUP D'OEIL. The *coup d'œil* of a general is the talent which great men have of conceiving in a moment all the advantages of the terrain and the use that they can make of it with their army. When you are accustomed to the size of your army you soon form your *coup d'œil* with reference to it, and habit teaches you the ground that you can occupy with a certain number of troops.

The *coup d'œil* is of great importance on two occasions. The first is when you encounter the enemy on your march and are obliged to choose ground on which to fight instantly. As I have remarked, within a single square mile a hundred different orders of battle can be formed. The clever general perceives the advantages of the terrain instantly; he gains advantage from the slightest hillock, from a tiny marsh; he advances or withdraws a wing to gain superiority; he strengthens either his right or his left, moves ahead or to the rear, and profits from the merest bagatelles.

The *coup d'œil* is required of the general when the enemy is found in position and must be attacked. Whoever has the best *coup d'œil* will perceive at first glance the weak spot of the enemy and attack him there. I shall have occasion to extend myself concerning this in the article on battles. The judgment that is exercised about the capacity of the enemy at the commencement of a battle is also called *coup d'œil*. This latter is the result only of experience.

THE DISPOSITIONS OF THE TROOPS. It is on exact knowledge of the terrain that is regulated the dispositions of the troops and the order of battle of the army. Our modern formations for combat, for the most part, are defective because they all are cast in the same mold: the infantry in the center and the cavalry on the wings. If an army is really to be camped according to the rules of war, it is essential that each arm should be placed in the locality where it can act. Infantry is most suitable for outposts; cavalry should always be in the plains or it becomes useless and cannot act. Thus, never encamp your cavalry near woods of which you are not the master, nor near impracticable marshes, nor in ravines parallel to your camp which prevent these troops from acting. For if the enemy intends to attack you and perceives your mistake, he will utilize these advantages.

He will oppose your cavalry with infantry and cannon, and he will rake them with rifle fire to the point that, provoked at seeing themselves killed uselessly, they take to flight. Therefore, without worrying about ordinary tricks, put all your cavalry on one wing! Put it all in the second line! Divide it equally between the two wings, or place it without observing the order of battle but according to the terrain that permits it to act.

As for Prussian infantry, it is superior to all rules. However, open country suits it best; I repeat it again. Never enclose it in villages and do not choose camps which are unassailable, but open enough so that you can attack the enemy. The power of the Prussians is in the attack, and I shall have farther on, when I speak of battles, occasion to give more illumination on this point. I observe that, regardless of circumstances, a corps of your army should always be destined for the reserve, even when you camp on two lines. The regiments which you intend to use for this purpose should be notified in advance. I shall have occasion to pluck this string in the article on battles, for rear guards are the safety of armies and often they carry victory away with them.

DETACHMENTS; HOW AND WHY THEY SHOULD BE MADE. There is an ancient rule of war that cannot be repeated often enough: hold your forces together, make no detachments, and, when you want to fight the enemy, reassemble all your forces and seize every advantage to make sure of your success. This rule is so certain that most of the generals who have neglected it have been punished promptly. Thus the great Prince Eugene was defeated at Denain because he did not have time to come to the support of Lord Albemarle's detachment. Guido Starhemberg also was defeated at Almanza through the fault of the English, who had failed to join him. The Prince of Hildbourghausen endured a similar affront at Banjaluka and Wallis on the banks of the Timoc, for being detached from the Imperial army, and finally the Saxons at Kesseldorf for not having called in Prince Charles of Lorraine, who was only a day's march distant. Likewise, we could have been defeated at Soor, if the exceptional courage of the troops and the skill of the generals had not pulled us out of the affair.

Thus the subject of detachments is extremely delicate. None should be made, except for good reasons, if you are acting offensively in open enemy country and are only master of some strong point. If you are actually waging war never throw out detachments except for convoys. In countries like Bohemia and Moravia, which are very mountainous, you will be obliged to leave detachments to guard the mountain gorges through which your convoys arrive, until the time when you have established your magazines in a fortified city. In such a case there are two precautions to take: the first is to choose strong encampments; the other, to place even these detachments where they are able to defend themselves against any eventuality until you can come to their help.

I do not call an army corps which is used as an advance guard a detachment, and as for other detachments, it is necessary to provide a secure retreat for them. I did this for ours in Upper Silesia, where, in case the enemy was too superior to them, they had a secure retreat in the fortresses of Neisse, Brieg, or Cosel. Officers who command detachments should be determined men, intrepid and prudent. Light troops should never be able to excite them, but at the unexpected approach of a large army corps they must look out for themselves, and they should know how to withdraw before a superior force and to profit in turn of the advantage of numbers.

Ordinarily, most detachments are made in defensive wars. Petty geniuses attempt to hold everything; wise men hold fast to the most important resort. They parry the great blows and scorn the little accidents. There is an ancient apothegm: he who would preserve everything, preserves nothing. Therefore, always sacrifice the bagatelle and pursue the essential! The essential is to be found where the big bodies of the enemy are. Stick to defeating them decisively, and the detachments will flee by themselves or you can hunt them without difficulty. Thus we abandoned Upper Silesia to the pillage of the Hungarians, and we hastened with all our forces to oppose the Prince of Lorraine; once he was beaten, Nassau purged Upper Silesia without difficulty of the Hungarians who infested it.

THE TALENTS THAT A GENERAL MUST HAVE, RUSES, STRATAGEMS OF WAR, SPIES. A perfect general, like Plato's republic, is a figment of the imagination. Either would be admirable, but it is not characteristic of human nature to produce beings exempt from human weaknesses and defects. The finest medallions have a reverse side. But in spite of this awareness of our imperfections it is not less necessary to consider all the different talents that are needed by an accomplished general. These are the models that one attempts to imitate and which one would not try to approach if they were not presented to us. It is essential that a general should dissemble while appearing to be occupied, working with the mind and working with the body, ceaselessly suspicious while affecting tranquillity, saving of the blood of his soldiers and not squandering it except for the most important interests, informed of everything, always on the lookout to deceive the enemy and careful not to be deceived himself. In a word he should be more than an industrious, active, and indefatigable man, not forgetting one thing to execute another, and above all not despising those sorts of little details which pertain to great projects.

The above is too vague; I shall explain.

The dissimulation of the general consists of the important art of hiding his thoughts. He should be constantly on the stage and should appear most tranquil when he is most occupied, for the whole army speculates on his looks, on his gestures, and on his mood. If he is seen to be more thoughtful than customary, the officers will believe he is incubating some project of consequence.

If his manner is uneasy, they believe that affairs are going badly, and they often imagine worse than the truth. These suppositions become the rumors of the army, and this army gossip is certain to pass over to the enemy's camp.

It is necessary, therefore, that the personal conduct of the general should be so well reasoned that his dissimulation will be so profound that no one can ever penetrate it. If he fears that he cannot master his expression, either he can pretend to be ill or he should make an excuse of some personal trouble to explain his appearance to the public. Above all, when he has received some bad news, he should treat it as a trifle and show the number of resources which he has to retrieve it. While never despising his enemy in the bottom of his heart, he should never speak of him except with scorn and compare carefully the advantages of our troops over the others. If some detachment is unfortunate in the war, he should examine the cause; and, after having determined the reason for the fault, he should instruct his officers concerning it. In this fashion a few minor misfortunes will never discourage the troops, and they will always preserve the feeling of confidence in their ability.

Secrecy is so necessary for a general that the ancients have even said that there was not a human being able to hold his tongue. But here is the reason for that. If you form the finest plans in the world but divulge them, your enemy will learn about them, and then it will be very easy for him to parry them. The general plan of the campaign should be communicated at most to the officer responsible for supplies, and the rest of the details should not be told to officers except when the time has come to execute them. When there are generals detached and you must write to them, the letter should be completely in code. If the enemy intercepts one you will not have betrayed yourself.

Since there are prodigious preparations to be made for war and some must be started early, secrecy may be betrayed thereby. But in this case you must deceive your own officers and pretend to have designs which you want the enemy to attribute to you. He will be notified by the indiscretion of your officers, and your real intention will remain hidden. And for surprises and sudden blows, well-thought-out instructions should be prepared, but they should not be delivered to the officers who are charged with the duty until the moment of execution. When you are planning to march, arrange everything in advance, so as to be able to act freely, always under other pretexts, and then do suddenly what you have proposed to yourself. It is absolutely necessary to change your methods often and to imagine new decoys. If you always act in the same manner you soon will be interpreted, for you are surrounded with fifty thousand curious who want to know everything that you think and how you are going to lead them.

The commander should practice kindness and severity, should appear friendly to the soldiers, speak to them on the march, visit them while they are cooking, ask them if they are well cared for, and alleviate their needs if they have any. Officers without experience in war should be treated kindly. Their good actions should be praised. Small requests should be granted them, and they should not be treated in an overbearing manner, but severity is maintained about everything regarding the service. The negligent officer is punished; the man who answers back is made to feel your severity by being reprimanded with the authoritative air that superiority gives; pillaging or argumentative soldiers, or those whose obedience is not immediate, should be punished.

The general even can discuss the war with some of his corps commanders who are most intelligent and permit them to express their sentiments freely in conversation. If you find some good things among what they say you should not remark about it then, but make use of it. When this has been done, you should speak about it in the presence of many others: it was so and so who had this idea; praise him for it. This modesty will gain the general the friendship of good thinking men, and he will more easily find persons who will speak their sentiments sincerely to him.

The principal task of the general is mental, large projects and major arrangements. But since the best dispositions become useless if they are not executed, it is essential that the general should be industrious to see whether his orders are executed or not. He should select his encampment himself, so that thereby he may be the master of his position, that the plan of it may be profoundly impressed on his mind, that he may place the cavalry and infantry guards himself, and that he may order on the spot the manner in which villages should be occupied. Afterwards, no matter what happens, he is able to give his orders with knowledge, and he is able to make wise dispositions from his information of the ground. The more that all these minor details are well thought out, the more he will be able to estimate in each place what the enemy is able to do and the more tranquil he will be, having foreseen everything and provided in his mind for everything that might happen to him. But all this is not done except by his own energy. Thus be vigilant and indefatigable, and do not believe, having made one tour of your camp, that you have seen everything. Something new is uncovered every day, and sometimes it is only after having reflected two or three times on a subject that good ideas come to us.

Skepticism is the mother of security. Even though only fools trust their enemies, prudent persons never do. The general is the principal sentinel of his army. He should always be careful of its preservation and that it is never exposed to misfortune. One falls into a feeling of security after battles, when one is drunk with success, and when one believes the enemy completely disheartened. One falls into a feeling of security when a skillful enemy amuses you with pretended peace proposals. One falls into a feeling of security by mental laziness and through lack of calculation concerning the intentions of the enemy. To proceed properly it is necessary to put oneself in his place and say: what would I do if I were the enemy? What project could I form? Make as many as possible of these projects, examine them all, and above all reflect on the means to avert them. If you find yourself unable (either because your camp is badly defended or because it is not in the locality where it should be, or that it is necessary to make a movement), put it right at once! Often, through an hour's neglect, an unfortunate delay loses a reputation that has been acquired with a great deal of labor. Always presume that the enemy has dangerous designs and always be forehanded with the remedy. But do not let these calculations make you timid. Circumspection is good only to a certain point. A rule that I practice myself and which I have always found good is that in order to have rest oneself it is necessary to keep the enemy occupied. This throws them back on the defensive, and once they are placed that way they cannot raise up again during the entire campaign.

If you wish to be loved by your soldiers, husband their blood and do not lead them to slaughter. They can be spared by shortening the battle by means that I shall indicate, by the skill with which you choose your points of attack in the weakest localities, in not breaking your head against impracticable things which are ridiculous to attempt, in not fatiguing the soldier uselessly, and in sparing him in sieges and in battles. When you seem to be most prodigal of the soldier's blood, you spare it, however, by supporting your attacks well and by pushing them with the greatest vigor to deprive time of the means of augmenting your losses.

Ruses of war are of great usefulness. They are detours which often lead more surely to the objective than the wide road which goes straight ahead. Animals have only one method of acting, but intelligent men have inexhaustible resources.

These resources are infinite in number. Their object is to hide your veritable design and to catch the enemy in the trap you have prepared for him. Thus the contrary of what one wishes to do is feigned. If you open the campaign, you have your troops march and counter-march, so that the enemy cannot learn the locality where you assemble. If it is a question of capturing cities, you encamp in a place which makes him fearful for two or three of his cities at the same time. If he hastens to one flank, you throw yourself on the other. If there are no cities to be taken but some defile you wish to seize, your ruses should tend to draw the enemy away from it, giving the appearance that you are moving in some other direction. If he falls into the snare, you throw yourself at top speed on the defile you want to master.

You outwit the enemy to force him to fight, or to prevent him from it. There are two means of forcing the enemy to fight; one is in pretending to fear it. His self-confidence becomes your accomplice; security lulls him and your cunning triumphs. That is what happened before the battle of Friedberg, where roads were made for the columns from Schweidnitz to Breslau, as if the army were to retire that way at the first approach of the enemy. They thought that they only had to show them-selves to chase us out. But things turned out otherwise, and they were the dupes of their preconception. The enemy is forced to fight by making marches which en-velop him, which force him to leave his camp and to move into localities where you are ready to smack him. When the Prince of Lorraine was in his strong camp at Königgrätz, he could have been forced to leave it, by making, as was possible, two marches toward Landskrom. He would have believed that his enemy had designs on Moravia, and, since he drew his food from there, he would surely have hastened toward it. Then, either while on the march or in some one of his camps, he could have been attacked. River crossings are in this class, but I shall treat them separately.

When it is desired to avoid battle, different ruses are used, and apparent war is made which has all the actions of the offensive and which, nevertheless, is of an opposite nature. It is your attitude that imposes on your enemy and the suspicion that you give him that you are forming the boldest projects against him. The attitude is maintained by not withdrawing easily before the enemy, and often the appearance that you are waiting for him will make him lose all desire to attack you. But if he does come, you steal away by a night march which you had planned long before. He thinks he has you, and the next day there is no one. If you only withdraw, you will be followed, but then it is necessary to take a position to the flank which will prevent him from passing you without running into great danger. This sort of war is the masterpiece of the Austrians, and it is from them that it should be learned.

There is another ruse, which is that if you find the enemy too strong to attack him, you help him with the means of dividing his forces at the end of the campaign and, in place of scattering your own winter quarters, you distribute them in such a fashion that in no time you can assemble the troops, and then you fall on the enemy, who are dispersed. Study the campaign that Turenne made in 1673 and study it often! It is the model of this sort of expedition.

In our times it is no longer possible to draw entire armies into ambuscades. This may have been good in other days; at present it suffices to profit from the enemy's faults. Ambuscades and other stratagems have remained useful for light troops whose fashion of fighting is favorable to this sort of ruse and who often owe their success only to the small numbers employed in them.

There is another type of ruse which is admirable; it is that of double spies. It is necessary to know them and then tell them with an air of good faith everything that you want the enemy to know. No one ever has gained greater advantage from betrayal than King William. Luxembourg had bribed the secretary of this prince; the King discovered it and made use of this traitor to give false information to Luxembourg, and this general nearly was surprised and defeated at Steenkerke.

It is essential to know what is happening among the enemy. Prince Eugene bribed the postmaster of Versailles, who opened the dispatches which went to the French army and sent him a copy. The best spies that one can have are those on the staff, or even the servants of the enemy's general. With the Austrians, it is difficult to receive letters from their camp because of the numbers of their light troops who infest the roads.

I am of the opinion that the best thing against the Austrians will be to bribe some captain or major of their hussars, by means of whom intelligence can be carried on with them. Catholic priests are the best spies that one can use, but they and the common people are so accustomed to lying that they exaggerate everything, and their reports cannot be depended on. In the countries where the people are opposed to you, like in Bohemia and Moravia, it is very difficult to keep informed of what is happening. If greed for silver does not work, it is necessary to employ fear. Seize some burgomaster of a city where you have a garrison, or some mayor of a village where you camp, and force him to take a disguised man, who speaks the language of the country, and under some pretext to conduct him as his servant in the enemy army. Threaten him that if he does not bring your man back, you will cut the throat of his wife and his children whom you hold under guard while waiting, and that you will have his house burned. I was obliged to employ this sad expedient in Bohemia and it succeeded for me. In general it is necessary to pay spies well and not to be miserly in that respect. A man who risks being hung in your service merits being well paid.

THE DIFFERENCE BETWEEN COUNTRIES AND THE PRECAUTIONS THEY REQUIRE OF A GENERAL. I am writing this work only for Prussian officers. Consequently, I only speak of countries and of enemies where we may wage war. There are three sorts of countries: our own, neutral, and enemy, and in enemy country there are

Catholics and Protestants. All of these things have their effect in war and require differences in conduct applicable to places and to circumstances. If one considers only glory, there can be no war more favorable toward acquiring it than in our own country; since the least action of the enemy is known and discovered, detachments can be sent out boldly and, having the country on their side, are able to accomplish brilliant enterprises and are always successful; because in the larger operations of war you find more aid and can undertake bolder deeds, such as surprises of camps and cities; and since the people favor you, it will be due to your negligence or to an unpardonable ignorance if you do not succeed.

In neutral countries it is necessary to make friends. If you can win over the whole country so much the better. At least form a body of your partisans! The friendship of the neutral country is gained by requiring the soldiers to observe good disciplnie and by picturing your enemies as barbarous and bad intentioned. If the people there are Catholic, do not speak about religion; if they are Protestant, make the people believe that a false ardor for religion attaches you to them. Use priests and the devout for this purpose. Religion becomes a dangerous arm when one knows how to make use of it. However, move more carefully with your partisans and always play a sure game.

In countries which are both enemy and Catholic, such as Bohemia and Moravia, no partisan group should be attempted. They will all be lost, the country being hostile to them. If you are projecting some sudden blow, it must be done by detachments. You are obliged to wage a closefisted war and to make use of your light troops on the defensive. My own experience has convinced me of this.

THE MARCH OF AN ARMY FORWARD OR IN RETREAT OR FOR BATTLE. MARCHES FOR RELIEF. The first thing that a general must think of after having provided for the security of his camp is to have the environs and all the places through which he may have need to march reconnoitered. This is done by large detachments who go to these places under other pretexts, while the quartermasters and the engineers and chasseurs reconnoiter to determine in how many columns you can march. They look over the situation rapidly and make their report. The chasseurs who accompany them will serve as guides to the columns on the march. The general makes his preparations on these reports.

If he is making an ordinary march forward, without fear of the enemy, this is how he disposes his command, presuming that there are routes for four columns: this evening at eight o'clock six battalions of grenadiers, a regiment of infantry, ten squadrons of dragoons, that is to say one or two regiments complete and two regiments of hussars, will form the advance guard, marching only with light baggage. The bulk of the baggage will remain with the army. They will march a mile ahead, where they will seize this defile, this height, this river, this city, or this village, and where they will wait until the army is close by to continue their march to the new camp.

The army will march tomorrow at three o'clock in four columns. The detachments return to camp as soon as the troops are to be sent into battle. Cavalry of the two right lines, marching by file to the right, form the first column; the infantry of the two right lines, marching by file to right, form the second column; the infantry of the two lines to the left, marching by file to the right, form the third column; the cavalry of the two lines to the left, marching by file to the right, form the fourth column; such and such regiments of infantry of the second line and the regiment of hussars of N. will be the rear guard to cover the baggage and the artillery. These will take the two or three best roads to follow the army. The adjutants N.N.N. remain near the baggage columns and will be responsible that the wagons are not strung out, and the officer who commands the rear guard will notify the general in time if he believes that he needs support. Three wagons loaded with beams, joists, and planks to make bridges over streams march at the head of the four army columns with the detachment of carpenters. Columns should not get ahead of each other but advance on the same front as far as is possible. The officers should observe distances exactly, and the regiments should be kept closed. If, for example, one or both the two columns of cavalry had to traverse some woods, it would be necessary to place several battalions of grenadiers at their head and even, if necessary, the cavalry could be placed in the center, assuming it is open ground and the infantry move through the woods.

If you wish to make such a march toward the enemy,

you would send all the baggage under an escort to the strongest city in your vicinity. Your advance guard would only precede you by a quarter of a mile, and you would march bridle in hand, always attentive of everything that passes and always observing the ground, so that you will always have a position ready in your mind, in case you should have to occupy one in haste. That is why you should always go on the heights, in these sorts of marches, as much as you are able without endangering yourself, to see the ground better and get detailed knowledge of it.

When you wish to make these marches parallel to the enemy's position, you march either by the right or left in two lines, which at the same time form your two columns, and you detach a body at the extremity of the wing by which you wish to march, which serves as an advance guard. You form your rear guard just about the same, following the rear of the army. This method of marching is the surest and easiest, and especially, when it can be used, it is the best before an action because you are formed in an instant. In all marches made in mountainous countries or in woods the infantry should march first. The cavalry should always go on open ground. It can act there. But in sunken roads or bushy woods you risk losing it because it is not able to fight and its weapons become useless.

RETREATS WITH COLUMNS REVERSED. When you are marching in withdrawal before the enemy, it is essential above all to disembarrass yourself of your heavy baggage. This done, you make your dispositions on the roads which you can use and the terrain that you occupy. If you are on open ground, the infantry withdraws first. If the country is broken, it is the cavalry that should precede. I shall presume that you have a defile behind you to pass through and that your camp contains a small plain; on this basis I would make the following disposition for two columns.

Six battalions of infantry under the orders of N. will proceed through the defile at seven o'clock this evening and post themselves on the other side, pointing their cannon and at the same time leaving the roads for the columns open. The army will march at four o'clock tomorrow morning. As soon as the troops are under arms and tents struck, the detachments, camp and village guards, etc., will withdraw and rejoin their organizations. The army will march in two columns, the cavalry of the right first, the second line of the right taking the lead, followed by the first line of the right, followed by the second line of infantry of the right, and this latter by the first line of infantry of the right, which will form one mixed column. The second line cavalry of the left wing will lead the second column, followed by the first line; the second line of infantry of the left will join the latter followed by the first line, the whole army filing by the right, six battalions of the first line sustained by ten squadrons of hussars.

This rear guard will range itself before the center of the army in two lines with intervals. When the whole army shall have left, the first line will withdraw through the intervals of the second and will place itself in battle formation not far from the defile. When it shall have established its front, the second line will withdraw, pass through the intervals of the first, and pass through the defile with the larger portion of the hussars. Then the first will follow in the same manner, and the enemy, who would like to attack them, is contained by the troops posted the evening before to sustain the defile. These latter should remain to the end and not place themselves in march except to follow the rear guard and file through in succession. However, a general can make changes in his dispositions in accordance with the terrain and circumstances he finds.

THE PRECAUTIONS THAT SHOULD BE TAKEN IN RETREATS AGAINST HUSSARS AND PANDOURS. No attack by hussars or irregulars need be apprehended in open country. Hussars fear fire and pandours, hand to hand combat. In this sort of march, if they are able, they will attempt something against the baggage. They are brave when they hope to win booty. But it is quite different in woods and mountains. There, the pandours lie flat on the ground and hide themselves behind stones and trees so that they are able to fire without your being able to see where the shots come from, nor to return the injury and harm they do. Thus I shall only speak here about how you can best secure yourself from them in retreats made in mountains.

We made two such retreats during the year 1745, one from the center of Liebenthal and the other from Trautenau to Schatzlar. At that time we placed detachments of from four to six platoons on the wings of the columns.

They occupied the heights which dominated the road, to turn aside these scoundrels, and the officers who were in command only had to have a few men fire against them. The rear guard also is always withdrawn from height to height following the army. But here is what happens as soon as one group abandons a height. The pandours run to it, seize it, and shoot you from there. For this I know of no remedy, and whatever a general does he always loses lots of men uselessly in this sort of a retreat. No matter how small a plain may be, have your hussars sortie out against the pandours! This turns them aside for a moment. But do not amuse yourself too much with them; otherwise your march will stretch out and you will lose prodigous numbers. Consequently, halts should not be made, and this type of difficult march should be made as rapidly as possible. But if the pandours imprudently occupy a small wood that can be turned, then hunt them down and have the hussars saber as many as you can.

How the Prussians Should Deal With Light-Armed Troops When We are on the Offensive. If you wish to seize a post held by hussars or pandours, march against them confidently and you will be sure to carry it. Your formation is too redoubtable for them. But if they appear more determined, you may suspect that their army is nearby and able to support them. Have all sides reconnoitered, then, to inform yourself, but you may always be certain that these people will not stop you a moment, whatever attitude they assume.

What A General Can Expect from the Move-

MENTS HE HAS HIS ARMY MAKE. Let no one imagine
that it is sufficient just to move an army about to make
the enemy regulate himself on your movements. A
general who has a too presumptuous confidence in his
skill runs the risk of being grossly duped. War is not
an affair of chance. A great deal of knowledge, study,
and meditation is necessary to conduct it well, and when
blows are planned whoever contrives them with the
greatest appreciation of their consequences will have a
great advantage. However, to give a few rules on such
a delicate matter, I would say that in general the first
of two army commanders who adopts an offensive attitude almost always reduces his rival to the defensive and
makes him regulate himself on his movements.

If you were to commence the campaign first and were
to make some march which indicated an extensive plan,
your enemy, who would be warned to oppose it, will be
obliged to adjust himself to you; but if you make a march
which gives him neither suspicions nor fears, or if he
should be informed that you lack the resources to execute
your project, he will pay no attention to you and on his
part will undertake some better considered actions which
will put you in a difficult place in turn.

Your first precaution should be to control your own
subsistence. If this is well arranged, you can undertake anything. The enemy likewise can be forced to
make large detachments by harassing his rear with light
troops, or by making demonstrations, as if you intended
to make a diversion in some other province of his realm
than that in which the war is being waged. Unskillful

generals race to the first trap set before them. This is why a great advantage is drawn from knowledge of your adversary, and when you know his intelligence and character you can use it to play on his weaknesses.

Everything which the enemy least expects will succeed the best. If he relies for security on a chain of mountains that he believes impracticable, and you pass these mountains by roads unknown to him, he is confused to start with, and if you press him he will not have time to recover from his consternation. In the same way, if he places himself behind a river to defend the crossing and you find some ford above or below on which to cross unknown to him, this surprise will derange and confuse him. I could write a lot more on this article, but what I have said should suffice and can furnish ample matter for the reflections of my readers.

RIVER CROSSINGS. I have said that the art of war is divided between force and stratagem. What cannot be done by force, must be done by stratagem. Thus if your enemy prevents you from crossing a difficult river and you are unable to cross near him, do like Caesar, Prince Eugene, and Prince Charles of Lorraine. They chose a distant and easy point where they planned to cross. If the river is large, a point should be chosen where some islands confine its course by dividing it; if there are no islands, find a point where the river makes a bend. Batteries are placed there; a crossing demonstration is made at an entirely different locality to draw the enemy, and, while he takes the bait, you build your bridges with all rapidity. You march there with all your forces and cross quickly. Entrenchments are absolutely necessary in these operations. The first troops who cross should instantly have their shovels in the ground or, if woods are available, make large abatis. For greater security, a general who commands such an enterprise should build a bridgehead on both sides of the river to retain it for the time that he advances into the country to push his advantage.

THE DEFENSE OF RIVERS. The defense of a river crossing is the worst of all assignments, especially if the front that you are to defend is long; in this case defense is impracticable. To dare undertake the defense of a river crossing, the front of attack should not be more than eight miles long at the most, and you should have one or two fortresses on the banks of the river at points where it is not fordable. In such a case, it is necessary to prepare against the enemy's enterprises some time in advance. I shall report the best of the expedients that have been used on such occasions.

You have all the boats and barges on the whole river collected and taken to one of your fortresses, to deprive the enemy of this help. Then you personally reconnoiter the two banks of the river; that on the enemy's side to note all the places that favor his crossing; that of your own side in order to have three or more big roads made from one end to the other of your front of attack so as to be able to march conveniently and easily in several columns. And when you have found the places that you consider favorable to the enemy's crossing, if you find there a small fort or a cemetery that he could use, have it destroyed and in each of these places form your troops in the order of battle and disposition you would use if you were going to fight, marking the principal points, at the same time, to be used at the right time and place.

After these precautions, camp your whole army in the center of your line of defense and make sixteen detachments, each consisting only of a few troops, and at the head of each place the elite of your officers. These detachments should be from hussars or dragoons. You will use them to scout the river bank all night. Each of these officers should be assigned a definite piece of ground for the security of which he is responsible. In the daytime it is sufficient to place mounted sentinels at the places on the banks where they are best able to observe the country. You should detach two generals from each of your wings to keep an eye on these detachments, to make certain that they will be as vigilant as such a mission requires. Officers should watch from the towers of the cities day and night to discover what is happening. Your two generals and the commanders of the cities make four reports to you a day. One should be sent at daybreak, another at ten o'clock in the morning, a third at four in the afternoon, and the last at ten o'clock at night. You put horses in relays from each of your wings to the quarters of these different generals and commanders so that in an hour and a half news from the most distant can reach you.

These detachments are only made to observe and warn. They will inform you as soon as the enemy crosses a large body on rafts and starts to build his bridges. Your duty is to attack the enemy then. To facilitate this, you will have sent all your heavy baggage to the rear and you will be camped with one foot poised. If the enemy crosses effectively at some point, you will have your army march instantly to this point, and, since all your dispositions have been made in advance, you have only to give them to your officers at once. You should prepare yourself for infantry combat; for if the enemy is clever, he will entrench the first troops who will have crossed. Have your dispositions well supported! Do not forget your reserves! Take advantage of the terrain and then attack him brusquely and you should be able to hope for the most brilliant success. If you are required to dispute the passage of small rivers, you will do it in the same fashion, only adding the precaution of destroying the fords with trees that you will have thrown into them with all their branches. If the heights are on your side, this will be a great advantage to you; if they are not, you have almost no hope of succeeding.

SURPRISES OF CITIES. Cities can be surprised when they are badly guarded, either by detachments which are sent against them by different roads or by introducing disguised soldiers into them, like Prince Eugene did at Cremone, or after a long seige has lessened the vigilance of the governor, like Prince Leopold of Anhalt at Glogau. Everything in war, but surprises especially, demands a great deal of information. To make your dispositions without knowing how a city is constructed within and without, is to order the tailor to make a suit without his knowing if the man for whom he makes it is tall or short, fat or thin. Therefore, procure extensive information before undertaking anything. Cities can be surprised by detachments, as happened at Cosel. Here an officer of the garrison deserted and disclosed to the Austrians that a part of the moat was more shallow than it should have been. They entered there effectively, and found the garrison too feeble to resist them.

The surprise of Cremone was an affair planned during the winter; it would have been a brilliant opening of the campaign if it had succeeded. In our neighboring countries we actually have only two cities to surprise. One is Wittenberg in Saxony, which is a paltry fortress; the other is Olmütz, but it will not be taken, I suspect, except by formal seige. When cities are large and lightly garrisoned, it is only necessary to attack them on all sides to master them. The garrison cannot resist everywhere, and the forcing of one point carries with it the loss of all the rest. It was thus that the Emperor Charles VII, seconded by the French and Saxons, made himself master of Prague. Little cities can be taken with firecrackers. Only observe, that if you bring up cannon to destroy the gates, the cannon should be covered so that the enemy's small-arms fire cannot kill the cannoneers.

THE ATTACK AND DEFENSE OF FORTIFIED PLACES. The art of conducting seiges has become a profession like those of the carpenter and shoemaker. The rules are so well known that it is not worth the trouble of repeating them. So many books tell of them, and everyone knows that a covered place is sought for the tail of the trench, that the first parallel is made as close as possible to the fort, and the work which is done in the following days is so minutely detailed and subject to such an exact calculation that it is almost possible to tell in advance the day that a fortification will be carried, at least unless this fort is singularly constructed and unless it happens to be defended by a man of distinguished merit. I shall not repeat everything, then, that Vauban and the late Prince of Anhalt have said on this subject. I shall content myself simply to add to it a few ideas which have come to me, both for the attack and the defense.

I have reflected on the attack of fortified places where the terrain allows the formation of several attacks, and also which have dry moats and few advanced works, like Olmütz and Wittenberg. If you lay seige to such a place, you will open the trench on one side and make a false attack on another. As soon as the enemy shall have taken all his precautions against these two points of attack and you have confirmed him in this opinion, why should you not order an assault at an entirely different point and have all your batteries open fire at daylight, as if one of these two attacks were intended to force a way through. You use this fire as a signal to notify the detachment which, during darkness, will have approached from another side of the city to scale it. I am convinced that little resistance will be encountered there and that the enterprise will succeed, at least if the dispositions have been based on knowledge of the place. The beseiged, thinking only of the avowed attacks, will without doubt strip all the rest of the fortifications. But to undertake such a blow you should have pressing reasons to become master of it quickly, and the beseiged must be so lulled that the idea of your design can never occur to them.

For the defense of cities nothing is stronger than mines and streams which are used to flood the trenches and fill up dry moats when the beseigers commence to make galleries in them.

The art of defending fortified places is that of putting off the moment of their reduction. Thus all the science of governors and commanders of fortified cities reduces itself to gaining time. It is gained by disputing the ground with the enemy. But the means that are employed to this effect are of different natures. Some officers think a great deal of sorties, and it is of them that I shall speak. I admit that I find it strange that mediocre garrisons hazard them, since a single man that they lose is more important than the loss of ten men to the beseiger. Therefore I believe that a commander should not make large sorties except when help is coming to drive away the attacker. In this case he should not spare his garrison and should regard the advantages that it gains over the beseigers like fortunate auguries of the battle which will follow. But if he is not expecting aid promptly, he can gain time in a more secure manner.

Everyone who has conducted seiges will have seen how the laborers become confused at the first shots of the enemy and how, once they have fled, the labor of the whole night is lost. This truth admitted, it follows from it that frequent small sorties, which continually alarm the beseigers, will be more successful and more sure to delay their work than large sorties, which you can never make without risking the loss of many men; and the consequence of the latter will be that you will have almost no garrison when it becomes time to defend your works. It is exactly for these works that the garrison must be conserved.

And now I shall say how I think this should be done. When you are expecting an assault against the exterior wall of the ditch, garrison it very weakly, but place your prepared fire on the works which are behind it, and in the laterals. When the assault is commenced make it hot for the enemy and, when he tries to enter, make two sorties against his two flanks; you will regain your counterscarp at once. If I were the commander, I would practice this maneuver as often as I could.

BATTLES OF ALL SORTS. SURPRISES OF ENCAMPMENTS. It is very difficult to surprise encampments in our days in view of the numbers of light troops used and the precautions which are universally in practice; for, when two armies camp close to each other, either their affairs are decided promptly by a battle or else one of the armies occupies a position so favorable that it can neither be forced nor surprised. It is, then, an event which can happen only rarely and, more probably, between detachments than between armies. However, since it is pertinent to speak of it, I shall detail the matters that should be observed in case an occasion is presented.

The first of your efforts should be devoted to gaining

all the information possible on the situation of the camp you wish to surprise; the second: to reconnoiter thoroughly the roads by which it can be reached; the third: to have assured and faithful guides conduct the column; the fourth: to observe secrecy inviolable and put the curious off the track; the fifth: to push all your light troops ahead under a specious pretext, but effectively to prevent some deserter from your own troops from betraying you, and to enclose the enemy in such a fashion that he cannot send his patrols out too freely; the sixth: to make good dispositions and instruct all the officers who are to execute it minutely; the seventh: to march at night without noise, with absolute prohibition against smoking or leaving ranks; the eighth: to form your line of battle not more than a quarter of a mile from the enemy camp and to attack half an hour before daylight.

If the ground permitted it, I would unleash a large body of light troops and cavalry in the camp to spread terror and confusion, and, on the side where the cavalry is camped, I would have infantry and cannon fire to spread confusion and to prevent the squadrons from forming. However, the more that darkness is avoided the better it is. Daybreak is favorable because you can recognize one another, you do not risk killing your own men, and the cowards, who think they can run away in the shadows, are not able to do it as well when the officers are able to distinguish them. Having carried the enemy camp, the cavalry should pursue the fugitives a certain distance. Above all, the soldiers should be pre-

vented from pillaging and getting drunk after this suc
cess, for the enemy may be able to recover from his
terror and profit from your confusion

How to Prevent Surprises. We are accustomed, as
I have said, to camp with a detached corps a certain
distance ahead of the army; we also garrison all the
villages up to a quarter of a mile away in front of the
camp; we place cavalry guards in the rear, then infantry
guards for the defense of the camp proper. Every night,
besides, eight or ten patrols are made on all sides around
the camp so as to be warned of what is happening. If
in spite of these precautions the enemy profits from the
negligence of some subaltern officer, the troops should
occupy their proper field of battle, the cavalry should
charge briskly whatever it finds in contact, and the infantry should limit itself simply to holding its ground
until daylight, when you can take measures which circumstances indicate to you as more or less favorable. In
general, I believe that night attacks are only good when
you are so weak that you do not dare attack the enemy
in daylight; it was this reason which obliged Charles
XII to attack the Prince of Anhalt during the obscurity
in the affair that he had with him on the island of
Rugen.

The Attack of Entrenchments. If you have resolved to attack an entrenched enemy, do it at once
and do not allow him time to perfect his works. The
principal point for success in your design is to know the
strength and weakness of the entrenchment thoroughly.
It is the general's *coup d'œil* that must decide this. If

you attack a bull by the horns your task will be difficult and perhaps it will not succeed at all. Ordinarily, the defects of entrenchments are either that they are not solidly enough supported, or they are too extensive for the number of troops to guard them. It is upon this knowledge that you should make your dispositions. In the first case, either the entrenchment, instead of pushing its trench and its parapet all the way to a river, does not reach it at all, or else the river is fordable and allows you to turn him.

Two entrenchments have been taken because of this same fault: those of the French in front of Turin where the right extended to the Doire without actually resting on it. The Prince of Anhalt, who was attacking on this side, noticed it, enveloped them, and the French gave way. The other of which I want to speak was that of the Swedes before Stralsund. The left of this entrenchment reached the sea; but Gaudi, a Prussian officer, and Köppen estimated that the ocean was fordable on this flank. The plans were made on this information, and the execution had all the success in the world, for the Swedes were driven out. At the battle of Malplaquet the allies lost 20,000 men unnecessarily because they chose their point of attack badly. After three hours of stubborn fighting they noticed that the abatis which covered the French left could be turned. They directed their forces in that direction, and the French were vanquished.

When the entrenchments that the enemy guards are too extensive, form your veritable attacks and feign some false ones to contain the enemy and prevent him from bringing help toward the point where you propose to make your principal effort. The formations of your troops can be varied infinitely. I shall limit myself to proposing one for an army of fifty battalions and one hundred squadrons. I first form a line of infantry of thirty battalions, with which I form a wing on the flank where I intend to make my principal effort. Of the twenty remaining battalions, I use twelve in the principal attack and eight in the secondary attack. I range these twelve battalions in two lines with all my infantry three deep, and my cavalry 300 paces behind the infantry, as the following figure shows.

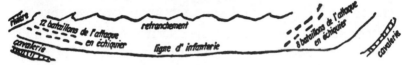

No. 1

riviere—river
12 bataillons de l'attaque en echiquier—12 attack battalions in checkerboard
retranchment—entrenchment
ligne d'infanterie—line of infantry
8 bataillons de l'attaque en echiquier—8 attack battalions in checkerboard
cavalerie—cavalry

In this order of battle you can see that my line of infantry holds the enemy in check and that it is ready to profit from the least false movement that he may make. Close by the battalions which attack I order workers and men who carry fascines to fill the ditch. If the infantry captures the entrenchment, I reinforce it with all my infantry with orders to hold the parapet without pursuing the enemy. Laborers make openings so that the cavalry can enter. The latter will form themselves according to regulations, under the protection of the infantry, and will then attack as the occasion and circumstances require.

DEFENSE OF AN ENTRENCHMENT. I have already said, and I repeat it, that I would never put myself in an entrenchment, at least unless a terrible misfortune, such as the loss of a battle or a triple superiority on the part of the enemy, forced me to do it. Even when inferior by half there are some resources of which I shall speak later. But supposing that very strong reasons should oblige a Prussian officer to entrench, it is essential that the front be contracted as much as possible so that the entrenchment can be garrisoned as it snould be. Furthermore, it is necessary to save two large reserves of infantry so as to be able to move them to points where they may be needed. The cavalry should be posted in a third line behind these reserves. First attention should be given to strong support of the entrenchment, as I have said above; second: to locating it so that its flanks are strong; and third: to constructing wide, deep ditches.

If you have time, you will increase the fortifications of your entrenchments every day, either with palisades, chevaux-de-frise, concealed pits, etc. Entrenchments are a species of fortification which, in consequence, should be subordinated to the rules of this art. These consist in using the terrain well, in obliging the enemy to approach you on a narrow front, and in limiting him

to points of attack which become only preliminaries
in his enterprises. This is done by pushing some salients
in advance which will take him in the flank if he attacks
between them. By these dispositions you will reduce
him to the point where he does what you want, and your
mind will be distracted by fewer objects in your de-.
fense. Here are two plans of entrenchments.

No. 2

batterie—battery
riviere—river
bois abattis—woods, abatis
abattis—abatis

You can see that the terrain in front narrows here.
The right is defended by a battery on the other side
of the river which lashes the flank. The center is defended by a redoubt and the left the same, and the entrenchment, making a bend behind the abatis, prevents
it from being turned. Necessarily, therefore, one of
these redoubts must be attacked. Consequently, they
are better fortified than the rest, and the enemy will run
his nose against him.

Here is the plan of another entrenchment.

377

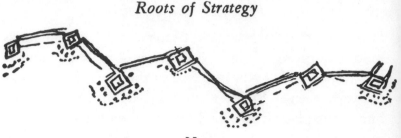

No. 3

You see that some redoubts advance in salients and that they are flanked by others behind them. You see that I fortify these redoubts better than the rest of the entrenchment. Here is the reason for it: these are the points that will be attacked. I have one reason more in placing these redoubts: it is that thorough fortification of a whole entrenchment requires infinite time, and seven or eight redoubts can be perfected more quickly. Observe furthermore that the plan of the entrenchment should be according to the terrain and that your redoubts should not be more distant than 400 paces from each other so that small-arms fire is able to defend them.

WHY MOST ENTRENCHMENTS ARE TAKEN. It is because whoever is enclosed in them is restricted to one ground and whoever attacks can maneuver freely; he who attacks is bolder than the one who defends himself; and because, furthermore, if a point in your entrenchment is forced, all the rest is lost on account of the discouragement that this occasions among the troops. However, I am of the opinion that the Prussians, with a resolute man at their head, could easily set right a misfortune of that type, especially if the general has conserved the resources of the reserves. Troops defending an entrenchment should fire continually, those attacking should not fire at all, but advance resolutely, gun on the shoulder.

LINES. HOW THE ENEMY CAN BE DEFEATED WITH UN-EQUAL FORCES WHEN YOU ARE THE WEAKER. A general should choose his ground with regard to the numbers and types of his troops and the strength of the enemy. If he is the stronger and has a great deal of cavalry, he will seek the plains, primarily because his cavalry can act best there and, in second place, because his superiority gives him the means to envelop an enemy on open ground, something he would be unable to do in broken country. If, on the contrary, you are inferior in numbers, do not despair of winning, but do not expect any other success than that gained by your skill. It is necessary to seek mountainous country and use artifices, so that if you were to be forced to battle, the enemy would not be able to face you with a front superior to your own, and so that you may be able definitely to protect your flanks.

If the terrain had not favored us in this fashion at Soor, we should never have defeated the Austrians. We were very weak in truth, but the enemy could not envelop us. Thus his numbers, in lieu of being useful to him, became a burden. Thus the terrain equalized between us that which force had decided in favor of the Austrians.

There is the first remark which concerns only the terrain. The second relates to the manner of attacking.

All weak armies attacking stronger ones should use the oblique order, and it is the best that can be employed in outpost engagements; for in setting yourself to defeat a wing and in taking a whole army in the flank, the battle is settled at the start. Cast your eyes on this plan.

You see how I fortify my right with which I want to make my principal effort. I have placed a body of infantry on the flank of the cavalry to fire from the woods on the enemy cavalry. I have three lines of cavalry and three lines of infantry, and my left is only for the purpose of containing the enemy's right wing, while all my forces act on the right. By this means one part of my army defeats the other, I am victorious, and I execute with one part what others do with the whole. In this battle I prefer to attack with my right rather than with my left because I avoid an attack of a village, which would cause too many casualties. Whenever you engage in a battle with one flank, you are the master of your army; you can stimulate or slow down the combat as you deem appropriate, and the whole wing which is not fighting acts as a reserve for you. Never forget to husband all the resources you are able on every occasion and to have, in consequence, reserves always at hand to repair disorder, if it occurs at some point.

BATTLES IN POSITION. Armies in position are attacked in the same manner that I have described here. It is necessary to observe that the first point is to know the locality well. However, I should advise avoiding, in so far as possible, beating against villages because this is

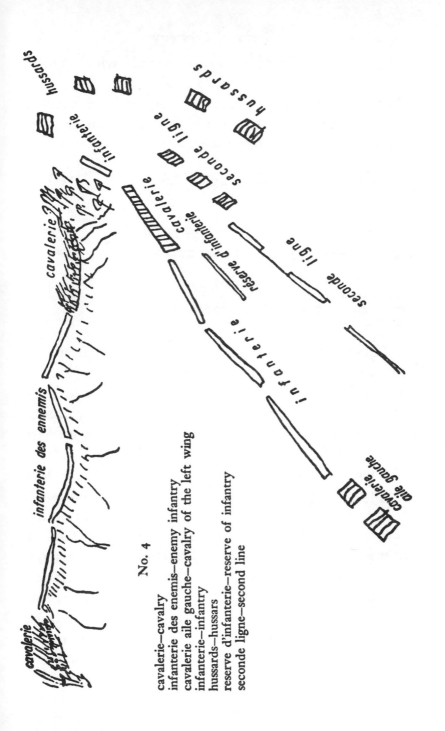

No. 4

cavalerie—cavalry
infanterie des enemis—enemy infantry
cavalerie aile gauche—cavalry of the left wing
infanterie—infantry
hussards—hussars
reserve d'infanterie—reserve of infantry
seconde ligne—second line

very deadly. There are some generals who maintain that an army in position should be attacked in the center. As for me I am of the opinion that it should be attacked at the weakest point. Here is the formation of those who want to attack the center.

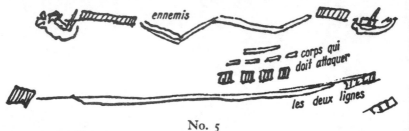

No. 5

enemis—enemy
corps qui doit attaquer—force which is to attack
les deux lignes—the two lines

They say that in breaking the center you separate the entire army and place yourself in a situation to gain the most brilliant advantages. As for me, I repeat it, I approve of all methods of attacking provided they are directed at the point where the enemy's army is weakest and where the terrain favors them the least.

Since the numerous artillery which is used these days frequently requires the attack of batteries firing case shot, I dare venture my opinion on this subject based on the reflections which similar attacks at Soor and Kesselsdorf have inspired. Nothing is more dangerous for the infantry than to carry hostile batteries, when fourteen or sixteen cannon, advantageously placed and supported by infantry, fire several successive discharges on the assailants. This upsets all the order of our troops. Case shot makes horrible ravages; a battalion is shot full of holes before it approaches the enemy; some entire platoons are carried away and often numbers of officers. And since the power of our battalions lies in their close ranks, and that each fills the place that he should hold, it is necessary to close the battalions in the act of attacking. While this is going on you endure a new discharge which, causing new confusion, sometimes awakens natural human fears too sharply. I am, therefore, of the opinion that if the enemy holds his position, assuming that his flank cannot be turned, that he cannot be assaulted and taken.

But I noted one thing at Soor and Kesselsdorf, which convinces me that it will always be the same. This is, that in these two battles, when the losses of our men made them give way in the first attack, the enemy, wishing to pursue them, left their lines. This made their

Attaque. je donne des intervalles aux bataillons, pour qu' ils puissent se retirer par là sans mettre la confusion dans les autres et j'y ajoute la cavalerie pour donner dans l' infanterie ennemie en cas ou 'elle sorte de son poste.

No. 6

Attaque. je donne, etc.—translation as follows:
Attack. I place intervals between battalions so that they can retire through them without creating confusion in the others and I add the cavalry to charge the enemy infantry in case it leaves its position.

artillery hold its fire, and as a result of this our men, mingling, so to speak, with the enemy, carried the batteries at once. I desire, therefore, that the first battalion should be ordered to attack weakly to induce the enemy to quit his position, to spare the blood of the soldiers, and to gain our ends more quickly. However, if the position can be turned, this is always the surest way. Here (No. 6) is approximately the order of battle for such an attack.

THE DEFENSE OF POSITIONS. I have often said that for Prussians I would choose only unassailable positions or else I would not occupy them at all, for we have too many advantages in attacking to deprive ourselves of them gratuitously. But since it is necessary to speak of this subject, I shall add only some reflections. The first is that it is essential that the wings should be so well secured that it is absolutely impossible to turn them; in the second place, that the cavalry should be in the second line; in the third place, that you conserve some reserves of infantry and fourthly, that indefensible villages should not be garrisoned, and that there is no good small, well-walled fort or a good cemetery which dominates the plain and which is able to resist cannon fire, or you will lose your troops. If, however, there are any villages on your front or on your wing, watch the wind! If it comes from the side or toward the enemy, set fire to these villages! You will save your men and make this place inaccessible to the enemy. I believe, furthermore, that if contrary to your expectations the enemy moves to attack you in such a position, you should not stick in it like a slave. Use it to confound him with your cannon and then march straight at him to attack. Such a decision will embarrass him greatly, and he will see himself, without knowing how, the assailant assailed. What should be watched especially is to place yourself in such a fashion that all your troops are able to act. Our camp at Grottkau was worthless because only our right wing could act. The left was behind a marsh and became useless. Villeroi was defeated at Ramillies as a result of having posted himself thus.

BATTLES IN PLAINS BROKEN WITH WOODS AND MARSHES. All these battles are basically of the same nature. Wherever the ground is broken, the country is made for artifice, and on such occasions I always favor battle for the reason that I have given previously. Whether it is with one of your wings, or with a body intended to attack the center, it all comes down to the same thing. In our ordinary battles I have prescribed that our first line of cavalry should only have a distance of four paces between squadrons; but in country where there are canals and ditches it is necessary to give them intervals of fifteen paces, so that if some squadron falls into a ditch this will not derange the whole line. The first line of infantry never has more interval between battalions than is required to allow the cannon to fire.

BATTLES IN THE OPEN FIELD. This sort of action should be general because you should keep your enemy occupied everywhere so that he cannot make movements that would be dangerous to you. The principal thing to watch is to block his wings. If you cannot block them both, I shall indicate the means to substitute. It is necessary, in addition, to reinforce the flanks of your infantry, so that in case one wing of cavalry gives way all your infantry will be able to support it equally. Here is my order of battle.

I place the infantry at the extremity of my wings to support the cavalry and to prevent the enemy from pursuing it, if it should be defeated. If it is victorious, I can use it with what I have on my flank to take the enemy infantry in the flank. I shall relate here what should be watched in the maneuver of all battles, especially in those in open field. If you march by wings, the platoons should keep equal distances so that your whole army may be formed against the enemy by a single movement. But if you march by columns in line, the platoons must be closed on each other. Then the battalions can form, and you make your order of battle in full march, the heads of the columns drawing off to the right while the tails of the first lines deploy equally.

It is a great advantage to be formed first on the day of action. Our troops will always have it because of the skill and promptness with which they maneuver. (I am speaking here of the last order of battle.) While the army is forming, all the cannon will fire as briskly as possible. Generals who command the wings will give particular attention to supporting them well; if this is absolutely impossible for one of the wings, the general of cavalry who commands the second line will extend the

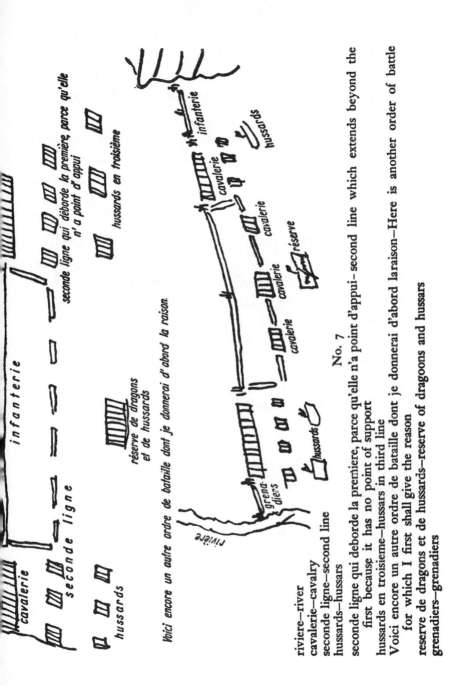

No. 7

riviere—river
cavalerie—cavalry
seconde ligne—second line
hussards—hussars
seconde ligne qui deborde la premiere, parce qu'elle n'a point d'appui
    first because it has no point of support
hussards en troisieme—hussars in third line
Voici encore un autre ordre de bataille dont je donnerai d'abord laraison—
    for which I first shall give the reason
reserve de dragons et de hussards—reserve of dragoons and hussars
grenadiers—grenadiers

first with two or three squadrons, and the hussars of the third line will extend the second with two or three. This will guarantee the flank of the cavalry in such manner that if the enemy were to fall on it they would be taken in the flank themselves.

Cavalry officers should always make this movement without even being ordered to. The infantry that is placed entirely on the wing of the cavalry should outflank the hostile army and fire enfilade on the hostile cavalry. I do not provide any interval for my cavalry because then each squadron would have two flanks, and a contiguous line has only one, which is its extremity. The attack of such a body thus becomes much more formidable. The duty of the cavalry on a day of action is to attack, as soon as ordered, in the manner that I have prescribed in my *Institutions Militaires*. It will certainly derange the enemy. They also should pursue when the enemy cavalry is entirely scattered.

The second line and the hussars should prepare themselves to cut the retreat of the infantry, which soon will have been scattered also. The cavalry battle will be entirely decided before the infantry can come into contact. The general who has already gained these premonitory signs of victory can then boldly bring up the infantry which covers his wing and the infantry on his flank, to outflank the hostile infantry, take them in the flank and envelop them, if he is able. The infantry will advance rapidly but in order. I do not want it to fire. Its menace will defeat the enemy. But in case it fires, the general should always make it continue the advance and, as soon as the enemy commences to eddy around their colors, have openings made in the first line to make way for the dragoons that I have placed between the battalions of the second line, as can be seen in the second order of battle. Then all the opposing infantry will be lost. Whoever attempts to flee before these dragoons will fall in the hands of your victorious second lines of cavalry, who await them and cut them off from the defiles. Thus your success will be complete.

I have not spoken yet of the reserve. It should be commanded by a skillful general and it should be placed in a locality where he can see everything. He should act on his own initiative and if he sees that one of the wings are in need of help, he should conduct a reserve there without being called. But if everything goes well, the general should employ the reserve in the pursuit. That is what I have to say on the subject of general actions, and I beg my officers to read it with attention and to impress it on their minds well.

PURSUIT AND WHAT TO DO AFTER BATTLE. The enemy is pursued to the first defile; all the harm possible is done to him, but you should not allow yourself to become so drunk with success that you become imprudent. If the enemy is thoroughly defeated, make several marches after him and you will gain a prodigous amount of territory. But always camp in accordance with regulations! Do not neglect the principles of foresight and know that often, puffed up with their success, armies have lost the fruit of their heroism through a feeling of false security. Think also of the poor wounded of the two armies.

Especially have a paternal care for your own and do not be inhuman to those of the enemy. The wounded are disposed of by sending them to hospitals, and the prisoners by sending them to a neighboring fortress under a strong escort. When an army has been defeated, it is permissible to make detachments, especially when it is a question of cutting it off or of taking two or three its cities at the same time. But it is the conditions of the time that should determine this operation, and there no way to prescribe a general rule.

OPERATIONS OF DETACHMENTS. What is practiced in armies is done on a small scale with detachments. I add that, in the one and in the other, if a little help reaches you in the action itself, it determines the turn of fortune for you. The enemy is discouraged and his excited imagination sees the help at least twice as strong as it really is.

RETREATS OF DEFEATED BODIES. A battle is lost less through the loss of men than by discouragement. I make my vows to Heaven that the Prussians never shall be obliged to make retreats, but, since I should touch on this matter, I shall state my opinions. For small bodies, and in large plains, the infantry should form a square protecting the remaining cavalry, thus gaining the first defile or nearest wood. If it is a large body, I should prefer retreat in checkerboard formation by entire lines which pass through each other; a general then can save his army if he seizes the first defile instantly, so that his troops posted there protect the retreat of the others through it. If his cavalry is discouraged, let it be sent away; for the rest of this day he will not be able to bring it against the enemy again.

How and Why Battle Should be Accepted. The man who does things without motive or in spite of himself is either insane or a fool. War is decided only by battles, and it is not finished except by them. Thus they have to be fought, but it should be opportunely and with all the advantages on your side. I call it opportune when it is a question of chasing an enemy out of your country; or of driving him out of a position in a locality which prevents you from penetrating into his; when you want to force him to raise a seige; or when you are unable to make one until you have defeated him; or, when it is a question of gaining superiority for yourself for a whole campaign, and the enemy, committing a fault, gives you the opportunity to take it from him. Finally, when the enemy is to receive reinforcements, you should, if possible, defeat him before their junction.

Advantages are procured in battles every time that you are determined to fight, or when a battle that you have meditated upon for a long time is a consequence of the maneuvers that you have made to bring it on. The best occasions that can be procured are when you cut the enemy off from his supplies and when you choose terrain favorable to the qualities of your troops and which forces the enemy to fight at the locality you choose. After this, what is most advantageous is to profit from a poor position of the enemy to push him out of it, but especially to occupy such positions yourself as enable you to cover a great deal of the country by small movements and so located that you will never be cut off from your own supplies nor from places which you should protect. The enemy should be attacked if he backs against a river, or if he has but a single bad defile behind him, because he risks a great deal and you risk little, even if you have bad luck.

REFLECTIONS ON THE HAZARDS AND MISFORTUNES OF WAR. When a general conducts himself with all prudence, he still can suffer ill fortune; for how many things do not cooperate at all with his labors! Weather, harvest, the officers, the health or sickness of his troops, blunders, the death of an officer on whom he counts, discouragement of the troops, exposure of your spies, negligence of the officers who should reconnoiter the enemy, and finally, betrayal. These are the things that should be kept continually before your eyes so as to be prepared for them and so that good fortune will not blind us.

When we wished to march from Reichenbach to Ottmachau in 1741, rains had impaired the roads so extensively that the pontons could hardly be hauled through the mud, which, slowing up our march by two days, made our plan fall through. The same day of the march a fog came up so thick that the village guards delayed us for four hours and did not join the army until nine o'clock in the morning. And there went a plan up in smoke because of a fog that could not have been foreseen.

If you form a project for an offensive campaign and the harvest fails in the country that you wish to subjugate, you easily could fail in your enterprise. If contagious illness spreads among your troops in the middle of a campaign, this will oblige you, if it goes far, to content yourself with the defensive, instead of acting with the vigor that you had proposed at the outset.

If your orders are misunderstood and some blunder occurs, accidents resulting can be decisive on days of action. I feared such an experience the day of Friedberg. Kalckstein commanded the second line. I detached him to support Dumoulin, who was on our right wing, and I sent an adjutant to Prince Charles to direct him to take command of the second line in place of Kalckstein. The adjutant misunderstood me and told Prince Charles to form the second line with troops from the first. Fortunately, I perceived this error and had time to remedy it.

If an important detachment is entrusted to a man of judgment and if this man should become sick or should be killed, there is all your business hung up; for no one should imagine that sound heads are common in armies. Offensive generals are rare among us; I only know a few, and, nevertheless, it is only to these that this sort of detachment can be entrusted.

If you have been obliged to withdraw repeatedly before the enemy, the troops get frightened. The same thing happens if you have suffered some check; even when a good opportunity presents itself to you, it must be allowed to escape as soon as you see any uncertainty in the troops. I have been fortunate enough never to have been in this situation with my whole army, but after the battle of Mollwitz I saw what defeated cavalry is like and how long it takes to reaffirm their courage.

If you have some spies on whom you count and the enemy discovers them, there is your compass suddenly lost, and you are obliged to conjecture and conduct yourself only on the reports of your own eyes. If some one of your officers who is supposed to be scouting is negligent, he can put the whole army in danger. That is how Neipperg was surprised at Mollwitz. He had entrusted all his security to a major of hussars who was supposed to make a patrol on the day of battle and did not do it.

Learn then to make dispositions in such a fashion that the fate of your army does not depend on the good or bad conduct of a single minor officer. Especially if you have a river to guard, place so many inspectors over the officers who make the patrols that you will never be exposed by their negligence, and that more than one person shall be responsible for the occurrence.

There is still something worse to fear; this is treachery. There is what made us lose Cosel; there is how Prince Eugene was betrayed in 1735 by General Stein, who was a spy for France.

Finally, in considering fortuitous events and the chapter of accidents, one can see that a general should be skillful and lucky and that no one should believe so fully in his star that he abandons himself to it blindly. If you are lucky and trust in luck alone, even your success reduces you to the defensive; if you are unlucky, you are already there.

THE REASONS FOR MINUTE CAVALRY AND INFANTRY MANEUVERS. You will have seen by what I have had occasion to delineate concerning war that promptness contributes a great deal to success in marches and even more in battles. That is why our army is drilled in such a fashion that it acts faster than others. From drill comes these maneuvers which enable us to form in the twinkling of an eye, and from this that speed in all cavalry movements. And as for cavalry attack, I have considered it necessary to make it so fast and so close for more than one reason: (1) so that this large movement will carry the coward along with the brave man; (2) so that the cavalryman will not have time to reflect; (3) so that the power of our big horses and their speed will certainly overthrow whatever tries to resist them; and (4) to deprive the simple cavalryman of any influence in the decision of such a big affair.

So long as the line is contiguous and the squadrons well closed, it is almost impossible to come to hand-to-hand combat. The squadrons are unable to mix, since the enemy, being more open than we are and having more intervals, is unable to resist our shock. The force of our shock is double theirs, because they have many flanks and we only have one which the general fortifies to the extent possible, and finally because the fury of our attack disconcerts them. If they fire, they will take themselves to flight; if they attack at a slow trot, they are overthrown; if they wish to come at us with the same speed with which we attack, they come in confusion and we defeat them, as it were, in detail.

As for the rapid step of the infantry and the attack, rifle on the shoulder, I have some very good reasons to prefer it to any other. It is not the greater or lesser number of dead that decides an action but the ground you gain. It is not fire but bearing which defeats the enemy. And because the decision is gained more quickly by always marching against the enemy than by amusing yourself firing, the sooner a battle is decided, the fewer men are lost in it. My system is based on the idea then that it is up to the infantry to expel the enemy and to push him, so to speak, off the field of battle, and that it is the cavalry which crowns the action and gives it brilliance by the number of prisoners that it is up to them to take.

THE CHAIN OF WINTER QUARTERS AND ALL THAT CONCERNS THESE QUARTERS. When the army returns from campaign it forms a chain of winter quarters, and this always is a continuation of the campaign. The location of winter quarters cannot be determined before the issue of the campaign is settled. To make my rules easier to understand, I shall explain the disposition of our quarters from 1744 until spring, 1745. The mountains which separate Bohemia from Silesia determined them. The quarters at Schneideberg were under the orders of Lieutenant General Truchsess. He had posts in Friedland, where he had a redoubt on the top of the mountain, and some small detached posts on the roads which run into Silesia from Schatzlar and Braunau. The positions were fortified with abatis. All the roads and trails were blocked; each small post had some hussars for scouting, and the main body which Truchsess commanded was properly the reserve of the detachments. The road and the post at Silberberg were occupied by Dessau's regiment. The Comté de Glatz was defended by General

Lehwaldt with a corps similar to that of Truchsess. He made abatis, blocking the roads from Bohemia, and these abatis were guarded by infantry detachments. Lehwaldt and Truchsess were within supporting distance. The Austrians could not attack the one without fearing that the other might land on their shoulder. Troppau and Jägerndorf provided our advanced quarters in Upper Silesia, and they communicated with Lower Silesia through the district of Neustadt. The remainder of the troops, which did not form part of this chain, were in winter quarters by brigades so that they could be assembled more promptly and in better order.

I should add that an army should never be separated except when it is certain that the enemy will be likewise. Chains of mountains often form barriers for winter quarters; at other times it is rivers. Neither one nor the other should ever be trusted, for mountains can be crossed wherever goats cross, and winter freezes most rivers, which then are no longer good for anything in the system of your defense. The best chain of winter quarters is composed of fortified places, such as the French and Allies have in Flanders. I note at the same time that skillful generals never occupy positions which lend themselves to many ruses, at least if they are important.

Troops are rested during the winter. I love to have them well nourished, but the soldier should not have any ready money. If he has a few écus in his pocket, he thinks himself too much of a great lord to follow his profession, and he deserts at the opening of the campaign. Here is how I have regulated the matter. He receives his bread free and is given more meat than ordinarily, that is to say a pound a day. The general commanding the army should see that the army is filled up. If the army is in enemy country, this country, in the nature of things, should furnish all the recruits. If this is impossible, it should give enough money to the captains so that they can raise them in the empire. It is on these occasions where an industrious general is an eagle and where a lazy one lets everything wither away.

The general should make sure that new uniforms for the army arrive in time toward spring, that the captains provide shoes, that the wagons, cannon carriages, etc., of the army are repaired, as well as the saddles and boots of the cavalry; in a word, he should enter into all these details and himself visit the quarters to see what is going on there, if the officers are drilling the recruits, if they are working, and to animate them with kind words and reprimands to make them do their duty. When it will soon be time to open the campaign, he should order all the governors and commanders of large cities to keep a lookout so that officers who are not sick return to their corps, and to send truthful lists of those whose health prevents them from fulfilling their service immediately. It should be said to the shame of young men that debachery and laziness often make them prefer ease to glory.

Before taking the field troops are put in cantonments. From that time the brigade order of battle should be formed and the troops should be in cantonments as if they were ranged under banners, placing the cavalry of the right under a general who receives the orders, the two lines of infantry of the right under a general, the infantry of the left under another, and, finally, the last commands the cavalry of the left. This shortens the orders so that whatever you want done will be executed with more exactness.

WINTER CAMPAIGNS. It is only absolute necessity and great advantages which can excuse winter operations. Ordinarily, they ruin the troops because of the sickness by which they are followed and because, remaining constantly in action, there is no time either to recruit troops nor to clothe them. An army that is employed frequently and for a long time in such a rigorous season assuredly will not keep up well. If, however, very important motives, such as we had in 1740, 1744, and 1745, require making winter campaigns, the best thing that can be done is to use all possible vigor so that they may be short.

Winter campaigns are made by marching between cantonments very close together. To make this possible, all the infantry is placed in one city, as was done by the Prince of Anhalt during his Saxon expedition. On the days of marching the army assembles and marches in columns, as usual. When the enemy is near, beds are under the stars. The troops make big fires. As these fatigues are prodigious, it is necessary to cut them short; either the winter quarters of the enemy are fallen on or their army is attacked to decide things promptly.

Winter expeditions should never be undertaken in case success depends upon making formal seiges. The season does not permit it. The advantage from this sort of war is that, if it is successful, the advance is prodigious. It would perhaps have cost us four ordinary campaigns to take Silesia if we had not profited by choosing the critical time. It was devoid of troops, and this gave us the means to advance and establish the theater of war on the banks of the Neisse, whereas if spring had been awaited to act we should have advanced only to Glogau.

I except reasons of this importance, but ordinarily my maxim is to leave the troops in repose during the winter and to employ this time in restoring all the corps of the army with all the assiduity of which you are capable, and rather to reserve for yourself the first appearance in the field the following spring.

MILITARY MAXIMS

of

NAPOLEON

INTRODUCTION

Napoleon fought more battles than Alexander, Hannibal, and Caesar combined. He is, beyond any doubt, the greatest of European soldiers. He never wrote his theories or principles on the conduct of war, although he often expressed the intention of doing so and remarked that everyone would be surprised at how simple they were.

Napoleon lived at a time when the possibilities of war had been increased enormously. Saxe had formed divisions in his army, consisting of two brigades of infantry and one of artillery, and had used them during an entire campaign. Marshal de Broglie had adopted a permanent divisional organization in 1759 and had concentrated his army rapidly by the assembly of these units. The divisional organization and marching in small columns of from 2000 to 4000 men, permitted rapid deployment on the battlefield, whereas the old precedures required six to eight hours to form a line of battle. Marshal de Broglie had developed the principle of dispersion with units in supporting distance, in camp and on the march, and concentration on the field of battle. Gribeauval had reduced the weight and increased the mobility of artillery so that it could maneuver with the infantry. Accurate maps were becoming general, an important matter in the handling of large forces.

The theories by which all these changes could be utilized had been expounded by Guibert, du Teil, and Bour cet. It remained for Napoleon alone, among the generals of his time, to seize all these possibilities to their full and develop from them a calculated system of strategy and a system of tactics calculated with equal brilliance. No other general of his time realized these possibilities until forced to learn by combating Napoleon.

He astounded his opponents by the crushing rapidity of his battles. He marched against the enemy and his plan of battle was a part of his plan of march. His strategical system, according to Capt. J. Colin and General Camon, were based on marching rapidly and secretly past the enemy's flank to get on the hostile line of communications. This forced his opponent to turn and fight at a disadvantage.

His tactical system, or scheme of battle, was based on a holding attack against the enemy's front to keep them occupied, a wide envelopment or turning movement on the enemy's rear with a small force to spread dismay and confusion in the defender's ranks, and then the decisive blow. This was given by a powerful attack, usually in the form of a close-in envelopment, which was prepared by concentrated fire of a mass of artillery.

Napoleon constantly added to the amount of his artillery. In 1800 he organized the horses and drivers of the artillery as part of the artillery batteries. Previous to this time the horses and drivers had been temporarily hired civilians, who hauled the guns up to the battlefield, left them there, and returned to get them after the battle was over. It is rather amusing that, even in recent days, one of the common criticisms of Napoleon has been that

he increased his artillery. This was ascribed to the de-
terioration of his infantry in his later career. The critics
overlook the fact that small-arms fire had improved and
that the old offensive charge had become increasingly
costly and less able to break the lines of the defenders
than it had been in the past. Napoleon used his artillery
in masses to break these lines, spread confusion, and prepare the way for his infantry. The result was a material
saving of lives for his infantry and enhanced chance of
victory.

Napoleon was the first great stategist of the western
world. His battles were the result of his stategical movements and were carefully calculated. The art of stategy,
as developed by writers for the past century, has its foundation in his operations. Baron Jomini was the chief
expounder of Napoleon's methods. Clausewitz' great
book, *On War,* was likewise an outgrowth of Napoleonic
studies. Jomini's work was the textbook for the conduct
of the American Civil War. It has been said that the
Civil War was fought with Jomini in the pocket of all
the higher officers. Clausewitz' influence was felt most
profoundly in the Franco-Prussian War of 1870 and in
the World War.

Many collections of Napoleon's maxims and precepts
have been made. The present collection is both the first
and the best selection of any small collection. It was
published in Paris in 1827 and almost immediately was
translated into German, English, Spanish, and Italian.
Stonewall Jackson carried these maxims in his haversack
throughout his campaign. "This little volume," states

Col. G. F. R. Henderson, Jackson's biographer, "contains a fairly complete exposition, in Napoleon's own words, of the grand principles of war."

In his introduction, General Burnod, the compiler of these maxims, states: "The art of war is susceptible of being considered under two titles: the one, which rests entirely on the knowledge and genius of the commander; the other, on matters of detail. The first is the same for all time, for all peoples, whatever the arms with which they fight. From this it follows that the same principles have directed the great captains of all centuries. The matters of detail, on the contrary, are subject to the influence of time, to the spirit of the people and the character of armaments."

The continuing interest and application of most of these maxims indicates that the original compiler succeeded in selecting Napoleon's most pertinent aphorisms of permanent value.

FIRST PART

1

The frontiers of nations are either large rivers, or chains of mountains, or deserts. Of all these obstacles to the march of an army, deserts are the most difficult to surmount; mountains come next; and large rivers hold only the third rank.

2

A plan of campaign should anticipate everything which the enemy can do, and contain within itself the means of thwarting him.

Plans of campaign may be infinitely modified according to the circumstances, the genius of the commander, the quality of the troops and the topography of the theater of war.

3

An army invading a country may either have its two wings resting on neutral countries or on great natural obstacles, such as rivers or chains of mountains; or it may have only one of its wings thus supported; or both may be without support.

In the first case, a general has only to see that his line is not broken in front. In the second case, he must rest on the wing which is supported. In the third case, he must keep his different corps resting well on his centre and never allow them to separate from it; for if it is a disadvantage to have two flanks in the air, the inconvenience is doubled if there are four, tripled if there are six;

that is to say, if an army is divided into two or three distinct corps.

The line of operations in the first case, may rest on the left or the right wing, indifferently. In the second case, it should rest on the wing which is supported. In the third case, it should fall perpendicularly on the middle of the line formed by the army in marching. But in all the cases above mentioned, it is necessary to have at every five or six days' march, a fort or entrenched position, where magazines of provisions and military stores may be established and convoys organized; and which may serve as a centre of motion and a point of supply, and thus shorten the line of operations.

4

It may be laid down as a principle that in invading a country with two or three armies, each of which has its own distinct line of operations extending towards a fixed point at which all are to unite, the union of the different corps should never be ordered to take place in the vicinity of the enemy, as by concentrating his forces he may not only prevent their junction but also defeat them one by one.

5

All wars should be systematic, for every war should have an aim and be conducted in conformity with the principles and rules of the art. War should be undertaken with forces corresponding to the magnitude of the obstacles that are to be anticipated.

6

At the commencement of a campaign, the question

whether to advance or not requires careful deliberation; but when you have once undertaken the offensive, it should be maintained to the last extremity. A retreat, however skillful the maneuvers may be, will always produce an injurious moral effect on the army, since by losing the chances of success yourself you throw them into the hands of the enemy. Besides, retreats cost far more, both in men and materiel, than the most bloody engagements; with this difference, that in a battle the enemy loses nearly as much as you, while in a retreat the loss is all on your side.

7

An army should be every day, every night, and every hour, ready to offer all the resistance of which it is capable. It is necessary, therefore, that the soldiers should always have their arms and ammunition at hand; that the infantry should always have with it its artillery, cavalry and generals; that the different divisions of the army should be always in a position to assist, support and protect each other; that whether encamped, marching or halted, the troops should be always in advantageous positions, possessing the qualities required for every field of battle—that is to say, the flanks should be well supported and the artillery so placed that it may all be brought into play. When the army is in column of march, there must be advanced guards and flank guards to observe the enemy's movements in front, on the right and on the left; and at sufficient distances to allow the main body of the arm to deploy and take up its position.

8

A general should say to himself many times a day: If the hostile army were to make its appearance in front, on my right, or on my left, what should I do? And if he is embarrassed, his arrangements are bad; there is something wrong; he must rectify his mistake.

9

The strength of an army, like the momentum in mechanics, is estimated by the weight multiplied by the velocity. A rapid march exerts a beneficial moral influence on the army and increases its means of victory.

10

When your army is inferior in numbers, inferior in cavalry and in artillery, a pitched battle should be avoided. The want of numbers must be supplied by rapidity in marching; the want of artillery by the character of the maneuvers; the inferiority in cavalry by the choice of positions. In such a situation, it is of great importance that confidence should prevail among the soldiers.

11

To operate upon lines remote from each other and without communications between them, is a fault which ordinarily occasions a second. The detached column has orders only for the first day. Its operations for the second day depend on what has happened to the main body. Thus, according to circumstances, the column wastes its time in waiting for orders or it acts at random. It ought then to be adopted as a principle that the columns of an army should be always kept united, so that the enemy cannot thrust himself between them. When for any reason this maxim is departed from, the detached corps should be independent in their operations. They should move towards a fixed point at which they are to unite. They should march without hesitation and without new orders, and should be exposed as little as possible to the danger of being attacked separately.

12

An army should have but a single line of operations which it should carefully preserve, and should abandon only when compelled by imperious circumstances.

13

The intervals at which the corps of an army should be from each other in marching, depend on the localities, the circumstances and the object in view.

14

Among mountains there are everywhere numerous positions extremely strong by nature, which you should abstain from attacking. The genius of this kind of war consists in occupying camps either on the flank or the rear of the enemy, so as to leave him no alternative but to withdraw from his position without fighting; and to move him farther back, or to make him come out and attack you. In mountain war the attacking party acts under a disadvantage. Even in offensive war, the merit lies in having only defensive conflicts and obliging your enemy to become the assailant.

15

In giving battle a general should regard it as his first duty to maintain the honor and glory of his arms. To spare his troops should be but a secondary consideration.

But the same determination and perseverance which promote the former object are the best means of securing the latter. In a retreat you lose, in addition to the honor of your arms, more men than in two battles.

For this reason you should never despair while there remain brave men around the colors. This is the conduct which wins, and deserves to win, the victory.

16

A well-established maxim of war is not to do anything which your enemy wishes—and for the single reason that he does so wish.

You should, therefore, avoid a field of battle which he has reconnoitered and studied. You should be still more careful to avoid one which he has fortified and where he has entrenched himself. A corollary of this principle is, never to attack in front a position which admits of being turned.

17

In a war of marches and maneuvers, to escape an engagement with a superior enemy, it is necessary to throw up entrenchments every night and to place yourself always in a good position for defense. The natural positions which are commonly met with cannot secure an army against the superiority of a more numerous one without the aid of art.

18

An ordinary general occupying a bad position, if surprised by a superior force, seeks safety in retreat; but a great captain displays the utmost determination and advances to meet the enemy. By this movement he disconcerts his adversary; and if the march of the latter evinces irresolution, an able general, profiting by the moment of indecision, may yet hope for victory or at least employ the day in maneuvering; and at night he can entrench himself or fall back on a better position. By this fearless conduct he maintains the honor of his arms, which forms so essential a part of the strength of an army.

19

The passage from the defensive to the offensive is one of the most delicate operations of war.

20

Your line of operations should never, as a general rule, be abandoned; but changing it when circumstances require, is one of the most skillful of military maneuvers. An army which changes its line of operations skillfully, deceives the enemy, who no longer knows where his antagonist's rear is, or what are the weak points to threaten.

21

When an army is encumbered with siege equipage and large convoys of wounded and sick, it should approach its depots by the shortest roads and as expeditiously as possible.

22

The art of encamping on a position is nothing else than the art of forming in order of battle on that position. For this purpose the artillery should all be in readiness and favorably placed; a position should be selected which is not commanded, cannot be turned, and from which the ground in the vicinity is covered and commanded.

23

When you occupy a position which the enemy threatens to surround, you should collect your forces quickly and menace him with an offensive movement. By this maneuver you prevent him from detaching a part of his troops and annoying your flanks, in case you should deem a retreat indispensable.

24

A military maxim, which ought never to be neglected, is to assemble your cantonments at the point which is most remote and best sheltered from the enemy, especially when he makes his appearance unexpectedly. You will then have time to unite the whole army before he can attack you.

25

When two armies are in order of battle, and one, if obliged to retire, must effect its retreat by a bridge, while the other can withdraw towards all points of the compass, the latter has greatly the advantage. A general so situated should be enterprising, strike vigorously and maneuver against the flanks of his adversary; and victory is his.

26

It is a violation of correct principles to cause corps to act separately, without communication with each other, in the face of a concentrated army with easy communications.

27

When you are driven from your first position, the rallying point of your columns should be so far in the rear that the enemy cannot get there before them. It would be the greatest of disasters to have your columns attacked one by one before their reunion.

28

No detachment should be made the day preceding a battle, for during the night the state of things may change, either by a retreat of the enemy or by the arrival of strong reinforcements, which would put him in condition to assume the offensive and render the premature dispositions which you have made ruinous.

29

When you have it in contemplation to give battle, it is a general rule to collect all your strength and to leave none unemployed. One battalion sometimes decides the issue of the day.

30

Nothing is more rash or more opposed to the principles of war than a flank march in presence of an army in position, especially when that army occupies heights at the foot of which you must defile.

31

When you intend to engage in a decisive battle, avail yourself of all the chances of success; more especially if you have to do with a great captain; for if you are beaten, though you may be in the midst of your magazines and near your fortified posts, woe to the vanquished!

32

The duty of an advance guard does not consist in advancing or retreating, but in maneuvering. It should be composed of light cavalry supported by a reserve of heavy, and by battalions of infantry, with artillery to support them. The advance guard should be formed of choice troops; and the generals, officers and soldiers, according to the requirements of their respective rank, should be thoroughly acquainted with the peculiar tactics necessary in this kind of service. An untrained company would be only a source of embarrassment.

33

It is contrary to the usages of war to cause your parks or heavy artillery to enter a defile, the opposite extremity of which is not in your possession; since, in the event of a retreat,, they will embarrass you and be lost. They ought to be left in position, under a suitable escort, until you have made yourself master of the termination of the defile.

34

It should be adopted as a principle never to allow intervals through which the enemy can penetrate between the different corps forming the line of battle, unless you have laid a snare into which it is your object to draw him.

35

The camps of the same army should be always so placed as to be able to sustain each other.

36

When a hostile army is covered by a river on which it has several bridgeheads, you should not approach it in front, for in doing so your forces would be too little concentrated and in danger of being broken into detached parts, if the enemy should sally from one of the bridgeheads. You should approach the river you wish to cross in columns disposed in echelon, so that there may be only a single column—the foremost one—which the enemy can attack without exposing his own flank. Meanwhile the light troops will line the bank; and when you have fixed on the point at which to pass, you must proceed rapidly to the spot and throw the bridge across. You must take care that the bridge shall always be at a distance from the leading echelon in order to deceive the enemy.

37

The moment that you become master of a position which commands the opposite bank, you obtain many facilities for effecting the passage of a river, especially if that position has sufficient extent to admit of your planting a large number of pieces of artillery upon it. This advantage is less if the river is more than six hundred yards wide, as the grape no longer reaches the other shore; and consequently the troops that oppose the passage can, by suitable precautions, easily render your fire of little effect. Hence if the grenadiers charged with the duty of passing the river to protect the bridge, succeed in crossing to the other side, they will be swept off by the enemy's grapeshot; as his batteries established four hundred yards from the termination of the bridge are near enough to pour in a very destructive fire, although more than a thousand yards distant from the batteries of the army which is endeavoring to pass. Therefore he has all the advantage of the artillery. So in such a case a passage is not practicable unless you either contrive to take the enemy by surprise, or are protected by an intervening island, or avail yourself of a deep re-entrant bend, which enables you to erect batteries crossing their fire just in advance of the point where a landing is to be effected. Such an island or re-entrant forms a natural bridge-ead and gives the advantage of the artillery to the attacking army

When a river is less than a hundred and twenty yards in breadth and you can command the opposite bank, the troops that are thrown over to the other side derive such advantages from the protection afforded by the artillery that, however slight the re-entrant formed by the river may be, it is impossible for the enemy to prevent the establishment of the bridge. Under such circumstances, the most skillful generals, when they have been able to foresee the designs of their antagonist and arrive with their army at the point at which he was making his attempt, have contented themselves with disputing the passage of the bridge. A bridge being in fact a defile, you should place yourself in a half-circle around its extremity and take measures to shelter yourself at the distance of six or eight hundred yards from the fire of the other bank.

38

It is difficult to prevent an enemy provided with bridge equipage from crossing a river. When the object of the army which disputes the passage is to cover a siege, the commanding general, as soon as he is certain that he cannot successfully oppose the passage, should take measures to arrive in advance of the enemy at a position between the river and the place whose siege he is covering.

39

In the campaign of 1645, the forces of Turenne were

hemmed in before Philipsburgh by a very numerous army.
There was no bridge over the Rhine, but Turenne established his camp on the ground lying between the river
and the place. This should serve as a lesson to officers
of the engineer department in regard to the construction
of bridgehea   as well as of fortresses. There should be
left, between the fortress and the river, a space in which
an army may be rallied and formed; as the entrance of
the troops into the place itself would endanger it. An
army pursued and retiring upon Mayence, must necessarily be in a precarious situation, since it would require
more than one day to pass the bridge, and the works
surrounding Cassel are too small to contain an army without crowding and confusion. Four hundred yards should
have been left between the works and the Rhine. It is
essential that bridgeheads before large rivers should be
constructed on this plan; otherwise they will be of little
utility in protecting the passage of an army in retreat.
Bridgeheads, as they are taught in the schools, are good
only before small rivers where the defile is not long.

40

Fortresses are useful in offensive as well as defensive
war. Undoubtedly they cannot of themselves arrest the
progress of an army, but they are excellent means of de-
laying, impeding, enfeebling and annoying a victorious
enemy.

41

There are only two modes of prosecuting a siege successfully. One is to begin by beating the hostile army
employed to cover the place, driving it from the field of

operations and forcing its remains beyond some natural obstacle, such as a chain of mountains or a large river. This first difficulty overcome, you must place an army of observation behind the natural obstacle until the labors of the siege are finished and the place is taken.

But if you wish to take the place in the face of an army of relief without hazarding a battle, you must be provided with siege equipage, ammunition and provisions for the time during which the siege is expected to continue; and must form lines of contravallation and circumvallation, turning, meanwhile, the peculiarities of the ground such as heights, woods, marshes and overflows to the best account.

As there is then no necessity for keeping up any communication with your depots, you have only to hold in check the army of relief. To this end you should form an army of observation which must never lose sight of the enemy and which, while shutting him out from all access to the place, may always have time to fall upon his flanks or rear, if he should steal a march upon you. By taking advantage of your lines of contravallation you can employ a part of the besieging forces in giving battle to the army of relief.

A siege therefore, in the presence of a hostile army requires to be covered by lines of circumvallation.

If your army is so strong that, after leaving before the place a body four times the number of the garrison, it is still equal to the army of relief, it may move to a greater distance than one day's march.

If, after making the detachment, it remains inferior to

the army of relief, it should be posted at one short day's march from the place besieged, so as to be at liberty to fall back on the lines or receive succor in the event of sustaining an attack.

If the two armies of siege and of observation, united, are equal only to the army of relief, the besieging army must remain altogether within or near its lines and employ itself in pushing the siege with all possible activity.

42

Feuquieres has said that you should never wait for the enemy in your lines of circumvallation, but should go out and attack him. The maxim is erroneous. No rule of war is so absolute as to allow no exceptions, and waiting for the enemy in the lines of circumvallation ought not to be condemned as injudicious in all cases.

43

They who proscribe lines of circumvallation and all the aid which the art of the engineer can furnish, gratuitously deprive themselves of auxiliaries that are never injurious, almost always useful and often indispensable. The principles of field fortification, however, need improvement. This important branch of the art of war has made no progress in modern times. It is even at this day in a lower state than it was two thousand years ago. Officers of the engineer department ought to be encouraged to perfect this branch of their art and raise it to a level with others.

44

When you have a hospital and magazines in a fortified town, and circumstances are such as not to admit of your leaving a sufficient garrison to defend it, you should at least make every possible exertion to put the citadel in security from a coup de main.

45

A fortified place can protect a garrison and arrest the enemy only a certain length of time. When that time has elapsed and the defences of the place are destroyed, the garrison may lay down their arms. All civilized nations have been of one opinion in this respect, and the only dispute has been as to the greater or less degree of resistance which the governor should offer before capitulating. Yet there are generals—Villars is of the number —who hold that a governor ought never to surrender, but that in the last extremity he should blow up the fortifications and take advantage of the night to cut his way through the besieging army. In case you cannot blow up the fortifications, you can at any rate sally out with your garrison and save your men. Commanders who have pursued this course have rejoined their army with three-fourths of their garrison.

46

The keys of a fortified place are ample compensation for permitting the garrison to retire unmolested, whenever the latter evince a determination to die rather than accept less favorable terms. It is always better, therefore, to grant an honorable capitulation to a garrison which has resisted vigorously than to run the risk of an attempt to storm.

47

Infantry, cavalry and artillery cannot dispense with each other. They ought to be quartered in such a manner as always to be able to support each other in case of surprise.

48

Infantry formed in line should be in two ranks only, for the musket cannot otherwise be used with equal effect. It is admitted that the fire of the third rank is very imperfect and even injurious to that of the first two.

But though the great body of the infantry should be drawn up, as has just been said, in two ranks, the absence of a regular third rank should be supplied by supernumeraries composed of one soldier out of nine or one every two yards.

49

The practice of mingling companies of horse and foot together is bad; it produces nothing but trouble. The cavalry is deprived of its capacity for rapidity of motion; it is cramped in all the movements; it loses its impulse.

The infantry, too, is exposed; for, at the first movement of the cavalry, it remains without support. The best mode of protecting cavalry is to support its flank.

50

Charges of cavalry are equally serviceable in the beginning, the middle and the end of a battle. They should be executed whenever they can be made on the flanks of the infantry, particularly when the latter is engaged in front.

51

It is a function of the cavalry to follow up the victory and prevent the beaten enemy from rallying.

52

Artillery is more necessary to cavalry than to infantry, because cavalry does not fire and can fight only in close conflict. It is to supply this deficiency that horse-artillery has been resorted to. Cavalry, therefore, should always be accompanied by cannon, whether attacking, resting in position or rallying.

53

The principal part of the artillery should be with the divisions of infantry and of cavalry, whether marching or in position, and the rest should be placed in reserve. Each piece should have with it three hundred charges of powder and ball, besides the contents of the ammunition-box. That is about the quantity consumed in two battles.

54

Batteries should be placed in the most advantageous positions and as far in advance of the lines of infantry and cavalry as is possible without endangering the guns. It is desirable that the batteries should have a command over the field equal to the full height of the platform. They must not be masked on the right or left, but should be at liberty to direct their fire towards every point.

55

A general should avoid putting his army into quarters of refreshment, so long as he has the opportunity of collecting magazines of provisions and forage, and thus supplying the wants of his soldiers.

56

A good general, good officers, commissioned and non-commissioned, good organization, good instruction and strict discipline make good troops independently of the cause for which they are fighting. But enthusiasm, love of country and the desire of contributing to the national glory may also animate young troops with advantage.

57

It is very difficult for a nation to create an army when it has not already a body of officers and non-commissioned officers to serve as a nucleus, and a system of military organization.

58

The first quality of a soldier is constancy in enduring fatigue and hardship. Courage is only the second. Poverty, privation and want are the school of the good soldier.

59

There are five things which a soldier ought never to be without: his musket, his cartridge-box, his knapsack, his provisions for at least four days and his pioneer hatchet. Reduce his knapsack, if you deem it n   y to do so, to the smallest size, but let the soldier always have it with him.

60

You should by all means encourage the soldiers to continue in the service. This you can easily do by testifying great esteem for old soldiers. The pay should also be increased in proportion to the years of service. There is great injustice in giving no higher pay to a veteran than to a recruit.

It is not by harangues at the moment of engaging that

soldiers are rendered brave. Veterans hardly listen to them and recruits forget them at the first discharge of a cannon. If speeches and arguments are at any time useful, it is during the course of the campaign by counteracting false reports and causes of discontent, maintaining a proper spirit in the camp and furnishing subjects of conversation in the bivouacs. These several objects may be attained by the printed orders of the day.

62

Tents are injurious to health. It is much better for the soldier to bivouack, because he can sleep with his feet to the fire, which quickly dries the ground on which he lies. A few boards or a little straw shelter him from the wind.

Tents, however, are necessary for the leaders, who have to write and consult the map. They should be given therefore to the superior officers, who should be ordered never to lodge in a house.

Tents attract the observation of the enemy's staff and make known your numbers and the position you occupy. But of an army bivouacking in two or three lines, nothing is perceived at a distance except the smoke, which the enemy confounds with the mist of the atmosphere. He cannot count the fires.

63

The information obtained from prisoners ought to be estimated at its proper value. A soldier seldom looks beyond his own company and an officer can, at most, give account of the position or movements of the division to which his regiment belongs. A general, therefore, snould not allow himself to be confirmed in his conjectures as to the enemy's position, by attaching any weight to the statements of prisoners, except when they coincide with the reports of the advance guards.

64

Nothing is more important in war than unity in command. When, therefore, you are carrying on hostilities against a single power only, you should have but one army acting on one line and led by one commander.

65

The effect of discussions, making a show of talent, and calling councils of war will be what the effect of these things has been in every age: they will end in the adoption of the most pusillanimous or (if the expression be preferred) the most prudent measures, which in war are almost uniformly the worst that can be adopted. True wisdom, so far as a general is concerned, consists in energetic determination.

66

There are certain things in war of which the commander alone comprehends the importance. Nothing but his superior firmness and ability can subdue and surmount all difficulties.

67

To authorize generals and officers to lay down their arms by virtue of a special capitulation under any other circumstances than when they constitute the garrison of a fortified place, would unquestionably be attended with dangerous consequences. To open this door to cowards, to men wanting in energy or even to misguided brave men, is to destroy the military spirit of a nation. An extraordinary situation requires extraordinary resolution. The more obstinate the resistance of an armed body, the more chances it will have of being succored or of forcing a passage. How many things apparently impossible have nevertheless been performed by resolute men who had no alternative but death!

68

No sovereign, no people, no general can be secure, if officers are permitted to capitulate on the field and lay down their arms by virtue of an agreement favorable to themselves and to the troops under their command, but opposed to the interests of the remainder of the army. To withdraw from peril themselves, and thus render the position of their comrades more dangerous, is manifestly an act of baseness. Such conduct ought to be proscribed, pronounced infamous and punishable with death. The generals, officers and soldiers who in a battle have saved their lives by capitulating, ought to be decimated. He who commands the arms to be surrendered and those who obey him, are alike traitors, and deserve capital punishment.

69

There is but one honorable way of being made a prisoner of war; that is by being taken separately and when you can no longer make use of your arms. Then there are no conditions—for there can be none, consistently with honor—but you are compelled to surrender by absolute necessity

70

The conduct of a general in a conquered country is

encompassed with difficulties. If he is severe, he exasperates and increases the number of his enemies; if he is mild, he inspires hopes which, since they cannot be realized, cause the abuses and vexations unavoidably incident to war only to stand out in bolder relief. A conqueror should know how to employ by turns severity, justice and leniency in suppressing or preventing disturbances.

71

Nothing can excuse a general who avails himself of the knowledge he has acquired in the service of his country to give up its bulwarks to a foreign nation. That is a crime abhorrent to the principles of religion, morality and honor.

72

A general-in-chief cannot exonerate himself from responsibility for his faults by pleading an order of his sovereign or the minister, when the individual from whom it proceeds is at a distance from the field of operations, and but partially, or not at all, acquainted with the actual condition of things. Hence it follows that every general-in-chief who undertakes to execute a plan which he knows to be bad, is culpable. He should communicate his reasons, insist on a change of plan and finally resign his commission rather than become the instrument of his army's ruin.

Every general-in-chief who, in consequence of orders from his superiors, gives battle with the certainty of defeat, is equally culpable.

In this latter case, he should refuse to obey; for an order requires passive obedience only when it is issued by a

superior who is present at the seat of war. As the superior
is then familiar with the state of affairs, he can listen to
objections and make the necessary explanations to the
officer who is to execute the command.

But suppose a general-in-chief were to receive from his
sovereign an order to give battle with the injunction to
yield the victory to his adversary and permit himself to be
beaten. Would he be bound to obey? No! If the general
comprehended the utility of so strange an order, he ought
to execute it; but, if not, he should refuse to obey.

73

The first qualification of a general-in-chief is to possess
a cool head, so that things may appear to him in their
true proportions and as they really are. He should not
suffer himself to be unduly affected by good or bad news.

The impressions which are made upon his mind suc-
cessively or simultaneously in the course of a day, should
be so classified in his memory that each shall occupy its
proper place; for sound reasoning and judgment result
from first examining each of these varied impressions by
itself, and then comparing them all with one another.

There are some men who, from their physical and
moral constitution, deck everything in the colors of imagination. With whatever knowledge, talents, courage
or other good qualities these may be endowed, nature has
not fitted them for the command of armies and the direction of the great operations of war.

74

To be familiar with the geography and topography
of the country; to be skillful in making a reconnaissance;

to be attentive to the despatch of orders; to be capable of exhibiting with simplicity the most complicated movements of an army—these are the qualifications that should distinguish the officer called to the station of chief of the staff.

75

A general of artillery should be acquainted with all the operations of the army, as he is obliged to supply the different divisions of which it is composed with arms and ammunition. His communications with the artillery officers at the advanced posts should keep him informed of all the movements of the troops, and the management of his great park must be regulated by this information.

76

To reconnoiter rapidly defiles and fords; to obtain guides that can be relied upon; to interrogate the clergyman and the postmaster; to establish speedily an understanding with the inhabitants; to send out spies; to seize the letters in the mails, to translate and make an abstract of their contents; in short, to answer all the inquiries of the general-in-chief on his arrival with the whole army—such are the duties which come within the sphere of a good general of an advanced post.

77

Commanders-in-chief are to be guided by their own experience or genius. Tactics, evolutions and the science of the engineer and the artillery officer may be learned from treatises, but generalship is acquired only by experience and the study of the campaigns of all great captains. Gustavus Adolphus, Turenne and Frederic, as also Alexander, Hannibal and Caesar have all acted on the same principles. To keep your forces united, to be vulnerable at no point, to bear down with rapidity upon important points—these are the principles which insure victory.

It is by the fear which the reputation of your arms inspires that you maintain the fidelity of your allies and the obedience of conquered nations.

78

Read over and over again the campaigns of Alexander, Hannibal, Caesar, Gustavus, Turenne, Eugene and Frederic. Make them your models. This is the only way to become a great general and to master the secrets of the art of war. With your own genius enlightened by this study, you will reject all maxims opposed to those of these great commanders.

SECOND PART

79

The first principle of a general-in-chief is to calculate what he must do, to see if he has all the means to surmount the obstacles with which the enemy can oppose him and, when he has made his decision, to do everything to overcome them.

80

The art of a general of the advance guard or of the rear guard is, without compromising himself, to contain the enemy, to delay him and to force him to take three or four hours to advance a mile. Tactics supplies the only means to attain such great results. It is more necessary for the cavalry than for the infantry, for an advance guard or for a rear guard, than for any other position.

81

It is exceptional and difficult to find all the qualities of a great general combined in one man. What is most desirable and distinguishes the exceptional man, is the balance of intelligence and ability with character or courage. If courage is predominant, the general will hazard far beyond his conceptions; and on the contrary, he will not dare to accomplish his conceptions if his character or his courage are below his intelligence.

82

With a great general there is never a continuity of great actions which can be attributed to chance and good luck; they always are the result of calculation and genius.

83

A general-in-chief should never allow any rest either to the conquerors or to the conquered.

84

An irresolute general who acts without principles and without plan, even though he lead an army numerically superior to that of the enemy, almost always finds himself inferior to the latter on the field of battle. Fumblings, the *mezzo termine* (the middle course) lose all in war.

85

A general of engineers who must conceive, propose and direct all the fortifications of an army, needs good judgment and a practical mind above all.

86

A cavalry general should be a master of practical science, know the value of seconds, despise life and not trust to chance.

87

A general in the power of the enemy has no more orders to give: whoever obeys him is a criminal.

88

The heavy cavalry should be with the advance guard, with the rear guard and on the wings and in reserve to support the light cavalry.

89

To wish to hold the cavalry in reserve for the end of the battle, is to have no idea of the power of combined cavalry and infantry charges either for attack or for defense.

90

The power of cavalry is in its impulsion. But it is not only its velocity that insures success: it is order, formation and proper employment of reserves.

91

The cavalry should compose a quarter of the army in Flanders or Germany; in the Pyranees or in the Alps, a twentieth; in Italy or in Spain, a sixth.

92

In a battle like in a siege, skill consists in converging a mass of fire on a single point: once the combat is opened, the commander who is adroit will suddenly and unexpectedly open fire with a surprising mass of artillery on one of these points, and is sure to seize it.

93

The better the infantry is, the more it should be used carefully and supported with good batteries.

Good infantry is, without doubt, the sinew of an army; but if it is forced to fight for a long time against a very superior artillery, it will become demoralized and will be destroyed. It is possible that a general who is more skillful and a better maneuverer than his adversary, having better infantry, will gain success during a part of the campaign although his artillery park is very inferior; but, on a decisive day in a general action, he will feel his inferiority in artillery cruelly.

94

A good army of 35,000 men should in a few days, especially when supported by a fortress or a large river, make its camp unassailable by an army double in force.

95

War is composed of nothing but accidents, and, although holding to general principles, a general should never lose sight of everything to enable him to profit from these accidents; that is the mark of genius.

In war there is but one favorable moment; the great art is to seize it.

96

A general who retains fresh troops for the day after a battle is almost always beaten. He should, if helpful, throw in his last man, because on the day after a complete success there are no more obstacles in front of him; prestige alone will insure new triumphs to the conqueror.

97

The rules of fighting require that a part of an army should avoid fighting alone against an entire army that has already been successful.

98

When a general has laid siege to a place by surprise and has gained a few days on his adversary, he should profit from this by covering himself with lines of circumvallation; from this moment he will have improved his position and will have acquired a new element of power and a new degree of force in the general framework of affairs.

99

In war the commander of a fortress is not a judge of events; he should defend the fortress to the last; he deserves death if he surrenders it a moment before he is forced to

100

Agreements to surrender made by surrounded bodies, either during a battle or during an active campaign, are contracts with all the advantageous clauses in favor of the individuals who contract them, and all the onerous clauses against the prince and the other soldiers of the army. To avoid peril oneself, while making the position of the rest more dangerous, is an act of cowardice.

101

Defensive war does not exclude attacking, just as offensive war does not exclude defending, although its aim may be to force the frontier and invade the enemy's country.

102

The art of war indicates that it is necessary to turn or envelop a wing without separating the army.

103

When they are thoroughly understood, field fortifications are always useful and never injurious

104

An army can march anywhere and at any time of the year, wherever two men can place their feet.

105

Conditions of the ground should not alone decide the organization for combat, which should be determined from consideration of all circumstances.

106

Flank marches should be avoided; and when they must be undertaken, they should be as short as possible and made with the greatest speed.

107

Nothing can be designed better to disorganize and destroy an army than pillage.

108

Praise from enemies is suspicious; it cannot flatter an honorable man unless it is given after the cessation of hostilities.

109

Prisoners of war do not belong to the power for which they have fought; they all are under the safeguard of honor and generosity of the nation that has disarmed them.

110

Conquered provinces should be maintained in obedience to the conquerors by moral means, such as the responsibility of local governments and the method of organization and administration. Hostages are among the most powerful means; but to be effective, they should be many and chosen from the preponderant elements, and the people must be convinced that immediate death of the hostages will follow violation of their pledges.

111

The geographical conditions of a country, life in plains or mountains, education or discipline, have more influence than climate on the character of the troops.

112

All great captains have done great things only by conforming to the rules and natural principles of the art; that is to say, by the wisdom of their combinations, the reasoned balance of means with consequences, and efforts with obstacles. They have succeeded only by thus conforming, whatever may have been the audacity of their enterprises and the extent of their success. They have never ceased to make war a veritable science. It is only under this title that they are our great models, and it is only in imitating them that one can hope to approach them.

113

The first law of naval tactics should be that as soon as the admiral has given the signal that he is going to attack, each captain should make the necessary movements to attack an enemy ship, take part in the combat and support his neighbors.

114

War on land, in general, consumes more men than naval warfare; it is more dangerous. The sailor in a fleet fights but once during a campaign; the ground soldier fights every day. The sailor, whatever may be the fatigues and dangers of the sea, suffers much less than the soldier: he is never hungry nor thirsty; he always has a place to sleep, his kitchen, his hospital and his pharmacy. There are fewer sick in the English and French fleets, where discipline maintains cleanliness and experience has discovered all the means of preserving health, than in armies. Besides the perils of battle, the sailor risks those of tempests; but seamanship has so much diminished the latter that it cannot be compared with those on land, such as popular uprisings, partial assassinations and surprises by hostile light troops.

An admiral commanding a fleet and a general com
manding an army are men who need different qualities.
One is born with the qualities proper to command an
army, while the necessary qualities to command a fleet
are acquired only by experience.

The art of war on land is an art of genius, of inspiration. On the sea everything is definite and a matter of
experience. The admiral needs only one science, navi-
gation. The general needs all or a talent equal to all, that
of profiting by all experience and all knowledge. An
admiral needs to divine nothing; he knows where his
enemy is and he knows his strength. A general never
knows anything with certainty, never sees his enemy
clearly and never knows positively where he is. When
armies meet, the least accident of the terrain, the smallest
wood, hides a portion of the army. The most experienced
eye cannot state whether he sees the entire enemy army
or only three quarters of it. It is by the eyes of the mind,
by reasoning over the whole, by a species of inspiration
that the general sees, knows and judges. The admiral
needs only an experienced glance; nothing of the enemy
force is hidden from him. What makes the general's
function difficult is the necessity of nourishing so many
men and animals; if he permits himself to be guided by
administrators, he will never budge and his expeditions
will fail. The admiral is never bothered since he carries
everything with him. An admiral has neither reconnais-
sances to make, terrain to examine nor fields of battle to
study. Indian Ocean, American Ocean or North Sea—it is

always a liquid plain. The most skillful will have no advantage over the least, except for his knowledge of prevailing winds in such and such coastal waters, by foresight of those which should prevail or by atmospheric signs: qualities which are acquired by experience and by experience only.

The general never knows the field of battle on which he may operate. His understanding is that of inspiration; he has no positive information; data to reach a knowledge of localities are so contingent on events that almost nothing is learned by experience. It is a faculty to understand immediately the relations of the terrain according to the nature of different countries; it is, finally, a gift, called a *coup de oeil militaire* (the ability to take in the military situation at a glance) which great generals have received from nature. However the observations that can be made from topographic maps and the facility which education and habit give in reading maps, can be of some assistance.

An admiral depends more on the captains of his ships than a general on his generals. The latter has the opportunity to take direct command of the troops himself, to move to any point and to repair false movements. An admiral can influence personally only the men on the vessel on which he finds himself; smoke prevents signals from being seen and winds change or vary over the space occupied by his line. It is thus of all professions that in which subalterns should use the largest initiative.

INDEX

THE ART OF WAR

● ● ●

THE MILITARY INSTITUTIONS OF THE ROMANS

BOOK I

THE SELECTION AND TRAINING OF NEW LEVIES

Roots of Strategy

BOOK II

THE ORGANIZATION OF THE LEGION

Index

● ● ●

MY REVERIES UPON THE ART OF WAR

● ● ●

THE INSTRUCTION OF FREDERICK THE GREAT FOR HIS
GENERALS, 1747

446

Index

● ● ●

THE MILITARY MAXIMS OF NAPOLEON